S0-AIX-951

WITHDRAWN

FIFTY YEARS OF
PRISON SERVICE

Patterson Smith Reprint Series in
Criminology, Law Enforcement, and Social Problems

A listing of publications in the Series *will be found at rear of volume*

PUBLICATION No. 61: PATTERSON SMITH REPRINT SERIES IN
CRIMINOLOGY, LAW ENFORCEMENT, AND SOCIAL PROBLEMS

FIFTY YEARS OF PRISON SERVICE

AN AUTOBIOGRAPHY

BY

ZEBULON REED BROCKWAY

Superintendent of the Elmira Reformatory from the
time of its opening in 1876, to the year 1900.

CARL A. RUDISILL LIBRARY
LENOIR RHYNE COLLEGE

Montclair, New Jersey

PATTERSON SMITH

1969

Originally published 1912
Reprinted 1969 by
Patterson Smith Publishing Corporation
Montclair, New Jersey

HV
92 72
. B85
196 9
14 7809
Nov. 1989

SBN 87585-061-8

Library of Congress Catalog Card Number: 69-14914

To
FRANK B. SANBORN
Co-worker, Counselor, Defender,
and
Life-long Friend
This Narrative is Devotedly Dedicated

EDITOR'S NOTE

WHEN the members of the International Prison Congress paused on their tour of inspection to visit the Elmira Reformatory and pay their respects to Mr. Z. R. Brockway, the first superintendent, I chanced to be among them. In a quiet moment Mr. Brockway, as an old friend, asked if, at my convenience, I would look over some memoranda he was preparing with reference to his share in the work of prison management in this country. Of course I gladly consented.

When the manuscript came to me I was amazed at the amount of labor he must have expended, for it consisted of more than 1600 pages, every word of which he had written with his own hand! Deeply impressed with its value as a human document I begged him to give it to the public, instead of leaving it only for the family archives. I offered to aid him in preparing it for the press if he would consent. This permission was rather reluctantly given, for it was hard to convince him that there were enough people interested to justify its publication.

If, in carrying out my part of the agreement, I have somewhat compressed the story, disjointed here and there the long sentences that he loves to swing, and occasionally replaced his words with others more to my own liking, I beg his pardon. My only excuse is that I wanted to have this remarkable story put in such phrase that a wide public may see how utterly Mr. Brockway has devoted his long life in the noblest spirit to the work of the reformation and rehabilitation of the prisoner and the protection of society. His life has followed an undeviating and uneventful course. His motto might well have been "This one thing I do" and surely he has done it well.

ISABEL C. BARROWS

New York, April, 1912

AUTHOR'S PREFACE

M Y ADULT life during the last half of the nineteenth century was so identified with the modern prison reformatory movement in the United States, my prison service was so unusually continuous, that numerous requests have been made for a record of the facts and lessons of such an experience. In complying with these requests, and performing perhaps a duty, I shall essay to write a chronicle perchance interesting, peradventure suggestive, — haply useful.

Retrospection now reveals more clearly than was seen while the years wore on, a mystic thread that joins events in one eventuality. Whether Fortune, Fate, or Providence, none can deny that the origin and the relations of the self are beyond the individual control. He who reads the following pages may discern, between the lines, that which open eyes discover in every life and in all things, — the rule of Supreme Will, determinant.

Both heart and sense of obligation prompt full mention of the interesting personalities of friends, — assistants of inestimable serviceableness, — and also of individual prisoners possessed of unusual characteristics. Incidentally, the rise and progress of reforms in the penal laws and changes in prison practice will be shown; and presentation given of the earlier conceived and finally conclusive views of sound penological principles as exemplified in the American Reformatory System. No apology is made for so much about myself in the narrative, for that is its avowed intention.

TABLE OF CONTENTS

APPENDICES

LIST OF ILLUSTRATIONS

PART I

CHAPTER I

INTRODUCTORY

ANCESTRY

THE New England branch of the Brockway family, from which both my maternal and my paternal ancestry are traced, was founded by Wolston Brockway, who was born in England about 1638 and, at twenty-four years of age, emigrated to America. He lived in the town of Lyme, Connecticut, near the mouth of the Connecticut River, where he died November 11, 1717, aged seventy-nine years. He was twice married and of his eight children William, the second child, was the progenitor of four sons and two daughters. The second son, John, born May 10, 1697, was the great-grandfather of both of my parents; thus my father and mother were second cousins.

This John Brockway, son of William, married Elizabeth Banning and produced a family of eight children. Their second son, also named John Brockway, married Caroline Reed: from these descends my mother's family. Their third son, Ebenezer Brockway, married Mary Butler, niece of Colonel Zebulon Butler of Wyoming, and from this pair my father's family descends.

My maternal grandparents were Reed Brockway and Mary Niles, and my paternal grandparents were Zebulon Brockway and Abigail Banning. My own baptismal names, Zebulon Reed, were doubtless derived from these grandparents' names.

My father, Zebulon Brockway, was born at Lyme, Connecticut, March 10, 1791; and died at Hadlyme, Connecticut, January 12, 1862, at seventy-one years of age. My mother, Caroline Brockway, was born at Susquehanna, Pennsylvania, March 22, 1801. At seven years of age her mother, Mary Niles Brockway, died and she was taken in charge and reared by Mrs. Caroline LaPlace of Lyme, Connecticut. When she was scarcely nineteen years old and my father twenty-nine, they were married, on the second of March, 1820. Mother lived to be eighty years of age. She died at my residence at the Elmira Reformatory, New York, July 3, 1881.

Seven children were born to my parents — four sons and three daughters — of whom (1912) three are living; namely, Semantha (Mrs. Comstock), aged eighty-six, Hadlyme, Connecticut; Fannie (Mrs. Fay), aged seventy, Chicago, Illinois; and myself, aged eighty-five. Wesley, first-born, died in infancy; Wilbur at the age of thirty-three; Hugh* when seventy-six; and Mary at the age of seventy-three.

My father was nearly six feet in stature, erect, and symmetrically formed. He weighed about 160 pounds, was of light complexion, large cranium (he wore a $7\frac{1}{2}$ hat), had strong rather than heavy features, and

---

* Hugh, whose full name was Hugh Blair Brockway, spent nearly all his mature life in the prison service, mostly associated with myself at Detroit and Elmira. For a time he was superintendent of the state institutions at Cranston, Rhode Island. Hugh served three years (1862-1865) in the volunteer service of the United States Army, Third Cavalry division of the Army of the Potomac, under the active command of Custer and Wilson in the army corps of General Phil Sheridan.

4

was athletic. In intellect he was superior as to strength and quality: he possessed excellent reasoning powers, a vivid imagination, and facility in expression.

This native mental superiority coupled with completest moral integrity and instinctive philanthropy, rather than any tinsel of wealth or circumstance, secured for him not only the uniform respect of his community and associates, but their fullest confidence and regardful esteem. Thus naturally he became the chosen arbiter of differences between neighbors and neighboring communities, and confidential counselor for the perplexed and worried, all of whom he gladly served without fee or reward. In business he was a merchant, gaining thus a comfortable living for himself and family, but he did not possess a mercantile mind nor strong desire to achieve accumulations. The large scope and contemplative character of his mind carried him constantly quite beyond the field of money making. Business was pursued because it was necessary for subsistence and never for business ambition.

Father was a man of importance in his time and place: a local magistrate, county commissioner, and state railroad commissioner; he was also for thirteen years one of the directors of the state prison. He held the rank of colonel in the state militia, by vote of the legislature and governor's commission — an appointment which, so soon after the war of 1812, was deemed a serious trust. In the decade of the 50's he was elected to the house of representatives and again to the senate of the state legislature. In the Fremont campaign he was candidate for presidential elector. Quite exceptionally, when nearly seventy years of age, he was admitted to the bar of the high court in order that he might as an attorney conduct an important litigation between towns, a case made familiar by his connection with it as magistrate and arbiter.

His native tendency and his ability for deductive reasoning, reinforced by intellectual as well as moral honesty, operated to withdraw him, during the middle and latter years of his life, from adherence to any of the religious denominations. For a time, in adolescence, it is said he connected himself with the Methodists; and three sons were named after admired Methodist university men and preachers — Hugh Blair, Wilbur Fisk, and the first-born named after Wesley. Though an irregular and rather indifferent attendant on stated public religious services, yet the grasp of his mind warrants the belief that he was alive to the great problems of Being and Knowing and to the mystery of the human relation to the Infinite. The dictum of professional dogmatists in theology and philosophy was not satisfying to his inquiring mind. He remained immune to their persuasions, and to the last retained in such matters his individual independence.

It is with filial approbation, not without admiration, that I record the following incident of the closing hours of my father's life. Yielding to solicitations he had consented to see the local clergyman, a cultured and lovable man. Only the concluding words of their conversation are known and can be here repeated. The clergyman, retiring, said his everlasting farewell, and expressed his regret at their difference of view and his hope that in the great beyond the truth disclosed there would reconcile the differences. My father, speaking with difficulty, replied: "It is of course possible that your thought may prove true. And possibly, you will

6

ZEBULON BROCKWAY
The author's father

CAROLINE BROCKWAY
The author's mother

concede, it may prove that my estimation of these hidden things may not be altogether unrealized. But the greater probability is that neither of us has correctly forecast the future; and, maybe, both of us are wholly wrong. However that may be, it is my preference, as it is my privilege, to take my departure maintaining *my own* opinions."

Mother was of medium height and shapely. She had black hair and eyes, florid countenance, nervo-sanguine temperament; was energetic, enduring, alert of mind and emotional, and yet remarkably self-controlled. Never in my knowledge of her entire life, with its trying incidents, do I recall a single instance of irritated impatience. She attributed her self-mastery to conscious superhuman support. She was devoutly religious. Sterling good sense held in leash her deep imaginative and emotional nature, but she dwelt much in transcendental spiritual consciousness. The Bible was my mother's book of books, her constant companion. I possess and lovingly cherish the well annotated copy she kept ever at hand and tearfully read; and also another copy of the Scriptures, given by my mother with her loving inscription when, at eighteen years of age, I first left home for extended absence. These keepsakes contribute to consciously connect my youth and old age, and they seem to perpetuate in fresh and tender remembrance the loving relation of mother and son in the earlier years of my life.

Her strong restful faith in the immanence and guidance of the Divine presence never faltered; and with rare insight she discerned the spiritual in the material, which accounts for her remarkable love of natural phenomena. This faith and consciousness supported her under the trials and exigencies of all her life. It was her habit to occasionally seclude herself for contemplation or, from open casement, to observe the earth and sky and moving clouds until, entranced, the common was replaced with the deeper spiritual appreciation. One summer morning shortly before her final illness I found her up and gazing from a window overlooking a charming landscape. Enraptured, she was unconscious of my presence. It was the first flush of dawn. The hilltops were touched with silver light; the deep shadows in the valley below were slowly disappearing — night consumed of day. It was the hush of early morning; diamond dewdrops everywhere, the lazy sway of leaf and branch in the freshening morning breeze, birds aloft calling mate to mate, awakening nature, the uprising sun: behold the day has come! Absorbed my mother sat, teardrops upon her cheek, her face aglow with inward happiness. How do I treasure that image! It is a precious memory and makes all the clearer that profound love for nature which in some degree her children have inherited.

The pecuniary circumstances of the family, if measured by the then New England standards, were comfortably sufficient. Our parents were not ambitious for wealth of worldly goods. Luxurious living, with sensuous enjoyments, did not attract them, and the social status was left to shape itself without their regardful thought. They were by nature above and beyond the field of current competition; they were satisfied with their merited neighborly regard and their own personal self-respect.

For her children the mother's longing was to see them possessed of religiousness like her own, willing then to

8

leave their earthly fortune and guidance to that Providence she herself so leaned upon. Father, with more rationalistic thought, relied on the ruling natural order of things and left his children to make their way according to their ability and circumstances, predetermined but unforeseen. They themselves — my parents — in all relations maintained the noblest standard. Recalling them for this brief genealogical sketch across the abyss of time that separates us, I estimate them and their lives as the best patterns of citizen and neighbor.

BIRTH, ENVIRONMENT, AND EARLY IMPRESSIONS

1827–1836

The family records show that the date of my birth was April 28, 1827; the place at Brockway's Ferry, Lyme, Connecticut, a road terminus, river landing, and ferry nine miles from the mouth of the Connecticut River where it empties into Long Island Sound. The house in which I was born occupied a terrace overlooking my father's store and the docks situated beneath the terrace on the river bank. The house and the store were red, with trimmings of white, nestled picturesquely under the nearby rocky bluff on the north and east. The river, here scimiter shaped, fully half a mile in width and nearly two miles in length between the bends, stretches out its silvery surface always in full view. On the southeast, at the river's sharp curve, rises a rocky promontory near whose summit, indented yet apparently projecting, was a rock flat and massive, where according to the local tradition King Joshua, an aboriginal Indian chief, was wont to seat himself and survey and rule his tribe. These "Joshua Rocks," the kingly seat with its legend, were always in the sight and mind of the children living near. The summit glistening in the noonday sun seemed a huge diamond, the sign of untold wealth beneath, and when suffused with moonlight witchery it was to our childish imaginations peopled with goblin or fairy forms. The weird impression was enhanced by the deep, dark, silent stream that submerged the mountain base and flowed on out to the ocean depths so near. The rocky prominence, the legend connected with it, and the river — its peaceful flow or strange activity when stirred with wind and tide; the marshes, the wooded shores and bluffs, the life upon its surface or in the depths; the sailing craft, fishing boats, and seines reeled or spread upon the sandy beach, — all together made and leave a memory image winsome and suggestive even now after the passage of the intervening seventy-five years; a witchery that brooded beneath and within; a subtle, spiritual, directing agency.

Our home was a hostage house for visiting preachers, some strong minded men, more of the evangelistic type, whose conversation of scriptural prophecy and fulfilment, of millenarianism, and of a spiritual consciousness, served, together with influences apparently trivial yet worthy of mention, to develop my maternal heritage of mystic tendency, useful as stimulating effort, strengthening in trials, but liable to excessive ideality. While not belittling the importance of religious impulsion to reformative efforts of later years, I am doubtless indebted for the avoidance of fanaticism to the counterbalancing paternally inherited tendency to rationalism.

Of the four of us born within the first ten years one, the eldest, Wesley, was from earliest infancy, by an accident, completely helpless until his death at nine years of age, myself then but six. Mother's burdens and devotion, her grief at his death, the funeral, and the little grave within our own grounds, have always been and now are most tender recollections.

Sally Joy, the housemaid and nurse, affectionate, faithful, and to my infantile sense sweetfaced and radiant, also made on me a lasting good impression. I was jealous of her lover, one Griswold, a sterling New Englander, a stoutarmed rower who on Sundays rowed his craft across the baylike river bend plain in sight for two miles. The boat, the man, the wake upon the water,— I seem to see them as I did then, and to feel the jealousy. Sally was never a "servant" proper but New England "help" instead. She matured into a noble woman, the mother of a numerous family, all worthy. She gained ownership of the homestead where once she helped and at eighty years of age died there. Never quite forgotten is the good savor that also came at this early period from casual contact with a stalwart common laborer, an unexpressed but emanative quality, the product of genuine religiousness and moral worthiness. This quality of his personality memorably affected me as back and forth from school or meeting, my hand in his broad palm, he led my steps.

A certain enduring conscious taste, or bias, is traceable for something of its source to the home of our grandparents where not infrequently we made visits. The hardby babbling brooklet, the woods, pastures, and animals of the farm; the spacious house with huge open fireplace, hearthstone, crane, utensils, and back log fire; our tall, calm, most kindly grandmother; the grandfather, his reserved, strong character (for even then I had a notion of his independence of opinion and disregard of current superstitions, a notion afterwards notably confirmed), — surely some formative influence originated amid these surroundings.

Another not unimportant permanent leaning, a taste and tendency, was formed when at eight years of age I was in love with the brunette elfin schoolgirl-mate with the euphonious name of Nancy Lay. Fascinated, I often ran away to her companionship causing worry and trouble at home. This was a genuine heart attachment, not to pass unnoticed, for it is not effaced and is now a pleasant recollection. Habitual high regard for women and maybe a preference for their society, finds here its root in this child love for Nancy Lay.

Then too began the discipline of conscious experiences, alternating joy and sorrow, the suffering of injustice and neglect, the hardening effect of futile punishment on the one hand and on the other the yielding responsiveness to love and to the proffer of sacrifice. Some remorse crept in and then came impressions and lessons from the knowledge of crimes committed and observation of criminals at large. The foregoing is perhaps too pretentious for the following recital of simple facts, but the activity of principles is shown by the occurrences, so the recital should proceed.

My parents gave me a live little watch; it ticked and the hands moved round. The sailors of a craft lying at my father's dock gave me a fullrigged toy ship three feet long. Here was happiness! Soon by accident the watch was lost and a thievish fellow stole my ship. Then came sorrow. At the " infant school" the teacher, through her ignorance, indiscretion, or arbitrariness, refused one day my most reasonable because necessary request. Then I bolted from the room, made resistance to the attempted punishment, and was expelled from school. Thus by means of unwise governance open insubordination began and the spirit of it was strengthened. Disobedience thus initiated in this private class showed later in the public district school, and truancy was added to the other faultiness. Punishments ensued but wrought no change of conduct. The sensitive but unyielding nature irresponsive to punishments derived nevertheless a certain benefit therefrom. Punishment served to heighten the contrast of love and persuasiveness and increased perhaps susceptibility thereto. Better behavior and consequent change of habitual mood, with later suggestiveness of a sound disciplinary principle, was produced when the district school teacher, a refined and lovely lady, having detained me after school hours, supposedly for punishment, surprised me with quite an opposite manifestation. Making no reference to my bad behavior, with sorrowful mien, tenderly, delicately, and in her womanly way, she revealed her genuine affectionate regard. This proved effective for the immediate object in view and left its abiding impression. Now as I write after so many years the memory excites feelings of gratitude for contact with this beautiful character in my obdurate childhood, and inextinguishable love for the treasured image of her charming personality. My efforts proved vain years ago to discover Miss Nichols or her descendants, that I might make some requital for her graciousness to me.

So too when my father had failed by floggings to change my behavior, and relentingly gave up the birch and insistently offered himself for vicarious castigation at my hands, the changed relation wrought immediately the desired effect, — not an instantaneously magical change of the native disposition, but the desired particular change of conduct. Of course the bettered habitual conduct in this one respect, the habit of obedience, thus begun tends to change of character but does not insure it.

The third item of salutary disciplinary experience is of quite a different character; it is the lesson of submissiveness to the inevitable which when well learned is scarcely distinguishable from faith in the dominance of Providence. In a schoolboy quarrel I was overcome and pinned to the ground by the combined strength and weight of three large boys lying across my slender frame. It was a memorable moment when the superior physical force stilled my struggles and compelled submission. This lesson of existent compulsive power beyond individual control proved a salutary lesson in prudence and avoidance of excessive presumption. For knowledge of a certain nameless corruption of character prevalent with prisoners, and the consequent need of precaution in the matter of permitted association among them, I am considerably indebted to the evil communications at this early period of my life of an older and vicious youth, a neighborhood acquaintance, from whose bad influence I myself was rescued by the removal of my family to the Hadlyme locality.

Another childhood experience which initiated lifelong sympathy with the friendless is the mental anguish I suffered when at seven years of age I was left alone

14

The Author's Birthplace. Brockway's Ferry, Lyme, Conn.
The "Joshua Rocks" at the right

and forgotten. On a bleak winter morning, on a country road deep-snowed and pathless, a bevy of us children, mittened and muffled, carrying our books and lunch baskets, were trudging on to school a mile away. In the road we met our gay young neighbor with sleigh and horse caparisoned with bells and robes and silver-decorated whip and harness. Generously he gathered in the children and drove them joyfully off to school, all but myself, inadvertently omitted. Not fear, or anger, but distress of desolateness came then, poignant and ineffaceable from memory. Throughout my mature life, when among the many thousands of the constant throng of offenders committed to my charge there came to my notice any who were abandoned by relatives, outcast, lost, or forgotten by their community, these have especially appealed to my sympathies, and all the more I truly believe because of this little incident.

Still earlier in infancy the consequence of my own rash act planted a memory germ that has always made for salutary self-restraint. In a baby quarrel with my sister, moved by impulsive childish anger I scratched her face with three sharp fingernails, leaving scars which well on to her middle life showed in the color of the cheek. Restraint of impulsive prompting and retaliation may be traced to that occurrence.

Finally, to these very early impressions, which through the whole of life have more or less affected my disposition and conduct, I will add one more. My father's store was entered by a burglar, one Moody, whose arrest, trial, and committal to prison made a permanent impression upon me. Larceny of the toy ship and malicious injury to other of my prized possessions by a worthless young fellow I knew, made real the hurt and injury of crime. Then the appearance on the road and wharf of Ferguson, a discharged state prison convict, whose long term of imprisonment had given to him the lockstep gait and servile demeanor of Wethersfield prisoners, engraved on my memory forever the miserable consequence of imprisonment and gave a decided bent to my mind.

FROM BOYHOOD TO YOUTH

1836–1845

In the year 1836 the family removed to Hadlyme, a river landing four miles north. There my father's business interests were extended to include a general merchandizing copartnership, ship chandlery, and a shipyard where coasting vessels were hauled out for repairs and new vessels built, rigged, and completely fitted out for service. The removal and the life at Hadlyme were beneficial, supplying more and better companions, better opportunity for school and church attendance, the improvement of incidental contact with the large business activities conducted with more enterprise and ability, and the ennoblement of the prevalent social moral tone of the community wrought by leading men through their personal worthiness, forehandedness, dignity of bearing, and a sense of what is honorable in public affairs. With these men in those days it was deemed disgraceful to be an office seeker or to be neglectful of pecuniary and public obligations. The formation of a standard of personal probity was emphasized doubtless by the presence of others in the community with contrary characteristics, — by the contrast thus presented. It is out of the heart that I add here in this memorandum of unconscious formative influences, seen clear in retrospect, that I owe much to my good parentage, — my father's recognized ability, integrity, and accepted moral rank in the community, and my mother's sterling qualities of character, her self-respect, her refinement, devotion, humanity, and her scrupulous, cheerful, though toilsome care of us all.

The following citation of incidents such as are common enough in the experience of youth, apparently unimportant in themselves considered, is made because, to my own sense of things, they reveal and confirm the abiding presence of a brooding protective influence, recall the existent communal sympathy, show subtle incentive and easy initiative to wrong acts, suggest consideration due to first offenders, "some soul of goodness in evil," and a useful lesson for restraint and ministering.

A giant insane negro who had been arrested was chained to the center of a vacant room awaiting the dilatory unorganized action of the town authorities. He seized me when thoughtlessly I was within his reach and would have crushed out my life but for accidental help and rescue by neighbors who were passing by. This insane man, the damage he had done and manifestly was liable to do, showed the need of systematic, effective care and treatment of dangerous individuals. Soon again there appeared a similar demand when a brutal, bloody fight with sheath-knives occurred between the sailors of a craft undergoing repairs in my father's shipyard. The shocking scene not only hurt my sensibilities but also seemed to change for a time the social atmosphere by the introduction into it of brutality and disorder. The fight and the scene it presented brought to my consciousness the fact that such bad characters are abroad and that governmental machinery is required for their restraint and treatment. This consciousness was accentuated too by knowledge of the depredations of a resident thievish family, so frequent and annoying as to create a general state of worry and some alarm.

Two surprising deliverances from death and an unusual rescue from other serious injury in the course of an indiscretion, occurred at this period.

In company with a lad about the same age (ten years) I was frolicking in the shallow water of a deep swift stream that nearby developed into a whirlpool. Beyond my depth, borne on towards the whirlpool, I had quit effort, lost consciousness, and sunk out of sight. When consciousness returned I lay on the bank of the stream in the sun-hot sand, my companion working over me. He had swum out and dived for my rescue and had borne my limp body to the bank, then rolled and rubbed me back to life. His name was Joseph Luther. To his presence of mind, bravery, and strength my life is due. In the summer of 1910, the skipper of a launch in which I sailed on the Connecticut River proved to be the son of Joseph Luther.

Again, another day, alone on horseback I rode unwittingly into a quagmire where both horse and rider floundered down beneath the surface. The swamp was near a lonely road, untraveled and sparse of habitations, yet strange to say two laborers chanced that way, saw my predicament, and saved me from the fatal consequence. The deliverance from moral disaster will be mentioned later.

The almost fatal illness of my eldest and favorite sister, away at boarding school, brought out such neighborly sympathy and helpfulness, both at home and at the school, and the unselfish devotion of the noble man who afterwards became her husband made so evident the reality of genuine human friendship and exalted personal love, that though the natural trend of my vocation would lead toward misanthropy, my distrust became and remains well tempered with a certain hopeful confidence in human nature.

Erelong an episode occurred which somewhat enlarged my experience. A mingled business and benevolent commission took me, a boy of about eighteen, to Indiana, a journey then rather formidable to my inexperienced youthful mind because it was my first important independent commission and the distance seemed considerable. The trip was made by sailing craft to New York, thence up the Hudson River to Albany, by rail (strap-rail-stringers and primitive cars of slow motion) to Buffalo. (The return over this route was on the Erie Canal in a packet boat.) By stern-wheel steamer I went from Buffalo to Toledo, Ohio, and by stage to my destination. I remember that during the discomfort of the railroad ride I had a vision of the luxurious appointments of modern travel, but not clearly enough to stimulate invention and fortune seeking. It was, however, an incipient exercise of mental forecast. En route I fell in with a former Connecticut acquaintance then in business at Austinburg, Ohio, the proprietor of an extensive mercantile establishment and a dealer in and shipper of cheese made on the Western Reserve. After duly fulfilling my particular commission I engaged myself in connection with his business in Austinburg, and served two years usefully there and advantageously to myself. On recovery from the illness that necessitated my return to Connecticut, another mercantile opportunity opened and engagement was made at Guilford in that state. An incident of my experience at Guilford warrants recital.

The continued and more varied mercantile life gave, of course, valuable experience of the dangers that beset young men who are living away from their own good homes. At Guilford Point, a summer resort two miles from the town on the Long Island shore, was the Hotel Pavillion, out of commission winters but whose caretaker furnished occasional entertainment for special small parties. Oysters quick from the beds beneath the ice-covered sea, hot roasted, served with wines and liquors; games of cards with trifling stakes (except sometimes in poker the stakes grew large) made up the entertainments. During the winter of my Guilford residence three several groups of chummy fellows visited the Hotel Pavillion for conviviality. Of all three groups I was a member and always treated as a favorite. Myself not loath, and tacitly induced by my employers for trade advantage, it came to pass that my convivial evenings at the Pavillion were very frequent. Late hours there, the feasts and frolicking, together with long hours at business, soon began to tell upon my general health.

Never over indulgent at the feasts, I did once get over interested in a game of poker, and except for the unusual stand taken by one older than the rest I might have been much embarrassed by the consequence. The game waxed hot that night and all of mine and some of my employer's money, — rightly in my possession but to be accounted for, — was in the pot and won by Captain Crampton. Had he retained the money, as well he might, I could no doubt have satisfactorily explained, but since then I have had custody of men for larceny and embezzlement committed under quite similar circumstances, whose minds at the moment of their crimes were as non-criminal as mine was then. A striking parallel case is related later in this narrative, in speaking of some notable prisoners in the Elmira Reformatory, of a clerk, once a college professor, who used his employer's cash, — the same amount precisely and in almost the same way. It is needless to say that after my own experience in Guilford in my earlier years, this prisoner's case, half a century afterwards, received the proper consideration. But Crampton did not retain the money. His offer to return it was of course at once refused, yet later, when he finally and soberly declared that he would never join us again if we persisted in our refusal and asked as a personal favor to himself that we would thus deliver him from the forced relation of a gambler, we could no longer refuse and each took back his money. That evening's experience ended forever for me all participation in games of chance with money staked. Impending injury to my health and habits was made so clear that I resigned my situation at Guilford and went home to await what next Dame Fortune might direct.

Let me ask the kind reader not to impatiently dismiss the recital of these apparently trifling incidents, for in truth they form a not unimportant part of the record of my life. To the unreflective they may seem trivial, as at the time of occurrence they were lightly passed or quite unnoticed. But no event in any human life is truly trivial. Character is but the sum and product of all impressions ever received, added to hereditary tendency. It is these simple experiences which develop positive tendencies of mind and lead to the formation and confirmation of opinions which help in the avoidance of evil and the execution of good. The belief that elements of individual character are thus largely formed, that in the incidents of a life beyond the individual control the choices themselves are predetermined, is the warrant for recalling such details.

Not long after leaving Guilford in 1848, at the age of twenty-one, I began at the state prison at Wethersfield the connection with prison service which continued almost uninterruptedly until 1900; first as guard, then clerk, then assistant superintendent at Albany, and as superintendent at Rochester, Detroit, and Elmira, — a service covering practically the last half of the nineteenth century.

CHAPTER II

WETHERSFIELD PRISON: THE PILSBURYS AS MANAGERS

THE Connecticut state prison is situated at Wethersfield, four miles from the city of Hartford, on a marshy tract of land which borders a cove or bay of the Connecticut River. The main buildings and the yard wall are of stone, but the cells and buildings within the enclosure are of brick. The cells, back to back like the shelves of a honeycomb, four tiers high, stand within a cell-house whose exterior walls are pierced with small window openings heavily grated with iron. The cells are small, 4 x 7 x 7 feet, and the doors were at first heavy oak plank with a small grated opening near the top, but later the modern round bar doors were substituted. The doors opened directly into narrow galleries on each tier. The whole establishment is of plain construction. It was rated originally as a good specimen of a small prison of the Auburn type, and was very satisfactory to the people of Connecticut, especially because it was so much better than the old Simsbury Mines prison from which the prisoners were removed to Wethersfield on September 28, 1827, the very year of my own birth in that state.

The following account of the two prisons is gleaned and condensed from a booklet by Richard H. Phelps,

1860.   It is here introduced to show the public sentiment relating to prisons and prisoners at the beginning
and during the first quarter of the last century.   This
cave prison at Simsbury was known in the time of the
American Revolution as Newgate, named after the
Newgate of England.   It was formed out of the Simsbury copper mines on Copper Hill.   Mr. Phelps says:

"The appearance of this place forcibly reminds the
observer of the walls, castles and towers erected for the
security of some haughty lordling of the feudal ages;
while the gloomy dungeons within its walls call to remembrance a bastille or a prison of the inquisition.
These caverns were first occupied as a place for the
confinement of Tories about the beginning of the
American Revolution, first used by the colony of Connecticut as a permanent prison in 1773, and established
as a state prison in 1790.   Some rude buildings covering
access to the caverns were constructed with an enclosure of half an acre or so built of planks with iron spikes
upon the top.   The passage down the shaft into the
cavern was upon a ladder fastened upon one side and
resting on the bottom.   At the foot of this passage
commences a gradual descent for a considerable distance, all around being solid rock or ore.   The passages
extend many rods in different directions, some of them
even leading under the cellars of the dwellings of the
neighborhood. . . .   On the sides, in the niches of
the cavern, platforms were built of boards for the
prisoners, on which straw was placed for their beds.
The horrid gloom of this dungeon can scarcely be
realized.   The impenetrable vastness supporting the
awful mass above impending as if ready to crush one
to atoms; the dripping water trickling like tears from
its sides; the unearthly echoes, all conspired to strike
aghast with amazement and horror. . . .   From
30 to 100 were placed together through the night,
solitary lodging as practised at Wethersfield afterwards

NEWGATE (SIMSBURY MINES) PRISON, CONN.

CONNECTICUT STATE PRISON, WETHERSFIELD

being then regarded as a punishment rather than a blessing to them. The punishments inflicted for prison offenses were flogging, confinement in stocks in the dungeons, being fed on bread and water during the time, double or treble sets of iron, hanging by the heels, etc. A bell summoning the prisoners to work brought them up from the cavern beneath through a trap door, in irregular numbers, two or three together, and sometimes a single one alone, when under guard of armed soldiers they were conducted across the yard to the smithy. The prisoners were heavily ironed and secured by fetters and being therefore unable to walk made their way by jumps and hops. On entering the smithy some went to the side of the forges where collars dependent by iron chains from the roof were fastened around their necks and others were chained in pairs to wheelbarrows. The attendants delivered pickled pork to the prisoners for dinner at their forges, a piece for each thrown on the floor and left to be washed and boiled in the water used for cooling the iron wrought at the forges. Meat was distributed in a similar manner for breakfast."

The intention of all this was not cruelty, but to make the prison an object of terror in the hope to deter from crime; and at the same time the burden and misery of such imprisonment was thought to be not unjust retribution for the civic and moral damage of crime. This deterrent and retributive purpose of public punishment, rooted in crude human nature, had been imported with the Puritan pilgrims accustomed to these ideas by the religious conflicts of Europe, and it prevailed in the early years of the century and still exists more or less, it must be conceded, at the present day. Doubtless the spread of rationalism with attendant human sympathy, and perhaps state pride wounded by contrast in the conditions of Connecticut prisoners as compared with those of other states and countries, considerably influenced the establishment of the Wethersfield prison to which the Simsbury prisoners were removed in 1827. After that they were in every way better cared for. It is believed, however, that the main consideration was that of economy, — more earnings from the labor of prisoners, and consequently a reduced cost to the state government for maintaining its prison establishment.

With the new Connecticut prison at Wethersfield there came into public prominence certain unusually successful prison managers, Moses C. Pilsbury and his son Amos Pilsbury. Louis D. Pilsbury, a son of Amos, was the first superintendent of New York state prisons (1877-1882) under the amended state constitution by which for inspectors of state prisons elected by popular vote was substituted a superintendent of prisons appointed by the governor and senate every five years.

The first warden of the prison at Wethersfield was Moses C. Pilsbury, previously warden of the New Hampshire state prison, to whose ability, with the influence upon public sentiment of the Prison Discipline Society of Boston, Massachusetts, much is due in the arrangement and system of the Wethersfield prison, then the acknowledged superior of other prisons in this country. He continued as warden for about three years and was succeeded by his son, Amos Pilsbury, who administered the prison some fifteen years, an almost continuous incumbency, broken by only a short interval. Moses C. Pilsbury was a man of most excellent character, a fair education, and good competency of means. Both education and means were

26

acquired under difficulties which called into play his native capabilities.   He served in the war of 1812 and held afterwards, until his death in 1848, some public office.   He was the first prison warden who caused the prisoners to earn their own support, the first prison keeper who introduced the practice of reading the Bible daily to the assembled prisoners, and he was the founder and head of the improvements in our prisons, at least in the New England states.

Amos Pilsbury followed and developed the principles his father had adopted and became famed for good management at Wethersfield and in New York, where, in 1845, the Albany County Penitentiary, the first large county industrial prison for misdemeanants in America, was established under his direction.   Mr. Pilsbury, as the superintendent, managed this prison continuously for more than thirty years.   The excellence of his discipline and the extraordinary financial results gave an impulse to the betterment of prisons throughout the country.   His impressive personality, administrative dignity, and high social standing in the community did much to elevate prison management to its later accepted high rank.

The excellent disciplinary and industrial basis for a prison system laid by Moses Pilsbury and his son, the enduring interest of their standards at Wethersfield, and my official association at the Albany Penitentiary with Amos Pilsbury seem to demand further mention, particularly of the latter.   Mr. Amos Pilsbury was essentially a large man, not tall but stout.   He tipped the scales at about 220 pounds.   He had a Roman nose, a strong symmetrical face, showing the roots of his close shaven dark beard up to the high cheekbone.   He had full gray eyes and was lion voiced, with peremptory manners. He was always well groomed and wore ruffled linen. He was of exact and sterling integrity, a man of honor and generous impulse; a strict disciplinarian, yet eminently just and sufficiently sympathetic. He was made warden of the Connecticut State Prison at Wethersfield, April, 1830, when he was but twenty-five years old. But because he administered faithfully for the public benefit, regardless of conflicting personal and partisan interests, he was assailed, and pending a legislative investigation in 1832 he was removed from office. The investigation excited unusual general interest throughout the state and resulted in a complete vindication and his restoration to the office which thereafter he held continuously until 1845, the date of his removal to Albany. This long tenure of office where partisan changes were frequent and individual hostility remained evinced great public confidence in the man and official. It is an interesting early historic instance of non-partisan prison administration and shows that Mr. Pilsbury was a pioneer in such deliverance.

During the brief period of his enforced retirement discipline was relaxed, disorder reigned, and when he resumed charge again open insubordination was anticipated. The night watchman, Hoskins, had been murdered, desperate attempts of prisoners to escape had been made, and industrial efficiency had been much diminished. On the day previous to his resuming control Mr. Pilsbury, accompanied by the board of directors, paid a visit to the prison. When they entered the shoeshop all there employed, at the instance of a leader, rose from their seats armed with their shoe-knives and demanded that Mr. Pilsbury should leave the shop. This he refused to do, telling the prisoners that though at that moment he had no authority over them he would not leave until they returned to their work. His bold attitude and strong personality so dominated them that one by one the men, including their leader and spokesman, resumed their seats and their work. But disciplinary troubles were not over. Outbreaks of boisterous disturbance afterwards occurred. The very next day, the day he resumed official control, all the prisoners in all the shops refused to return to their cells. After some parley they relented, but marched to the cell-house, singing, shouting, besmearing the walls with the mush in their ration pans which they were carrying for supper, then drumming on and tossing and smashing the pans. It was fiendish uproar. Such disorder continued at intervals for many weeks but after a time was suddenly and effectually quelled. One day when visiting the Sing Sing prison of New York, Mr. Pilsbury saw on a windowsill the cat-o-nine-tails, which instrument was presented to him by the warden. Arriving at the Connecticut River landing at Wethersfield at early dawn the next morning, with the little instrument in his gripsack, he heard, though a mile away, the matinal convict disturbance. On reaching the prison at that very early hour he summoned his deputy and at once, within the hearing of all, he made use of the instrument he carried on the first disturber he discovered. The effect was magical. From that day the disorder ceased, good order was restored, industrial efficiency returned, and salutary discipline was reëstablished. The cat-o-nine-tails was relegated to a windowsill in the Connecticut State Prison and was rarely used afterwards, and then merely for the recovery of some recalcitrant individual prisoner who had proved insusceptible to reason and persuasion. The mere presence of the instrument seemed almost effective enough.

Any sufficient explanation of the marked institutional change of tone wrought by the means thus used would involve a psychological disquisition inappropriate here, but the suggestion may be ventured that the effect was somewhat due to an impression of increased certitude and celerity of consequences; and as to the individuals who had been irresponsive to reason and persuasions, the beneficial effect may be attributed to the more direct appeal through bodily sensations.

The main reliance to amend the behavior and morals of prisoners at that period, based on unrest occasioned by the pains of imprisonment, was the influence of religious ministrations. These at the Wethersfield prison included daily scripture reading and prayer in the presence of the assembled prisoners, a Sunday Bible class, and preaching and visits at the cell door by the chaplain for the purpose of conversation and exhortation. The wardens, not themselves regardless, but vaguely superstitious, left the moralities of prisoners to the official chaplain, who supposedly was the intermediary agent of spirituality. Even today, in spite of the advance in theological ideas, the wardens of prisons and reformatories are too apt to shirk their scientific duty in this regard by devolving it on the chaplain.

Prison management by the Pilsburys always held predominant the aim and the inspiration of the economies. Profitable employment of prisoners, so that the cost of supporting prisons should be defrayed out of the products of their labor, was a tenet instilled by Moses Pilsbury, made remarkably effective by Amos Pilsbury at Wethersfield and at Albany, and afterwards by Louis D. Pilsbury in his management of the state prisons of New York.

The second year of Amos Pilsbury's wardenship at the small Wethersfield prison a handsome profit was derived from the inherent income alone. Governor Peters in his message to the legislature, May, 1832, said, "The friends of the penitentiary system have great reason to rejoice at the Connecticut State Prison during the first year. After paying every expense incurred for the support and management of the establishment there remains a balance in favor of the institution of $8,713.53." Hon. Roger Sherman in a later published report on the state prison said, " Instead of being a charge on the treasury it is a source of revenue. In ten years the net earnings above all expenses have been sufficient to pay every expense of its erection, support, and management, and leave a surplus on hand of over $10,000." Mr. Sherman adds, "The state is greatly indebted to the Messrs. Pilsbury for their superior skill in conducting the institution. By one who was competent to judge and had made extensive inquiry in this country and in Europe, they have been pronounced the best prison people in the world."

From a report made to the legislature, May, 1844, it appears that during the seventeen years the prison had been in operation the net income of profits thereof, after defraying every expense for support and management of the convicts, amounted in the aggregate to $93,000. These financial results of prison management were in that state, at that period, considered very important, and contrasted well with the cost of maintaining the old Newgate Prison where from 1810 to 1827 — a like period of seventeen years — upwards of $125,000 over and above the earnings were taken from the public treasury. These results were specially gratifying to the good people of Connecticut and served to call public attention throughout the country to the subject of a better prison administration. The motive was not narrowly nor merely mercenary. Mr. Pilsbury encouraged the building of improved county jails in each of the counties of the state, and on his recommendation some of the surplus earnings were by act of legislature so applied. He also urged that some portion of the surplus earnings should be devoted to providing and supporting an establishment for criminal and pauper lunatics.

Most of the mature life of Amos Pilsbury was spent in the management of the Albany County Penitentiary. He originated it and made it the pattern for others subsequently established in New York and several of the other states. By his influence it became practically a district penitentiary where under contract, for payment of a small weekly stipend, misdemeanants under sentence of a few days or weeks were received from the county jails of surrounding counties. The income thus derived, together with the earnings from the prisoners' labor, met the cost of maintaining the penitentiary and contributed annually a considerable sum to the county treasury.

Louis D. Pilsbury during his five years as the first state superintendent of prisons showed his inherent ability for good prison management. He saved the

Amos Pilsbury

Louis D. Pilsbury

state millions of money. He exacted the best of discipline throughout all the prisons in his charge, and on his retirement left them greatly improved.

The Pilsburys, while giving dominance to economic excellence of management, builded at the same time broader and better than they knew. The Pilsbury standard made a demand for capable prison governors who were honest and honorable in character. The requisite efficiency of the prisoners insured good prison discipline which possesses, at least incidentally, a certain cultural civic value. The necessary physical vigor and mental willingness involve good careful attention to hygiene. Sustained productive work by the prisoners, though at first involuntary and always wageless, could not be wholly valueless for habit forming. And doubtless some, if insufficient, skill of industry was occasionally acquired by prisoners. It is true, the Pilsburys in the prisons of their control did not practically adopt the scientific reformatory methods of the last half century, but the movement had their approval, sympathy, and effective aid.

Amos Pilsbury was one of the original commissioners for locating and building the reformatory establishment at Elmira. He was present at the Cincinnati National Prison Congress in 1870 and agreed with the formulated principles adopted by that remarkable assembly; and he said to me there that when he should reach home at Albany he would commence such improvements in his penitentiary management. In his sick room, shortly previous to his death, with deep feeling he expressed his regret that he had ever paid into the public treasury the earnings of prisoners instead of using such surplus funds for the prisoners' benefit. His son, Louis D.

Pilsbury, was a member of the first board of managers of the Elmira Reformatory. It was at his instance that I was called to the superintendency, and great was our indebtedness to his influence which enabled us to secure the adoption and development of the reformatory system in that institution.

For the sake of emphasis it should be repeated that the Pilsbury system of prison management, exemplified at Wethersfield, at Albany, and later at the state prisons in New York, as relates to the economies and discipline constituted a sound and invaluable basis for building the "Ideal Prison System for a State."* The stringent discipline maintained by the Pilsburys is necessary for the desirable institutional and individual prison economies and is indispensable in any really effective reconstructive formation of the character of adult criminals. The degree of stringency needful for the purposes named, so salutary for the bulk — the susceptible prisoners — brings to the surface in certain exceptional prisoners their lurking defectiveness and devilishness which under a more lenient discipline would remain concealed. Reformatory disciplinary training devoid of some friction is by that sign shown to be fallacious.

In concluding this account of the Wethersfield prison with a recital of frictional incidents, tragical occurrences, and interesting though troublesome prisoners confined during my service there — which ended about the middle of the century, I must ask the kind reader to avoid forming the opinion, natural

---

* For abstract of paper under this title prepared by the author for the National Prison Congress at Cincinnati, 1870, see Appendix I, page 389.

enough but erroneous, that the treatment of prisoners was censurably severe. Such was not the case. I gladly attest on my own knowledge that Amos Pilsbury's administration both at Wethersfield and at Albany was humane, considerate, and conscientious. He was a high-minded man not improperly swayed by his feelings. Dominated by his sense of duty, difficulties never dismayed him, nor was he too complaisant toward the demand of an always existent unreasonable and importunate sentimentalism.

Very early in the history of the Wethersfield prison — about 1832 — occurred the previously mentioned murder of a night watchman. On a night of boisterous weather outside, that shook the old loose windows so as to hide a lesser noise, two prisoners, Scott and Carr, sawed their cell door bars, reached the corridor, surprised the watchman, Hoskins, and with an iron bludgeon beat out his brains, but did not effect their escape. Scott, the leader, was an experienced criminal of desperate character. He had been previously imprisoned in the Sing Sing prison of New York, and in the prisons of some other states. At Wethersfield he was serving a sentence of fifteen years. Once while in this prison, when he had refused to work or submit to the regulations and was disciplined therefor, he cut off one hand at the wrist in order to disable himself. When on his recovery he was assigned to steadily turn a grindstone crank with the remaining hand, he openly threatened to kill the warden at the first opportunity. A barber by trade, Scott was one day assigned to assist in shaving his fellow prisoners. While thus engaged the warden, Mr. Pilsbury, who knew of the threat, came in and seated himself in the barber's chair to be himself shaved. Though greatly agitated, the prisoner performed the service well and remained afterwards an obedient prisoner until Mr. Pilsbury's forced retirement and the attempt to escape in 1832. For the murder of Hoskins he was hanged at Hartford in 1833.

One of the risks of the prison service is liability to injury from the sudden display of concealed homicidal impulse in prisoners not adjudged insane, and the reckless use of murderous instruments unexpectedly. For instance, a quiet prisoner in the carpenter shop suddenly seized a hammer and remarked, "I am going to kill Pilsbury," and ran from the shop. When they met, the alertness of the warden and his heavy cane just saved his life. Mr. Pilsbury never quite recovered from a wound 15 inches long diagonally across his back made by a prisoner whom he was interviewing in his cell.

Among the tragical traditions of that prison are the following: Deputy Warden Walker, a noble man and excellent officer, carried to his death a long deep scar inflicted by a prisoner. When making his round of daily inspection Mr. Walker entered the area between a factory building and the enclosing outside yard wall on which armed guards were always stationed. A prisoner working there, splitting kindling wood with an axe, without word or warning suddenly slashed Mr. Walker's forehead, felled him to the ground, and stood over him with raised axe for the final fatal blow, when the guard upon the wall shot, dexterously wounding the prisoner in the hip and saving the warden's life. Years afterward, when he was deputy warden at the state prison at Charlestown, Massachusetts, a prison where two wardens were killed by prisoners in quick succession, Mr. Walker was stabbed to death by a prisoner while in attendance in the chapel on official duty. The guard, Mr. Brown, who saved his life at Wethersfield, was soon promoted to the charge of prisoners in a factory and was himself killed by a prisoner of his gang who was still in custody and under sentence for life during the period of my service there.

In a separate department of the prison there was an interesting criminal, probably insane, by name Rabello, a native of the Cape Verde Islands. He was of medium stature, well knit frame, strong handsome features, always of princely bearing, and his personal habits showed much refinement. The son of a wealthy wine merchant, Rabello had never engaged in any business occupation or profession, but had spent his years in travel for pleasure and information. Returning after long absence from home he learned of his father's death, that his brothers had absorbed the property, and, worst of all, that his fiancée now rejected him. In his dejection he emigrated to America and took employment temporarily as choreman on a farm at Branford, Connecticut. In the twilight of a summer evening, when splitting wood at the wood pile, the farmer's toddling boy while frolicking accidentally hurt Rabello's foot. Enraged, he chopped the boy as he had chopped the wood. It was for this crime that he was committed to prison and kept in separate confinement. An insane jealousy of his personality continued after his committal. While ordinarily he maintained a reserved manner, distant, disdainful, regal, he seemed not irrational until intruded upon. Then his rage was fearful. After years of such seclusion Rabello died in the prison hospital, where for weeks preceding his death he was rational, and by his gentleness, considerateness, and continued tranquillity, he proved to be a most attractive personage. This man, who was of good lineage, good bodily symmetry and quality, good native intellectuality, cultured by sufficient systematic education and by travel, a man of refined tastes and personal habits, apparently normal but for his aloofness, was subject to paroxysms of passion excited by trivial occurrences. Acquaintance with Rabello and with other abnormal characters at the Wethersfield prison contributed to my lifelong reflective inquiry as to individual responsibility for conduct.

Prisoner Lamphere, epileptic, was a very dangerous prisoner. Shortly preceding and for days after the epileptic seizure, Lamphere was morose and frequently boisterous and homicidal. He was extraordinarily powerful when aroused, in physical strength a match for several ordinary men. Once he nearly severed the arm of a prison officer who was trying to move him from his cell to other quarters. Here plainly there was physical derangement, epileptic diathesis that determined the bad conduct casting its shadow of doubt about responsibility.

Traditional accounts of tragical events at this prison cast a gloomy shadow which impressively affected the spirits, opinions, and attitude of the novice. For instance, night watchman Shipman was shot and killed on a gallery of the corridor by one of two prisoners who emerged from their cells and had possession of a revolver. By means of false keys and cutting the bars in the doors they had effected their exit, but how they obtained the gun was never certainly ascertained. After due trial by the court both prisoners were hanged for the murder. At another time the warden, Mr. Willard, was killed by a prisoner named Marshall. Marshall had previously been a prisoner at Wethersfield when Mr. Willard was a deputy warden. He made an attempt to escape but was thwarted by Willard. Incensed by the failure and by the disciplinary consequences of that act he openly declared and nursed for years the purpose to kill Mr. Willard. After serving out that first term he was committed to the Michigan State Prison at Jackson for fresh crimes, but escaped from there in the winter, when the toes of both feet were frozen and amputated. Years elapsed and for another felony in Connecticut Marshall was again committed to the Wethersfield prison. Willard was now the warden and manager-in-chief. Marshall was restless and troublesome and was changed from one industrial department to another until he reached the shoeshop, so prolific of disciplinary troubles. He purloined the sharp point of the blade of a shoeknife, secreted it between the soles of one of his shoes and in his room fitted it into the end of a cane which he was allowed to carry on account of his lameness. Armed thus with the apparently innocent but secretly dangerous sword cane, he requested on a Sunday morning an interview with the warden at the cell. Mr. Willard graciously responded to this request, and prisoner and warden faced each other within and without the open-grated cell door. Through the bars of the door Marshall passed his slate on which was written, "Look on the other side." While Mr. Willard's attention was occupied Marshall through the grating fatally stabbed him in the abdomen with the knifed cane. For this murder Marshall was hanged, but in the county jail on the night before his execution he attempted suicide by thrusting into his skull a pointed wire withdrawn from the rim of his ration pan. The wire was discovered at the postmortem examination. It had penetrated half an inch and broken off.

Mr. Willard's successor as warden, Mr. Webster, was also killed, by a prisoner named Brennan who belonged to the shoeshop gang. Many of the prisoners then, indeed most of them, were tractable enough as relates to disciplinary control, but were not promising for future free citizens. The prison population, viewed as a whole, subjected only to punishment and religious ministrations, constituted a forbidding and wellnigh hopeless mass of fullgrown men. Enough of them were dangerous and manifestly incorrigible to check foolish sentimentalism and to impart to the whole matter of crime and criminals a grave significance.

ON DUTY AT WETHERSFIELD

1848–1850

My connection with the prison at Wethersfield began in 1848, when Elisha Johnson was warden, and continued into the period of the wardenship of Leonard Wells, a brother-in-law of Amos Pilsbury. Both Johnson and Wells carried on the prison in the way it was managed by Mr. Pilsbury. Thus my earliest serious impression of what a prison system should be was derived from contact with the most exactly administered "Auburn system," adapted for the treatment of men who were of mature age convicted of high crime, men of the deeper dyed criminous character; a prison system administered according to the Pilsbury standard.

40

This valuable first experience was succeeded by my service at the Albany Penitentiary as the deputy, or first assistant, to Mr. Pilsbury himself, who must be accredited as the Nestor of the Auburn prison system in America.

When serving as clerk of the Wethersfield prison my duties, under the close Connecticut economy of that time, included, besides keeping the accounts and records, assistance to the warden in purchasing supplies and in the details of the general and departmental management. The clerk was also commissioned to bring in sentenced prisoners from the place of conviction at the several county seats throughout the state. This latter duty devolved by law on the prison authorities and saved to the state an otherwise large expense for sheriff's fees. Removal of the prisoners was sometimes made by railroads but oftener by open conveyance over the country roads. It now seems almost incredible that, stripling as I was, I should have been sent on those country road journeys, which often extended to late evening hours, unarmed, without an attendant guard, yet conveying at one time several prisoners to serve long, even life sentences. Fortunately I never lost a prisoner in such transit nor was any attempt to escape ever made, and no accident or troublesome contumacy of prisoners ever occurred.

The ineffaceable impressions of experience, observation, and suggestions derived at Wethersfield, where only veritable criminals were confined, laid a good foundation for my career. The seriousness of the prison problem, its great public importance, and the indispensableness of thoroughness in every relation, were there stamped in. This initial prison service was useful too for afterwards properly estimating the misdemeanants and mixed prisoners of the Albany penitentiary, and has been serviceable always for the study and treatment of the various types of anti-social inhabitants in the institutions and communities of my acquaintance.

CHAPTER III

AT ALBANY: PENITENTIARY AND ALMSHOUSE

1851–1853

M Y APPOINTMENT and entrance upon service at the Albany County Penitentiary as deputy, or in nautical phrase, the first officer, occurred in the year 1851, when I was twenty-four years old. I had only casual acquaintance with Mr. Pilsbury incident to his occasional visits to his brother-in-law, Mr. Wells, the warden at Wethersfield, where there hovered a savor of his imperiousness during his own incumbency as warden. It was at his invitation that I paid a visit to the penitentiary at Albany to confer about the appointment. A trifling incident at that conference so shows Mr. Pilsbury's egoism and my own over-sensitiveness, and proved such a salutary regulator of our intercourse, promoting our friendship, that I deem it worth mentioning. After a day spent in looking over the institution Mr. Pilsbury towards bedtime broached the subject of my employment there. Having in mind his Wethersfield reputation for arrogance I ventured to say that however desirous I might be to remain complaisant under imperious direction I was so constituted that I could not; that I hoped he would appreciate my motive in this reference, which was to guard against annoyance to himself and injury to me which might result from a sudden and not unlikely disruption of any prospective relations. He did not take it kindly but haughtily replied that he would not consult his employes as to his manner of addressing them, and terminated at once our evening interview. My early departure next morning was without the appearance of my host or any adieu from him, but when our conveyance to the train had nearly reached the outermost limits of the extensive grounds the driver was halted by the remote stentorian call of Mr. Pilsbury himself who, following in dressing gown and slippers, came near to inquire if I would accept his offer. Under the circumstances I responded affirmatively. Never but once afterwards was there any jar to our pleasant relations. Then, quite mistaken as to the fact in question, he haughtily addressed me from a distance and immediately withdrew from sight and earshot. Momentarily incensed, on passing the guard room on my way to the noonday luncheon I threw away my cane — the emblem of office — so that it fell beneath a heavy piece of furniture, with which act I expected to terminate my service. After luncheon I was surprised to find my cane returned to its usual noonhour repository. The doorkeeper said Mr. Pilsbury himself had picked the cane up and returned it to its place. This impulsive pantomime performance, the only friction in all our relations, would surely but for his action have resulted in the severing of our connection and no doubt given a very different direction to the activities of my whole life.

The change from Wethersfield to Albany made a memorable epoch in the training and development for

44

my future prison service. The same degree of thoroughness and exactitude that characterized the prison management at the Connecticut prison pervaded the Albany penitentiary, but in other respects a marked difference was observed. The prevalent atmosphere, or tone, of the institution at Albany was better, or at least more agreeable, and more healthfully inspiring. The entire structure was comparatively new and it was charmingly situated. The material was brick, the façade painted a light gray. The walls were pierced with as many great windows as could be. The architectural form was slightly renaissant, without the cold repellent effect of the plain straight stone façade and loopholed windows of the front at Wethersfield.

The penitentiary is in the southwest suburb of the city and fronts on ample, well laid out grounds ornamented with trees, shrubs, and flowers, with a meandering brooklet and winding driveways and paths of approach. The view commands the hills across the Hudson River away towards Massachusetts. The whole is picturesque and suggests rather an institution for an educational or charitable purpose than a penitentiary. Within is great abundance of light from the large corridor windows. The walls and ceilings were always snowy white. Scrupulous cleanliness reigned everywhere. The inner court or prison yard, surrounded by factory buildings, had paved or graveled walks, grass plots, and beds of flowers. The first impression of the inside was of a cheerful, animated, busy, thrifty New England manufactory. There were of course well-appointed hospital apartments and medical attendants for the care of the sick, a chaplain, and a commodious chapel and auditorium for stated religious observances where occasional musical and oratorical entertainments and instructive exercises were given. Mr. Pilsbury himself made it a point to be present at all such assemblages of the prisoners.

The number of prisoners confined at Albany, — some six hundred, — twice the number at Wethersfield, seemed when viewed en masse to be of a different class. While it is true that a few years afterwards some felons from the state courts were received, and still later, under a profitable contract made with the United States government for their maintenance, felons from the federal courts were admitted (among them many Negroes from the southern states) — a policy that after a time changed the characteristic of the prison to similarity with the common state penitentiaries such as that at Wethersfield — the prisoners confined at that stage of the Albany penitentiary were all of them misdemeanants. They were adults, men and women of low type, habitual drunkards, common prostitutes, local and migrant vagabonds, professional gamblers, petty thieves, bruisers, and other similar characters from the social scum of the cities of Albany, Troy, and from the populous towns of surrounding counties. The mass here differed from that at Wethersfield in being devoid of a certain subterranean, menacing quality, attributable largely to the long sentences and to the larger ratio of desperate characters there confined, and there was less necessity for intensive guarding. The stringency of control maintained at Albany was not so much for safety as it was for the sake of serviceable industrial efficiency, the increase of prison earnings.

46

It is true that most felons come out of the class of misdemeanants, and in the misdemeanor prisons are to be found always some men and women prisoners who are experienced in heinous crimes. But most misdemeanants do not become felons; they remain "rounders" — out and in over and over again, short-term prisoners. In a state like New York the annual committals to prisons are estimated to be 95 per cent misdemeanants and 5 per cent felons. Close acquaintance with the characteristics of the individual prisoners of both classes diminishes the sense of difference and suggests that probably both felons and misdemeanants are what they are accidentally and by force of habit much more than by any difference of intrinsic depravity. It is believed that if the worst prisoners, about 10 per cent of the whole, were to be withdrawn from the felonious population of the Wethersfield prison, and if at the same time their sentences were shortened equal to the sentences of the misdemeanant population at the Albany penitentiary, there would wellnigh disappear as between each mass any observable difference of characteristics. Familiarity with the prisoners at Albany after my contact with those at Wethersfield, opened a vista of crime cause, pointed to the classes and conditions in society from which spring the serious offenders, and showed the great need in this larger field of good preventive prison management.

The employment of the prisoners at the Albany prison, aside from the usual domestic and prison duties, was in making rattan chair seats, braiding willow covers on bottles and carboys, and shoemaking. The system was partly by contract per day for each prisoner's time, and partly by the piece for work actually and satisfactorily performed. Early rising and work before breakfast were the habit at this prison as erstwhile in New Hampshire, the state from which the Pilsburys came, and in general in New England. Rising before dawn, waiting for light enough to see the factories across the prison yards, the establishment was astir at the earliest moment. The prisoners, officers, and guards, were all turned out often on summer mornings before five o'clock, in again for breakfast, and again at work at seven o'clock for the allotted full ten hours.

The exact data that showed in dollars the financial result of this then unprecedented prison management proved that in directing the employment of such worthless prisoners, serving short sentences, the institution was made self-sustaining and even profitable. The city and county were not only saved from any expense in caring for local offenders in the penitentiary but they received annually into the treasury considerable sums from the surplus earnings. The surrounding counties by boarding their prisoners at the Albany penitentiary incurred no additional cost above that of the home jail custody, and at the same time avoided the evil of the discharge of itinerant and other prisoners into their own immediate community. Also, very decided improvement in the conditions of the prisoners was effected by their removal from the county jails to the penitentiary. Instead of idleness, corrupting communications, and the degrading influence of jail confinement, prisoners in the penitentiary were under good hygienic conditions. Corrupting communications among them were almost entirely prevented and their minds and bodily energies were healthfully engaged in useful industry.

Everybody readily appreciated the economic benefit, and thoughtful influential individuals were gratified at the bettered condition of the prisoners. Mr. Pilsbury therefore was a recognized public benefactor. This, together with his high character, sincere devotion, and impressive personality, naturally extended his influence, with the result that similar penitentiary establishments were created at Allegheny, Pennsylvania; Cleveland and Cincinnati, Ohio; Chicago, Illinois; Milwaukee, Wisconsin; six in New York state; and notably the house of correction at Detroit, Michigan, to be hereafter particularly described. Mr. Pilsbury's inspiration and the impulse of his good management at the Albany penitentiary stimulated jail management in Connecticut and Massachusetts, where in the larger jails systematic labor and better general conditions were introduced and established. This admirable movement, which at the time was so promising, for alleviation of the crying evils of the common jail system — evils which since Howard's efforts in the last years of the eighteenth century have been unceasingly denounced by philanthropists and publicists yet exist today substantially as they existed then — came to an end as relates to the penitentiaries in New York in the last years of the nineteenth century. Agitation of the prison labor question by labor organizations, aided by petty politicians, induced legislation prohibitive of the usual productive prison employments, and since the authorities that controlled the county or district penitentiaries did not supply any compensative plan of occupation, the penitentiaries have deteriorated until they are again substantially large common jails not very much better than was the original county lockup.

The two years spent at the Albany penitentiary was a period of severe but serviceable training. The daily duties extended over many hours of ceaseless activity and intense application. These duties included close scrutiny of the prisoners collectively and separately with some discretion as to discipline; the care of institutional sanitation, of the industries and economies, — indeed, all the details of conducting and developing that new and most interesting institution. The performance of the duties, the exercise of authority with its responsibilities, all under tutelage of that master manager, bred self-confidence, born of knowledge and of the lessons of experience.

During that period Mr. Pilsbury recommended my appointment to the wardenship of the Rhode Island prisons. On request I appeared at Providence before the appointing board of which President Francis Wayland of Brown University was the chairman. But the appointment went to Mr. Willard, deputy warden of the state prison at Wethersfield, an applicant for the place, the same Mr. Willard who, after he returned to Wethersfield as a warden, was killed by prisoner Marshall as related. Mr. Willard was older and was adjudged more religious than myself, which considerations mainly influenced his selection. Not at the time nor ever afterward was the decision of the Rhode Island board in preferring Mr. Willard very much of a disappointment to me. It was soon deemed good fortune, and now in retrospect it seems to have been the guidance of good providence to a different destination.

Z. R. BROCKWAY, 1853

JANE WOODHOUSE, 1853

THE MUNICIPAL AND COUNTY ALMSHOUSE AT ALBANY

1853–1854

Ere long, unsolicited and quite unexpectedly, an opportunity opened enabling me to become better acquainted, through study of specimens, with the various classes, numerous in the larger cities, composed of diseased, defective, and dependent denizens who furnish the perennial supply of misdemeanant offenders who people the jails and short-term prisons. The Albany authorities applied to Mr. Pilsbury for his recommendation of a suitable superintendent for the city and county almshouse and infirmary, an establishment situated half a mile from the penitentiary. On his recommendation I was appointed and entered upon my duties there in the year 1853. The intention was to renovate things, to introduce suitable systematic industries and to generally reorganize the whole place with the view to reduce the size of the institutional population and diminish the annual cost of maintaining it. The plant consisted then of two hundred or more acres of fertile land, with buildings stocked with farm utensils and animals. The buildings for the inmates were around an open court, but the hospitals were isolated. One was a general hospital of a hundred beds, a hundred yards away. This was occupied then by ship fever and cholera patients. Another, a smaller building, situated in a field, had twenty smallpox patients. A centrally located commodious building was set apart for offices and the superintendent's residence.

The total composite institutional community numbered more than one thousand. Aside from the occupants of the hospitals there were thirty insane, but these were not provided for in separate quarters. ˙The bulk was made up of women, children, and enfeebled men, abandoned, destitute, and pauperized. Some were young strong women who had been stranded, now comfortably housed, fed, and clothed at the public expense. In addition there were fully a hundred ablebodied men of various nationalities and tongues, housed temporarily at the Albany institution at the instance of the commissioners of immigration at New York City. The immigrants were soon disposed of by putting them to work that winter clearing the docks along the river from great piles of ice which had been forced up and were obstructing business by the breakup in January. After some of the recalcitrants had been committed to the penitentiary, others scattered and found ways to support themselves by work for wages.

The young women went away to work for themselves when they were required to work every day in the almshouse braiding chair seats and doing other systematic service, and all able-bodied inmates soon found the new régime so irksome that they left, singly or in groups. Many hied to the city hall complaining to the authorities there of the bustle and requirements of the almshouse. Within a few weeks from the date of my appointment and my assuming charge the population was reduced from about eleven hundred to less than three hundred real objects of charity, with a corresponding reduction of maintenance expense.

When the city and county governments were apprised of the pitiable state of the insane at the almshouse, an appropriation of money was promptly made to provide a separate building for their care. This building, which was constructed 'under my supervision, I believe to be the first county hospital for insane almshouse patients. Afterwards in New York and in other states similar provision was made for the care of such patients. But the county care plan was hotly opposed by alienists who were in charge of the great state hospitals for the insane. It was, however, no part of our plan at Albany to institute a system of county care for the insane, but simply to relieve at once the distress of the insane in our institution and perhaps provide proper quarters for that moiety of pauper insane liable always to be kept at the county infirmaries.

During that year, 1853, an epidemic of cholera occurred, and many cholera patients were treated in our hospital. The number of deaths from all causes, in six months, reached two hundred and eleven. I myself suffered in July from an attack of incipient cholera and very much more seriously from a run of typhoid fever contracted from the ship fever contagion. My recovery from the typhoid attack was to physicians and all so surprising, and so great is my gratitude, that I must not omit to mention some favorable contributing circumstances. The sick chamber was large and airy and the residence was remote from disturbances. Dr. Thomas Hun of Albany, Dr. Reed Bontecou, my cousin of Troy, and Dr. Rogers, the resident physician, supplied the best possible medical attention. "Ellen," though untrained, was an excellent natural nurse for the days, and "Richard," one of the inmates, a trained nurse from the hospitals in France, supplied the skilful night nursing. Having married in the

April previous to this sickness, the wife's distressful anxiety would have been too painful to be borne but for the presence with us through several weeks of Henry T. Comstock, my brother-in-law, of Connecticut, who suspended his business and came to us and remained through the most trying period, giving the support of his strong, generous character. Except for the happy combination of situation, medical proficiency, skilful nursing, and complete relief from worry, I certainly could not have survived.

Among the inmates was one whose character and career are well worthy of recital; and in addition, my tender remembrance of him prompts me to the narration. He was a natty young Englishman who passed under the name of John White. In appearance he was of gentlemanly bearing, orderly by instinct, and a man of good taste. He was an excellent clerk and unusually inventive and resourceful in details of institutional arrangements and repairs. In short, he was an intelligent and well-disposed man. For the offense of public intoxication he had served a short term in the Albany penitentiary and now, again under arrest, at my solicitation was committed to my custody by resort to an antiquated statutory provision specially resuscitated for the purpose. He was committed for the period of two months. Assigned to clerical duties, he performed them so well during my sickness that on my recovery and at the expiration of his committal, I appointed him assistant superintendent. White continued his faithful and efficient service after his promotion until the time of my resignation preparatory to removal to Rochester, when he took to his cups again and after squandering all but a remnant of his means went home to England. After a brief visit there he re-embarked and returned to America. On shipboard, returning, he discovered his former, but unwon, sweetheart voyaging to America in the service of an English family as governess, — an educated, attractive, and most worthy English maid. The fires of the early attachment were now relighted. White's sobriety and good behavior on shipboard regained her confidence and immediately on reaching New York they were married, going at once to Albany, where White expected to find suitable employment. Disappointed, he took to drink and was soon destitute of means. In this extremity, leaving his new-made wife on charity at Albany, he made his way to me at the penitentiary in Rochester. Half drunk and bedraggled, he appeared at my office one morning. Fortunately I was able to give employment to both himself and his wife on the staff at the penitentiary, where they rendered admirable service for full six years.

In the year 1861, when I took charge of the house of correction in Detroit, White, intending to enter service with me there, shipped his household goods and left Rochester for Detroit, preceding Mrs. White to prepare a place for her. But for some weeks he did not report for duty nor could he be located. Finally, he was found locked in a room over a saloon in Detroit, his money gone, goods and clothing pledged for drink, and himself on the verge of delirium tremens. However, I employed him again and Mrs. White came on to Detroit, where for several years they lived happily, giving the same excellent service they had rendered at Rochester. Then, suddenly, much to my discomfiture and ruinously to himself, he appeared one day within the prison intoxicated and boisterous, and committed an atrocious assault upon an inoffensive youthful prisoner. For this he was necessarily discharged, and with my aid he went with Mrs. White back to England, to the home of his father, who was an influential man of means. On the death of his father, which occurred about five years after White's return, he succeeded to a considerable estate, of which, by his sustained probity, he had shown himself worthy. He was a total abstainer, a radical and prominent temperance advocate, and gained public confidence as shown by his appointment to a responsible borough office. He died in 1901, aged eighty-five years. Mr. White remained always grateful for the forbearance and aid he received in America. For twenty-five years preceding his last illness, and until physically unable to write, he every week mailed to my address, superscribed in his perfect chirography, some English newspaper or publication, and irregularly but frequently sent letters, always freighted with grateful expressions of his appreciation.

Now, having had at Wethersfield and at Albany contact with and observation of three several divisions of anti-social inhabitants — heinous criminals, misdemeanant offenders, malingerers, together with unfortunate and worthier dependents; inspired anew by gratitude for the three instances of remarkable preservation from accidents and sickness, my inclination toward this field of philanthropic occupation was greatly strengthened. Increased confidence and encouragement were derived from administrative experiences. The wife and little daughter served to settle domesticities so that I was ready and eager for advancement to new opportunities and enlarged responsibility. On recommendation of Mr. Pilsbury, I was appointed by the board of supervisors of Monroe County, superintendent of the new county penitentiary at Rochester, not then completed nor open for the reception of prisoners. In the autumn of 1854 I entered on duty there. I was then twenty-seven years of age.

CHAPTER IV

AT ROCHESTER: MONROE COUNTY PENITENTIARY

1854–1861

IN THE bearing on my subsequent career, the
seven years from 1854 to 1861 spent at Rochester in charge of the penitentiary there was
a period of enlarged experience in management, of
contemplative penological inquiry, and of the emer-
gence of deep religious feeling and the formation of a
remarkable personal friendship.

The Monroe County Penitentiary establishment,
though certified completed, was not yet in commission.
It was therefore my duty and privilege after furnishing
and provisioning it to open the institution by receiving
prisoners and instituting the governance, — an agreeable function exercised again afterward at the Detroit
House of Correction and at the Elmira Reformatory.
The state laws and the local legislative authority — the
board of county supervisors — gave to the superintendent large discretionary powers; and the three
official inspectors, who were inexperienced in prison
matters, lived remote and held only quarterly meetings.
They were kept well informed about everything, but
wisely did not assume the direction of affairs. The
inspectors never interfered with the selection of sub-

ordinate officers or in the distribution of patronage. From the very beginning at Rochester, as was equally the case at the Albany penitentiary, the supervisory managers held aloof from competitions of personal or partisan benefits and fully sustained the superintendent's impartiality.

Imbued with the notion that prisons should be made self-supporting by productive employment of prisoners, that public expenditure for prisons should be limited to the cost of providing the plant, the matter of selecting and organizing the prison industries became at first and naturally the central purpose of management at this new county prison. Even now, in the light of the reformatory purpose which latterly has so much replaced the economic consideration, the moving principle — profit from industries — should not be decried, for it was then, and in the last analysis is now, the mainspring of civic advancement, the foundation of individual development, and good economies are demanded by local public opinion and needful to insure popular support. For the sake of profit from their labor and income from the small weekly stipulated sum for their care we solicited and induced the surrounding counties to send their jail prisoners to our penitentiary, as was already authorized by law and was the practice at Albany and the surrounding counties there.

For the purpose of making such an arrangement and executing contracts, the superintendent of the penitentiary visited the several counties during the sessions of their supervisors to explain and advocate the plan. This for me was a new and useful exercise of personal persuasion. No very troublesome opposition to prison employment from labor organizations or others was encountered. Agitation about the different systems — the contract, public account, piece plan, and state supply systems — was not then afoot. But serious embarrassment to our prison employments was soon experienced, growing out of the general business depression that occurred. The contractors who were paying us a day wage for prisoners at work in the prison factories suddenly abandoned their contracts, creating the alternative either to suffer incident disorganization and demoralization, the product of idleness, or proceed without any appropriation for capital to carry on manufacturing on public account.

Here it should be remarked that the plan for occupying the time and the energies of the prisoners without achieving earnings, which thirty years later was adopted at the Elmira Reformatory, had not yet been conceived, nor in the then state of public sentiment could it have been undertaken. It was also thought useless to convene an extra session of the supervisors with a view to procuring from that board the necessary operating capital, so that after conference with the inspectors it was decided that the superintendent should shift for money and credit as best he could and carry on prison industries as he might be able to do.

By means of borrowing here and there on my note, endorsed by Mr. Conkey, a wealthy and financially responsible man of our board of inspectors; by the accommodation of payments in advance for goods to be made and delivered; by purchase of raw materials on long time credit and renewal and extension of matured obligations, the industrial interests of the penitentiary were kept alive through the period of business depression. But the burden of providing thus the business capital, foisted upon the management throughout the whole period of my incumbency, was a questionable policy. However, the experience of such financing, buying, and selling; of manufacturing profitably with the labor of short term prisoners — men and women — of the worthless class in the community; the selection and direction of assistants, provisioning, and disciplining, — the personal attention to all the current details of this comparatively small prison, — supplied, I believe, the most valuable preliminary practical training I could possibly have had for the future managerial duty for which I was destined. Fortunately, the economic result was satisfactorily successful; the prisoners' earnings, together with income from other counties for care of their prisoners, were sufficient here, as similar resources were at Albany, to defray all the cost of maintenance and to leave a considerable margin of surplus. This feature more than any other attracted outside attention and additionally stimulated founding such misdemeanant prisons in other states. It was also, perhaps, the main consideration that induced the municipal authorities of Detroit, Michigan, to tender me the position of superintendent of their new unfinished house of correction — an appointment which in 1861 I accepted.

Besides the benefit to myself of successfully contending with the depressed, even panicky, business conditions of the time, establishing and preserving the industrial and general integrity of the institution, I had the further advantage of having an adverse unjust criticism promptly refuted. In the year 1858, when we were soliciting from the board of county supervisors an appropriation of money for additional buildings and manufacturing facilities, and I was devotedly and somewhat anxiously engaged in working out the good results which were finally achieved, there appeared in the daily press the first and second of an intended series of articles, signed "Tax-Payer," offering objection to furnishing the money and opposing, generally, the policy we had adopted. The author of the articles was known to be an educated man living on his farm within the county, supposed to be emulous of local political preferment which he hoped to effect by posing as watchful of public expenditures. In the articles he attacked the business management of the penitentiary, arguing from my published reports, which he either garbled or erroneously quoted. He alleged that my reports were intentionally illusory; an intimation of disingenuousness that wounded my sensibilities and instigated the reply which brought to a sudden termination the projected series of articles. The attack seems now of very trifling consequence, scarcely worth mentioning, but at the time it seemed otherwise. And, indeed, it was important to me, being the first of numerous similar experiences to which I was destined; experiences quite sure to be suffered by any prison official who remains a long time in the service.

I have said above that the result of our early efforts at this penitentiary was "fortunate." The word is well chosen, for, though the policy pursued was justifiable, — nay, inevitable, —yet except for favoring circumstances apparently beyond any human determination, my prison managing career would then, no doubt, have been brought to its close.

Now, under the prompting of duty to be faithful in this record of events and experiences and in consideration of my later work with prisoners, I feel that I am warranted, in spite of instinctive reluctance, in alluding to a personal experience during those years at Rochester which ordinarily would be held sacredly private. That "City of Revivals" was profoundly moved under the religious ministrations of Charles G. Finney, a notable evangelist of that time. The slumbering religiousness of many people, including men of the learned professions and others recognized as intellectually able, was developed to open demonstration. At first and for a considerable time I refrained from participation, but later, partly influenced by the prevalent mental and moral contagion and in compliance with the request of a much loved friend, I attended some of the public religious services. The mind and methods of Mr. Finney, his logical reasoning and his restrained fervor, made strong appeal to my native tendencies, with the result that I, too, openly espoused Christianity and united myself with the Plymouth Congregational Church. My wife also joined, and our children were baptized.

This epoch was, naturally, followed by religious activities according to commonly accepted orthodox methods. After serving a while as teacher of a class in the Plymouth Church Sunday school I was made superintendent. Several of us, newly interested in religion, organized and conducted a cordon of mission Sunday schools in the suburbs of the city. Neighborhood house to house religious meetings were held.

Soon there appeared at the mission Sunday school centers, simultaneously, an unusual revival in religious interest. Naturally, too, dating from this epoch, new interest was aroused in the moral welfare of the prisoners of my charge; an interest which then at Rochester and afterwards for the first few years at Detroit took on and was limited to the usual evangelistic forms and methods. But later at the Detroit House of Correction evangelizing effort was supplemented with rational educational endeavor; and still later, notably at the Elmira Reformatory, a scientific cultural system of regeneration was substituted for evangelistic efforts. It is needful now, in order to avoid misapprehension, to say that, through all the years since the arousal at Rochester of quickened religious sensibilities, beneath and permeating investigations, experimentations, and any apparent radical change of opinion or of attitude relating to religion and reformations, I have suffered no abatement of faith in the existence and immanence of the Infinite-Creative-Formative-Force by which all things are, and move, and have their being. The change of view that has wrought change of attitude and of methods relates only to the theologies, ecclesiastical ceremonies, and to professionalism.

For friendships formed in my early middle life I am much indebted, particularly for two, to the religious awakening in Rochester and another at Detroit. Both of these friendships I shall mention in the course of this narrative, for without such mention these notes would be seriously marred and quite deficient. To such friendships is attributable my rescue from misanthropy, the effect of long close contact with criminals who were selfish, pitiless, degenerate, and utterly untrustworthy. The misanthropic mood if entertained would have discouraged, disqualified, and probably have turned me away from my vocation. The intimacy of personal friendly relation maintained these fifty-seven years with William R. Seward of Rochester, New York, is, as an oasis in the desert, restful, refreshing, and redeeming.

Mr. Seward, five years my junior, was a banker (now retired). He co-operated in the early religious activities before referred to. Our mutual confidences and similarities of sentiment soon cemented the unusual and enduring friendship that still exists. He inherited his religiousness, as a very Samuel, and from his childhood developed in the family and elsewhere remarkable spirituality of mind with love for and practice of religious observances and persuasions. Besides his daily ministrations of considerate kindnesses all through his life he has used his banker's knowledge and opportunities, without fee or other reward than his inner consciousness of benevolence, to aid widows, orphans, and other inexperienced and easily fleeced persons to invest safely and profitably, thus gaining for them comparative pecuniary independence in place of penury and distress which otherwise might have been their lot. I myself through his agency have been similarly benefited. His combination of qualities — excellent banker's ability, with uniform practical benevolence — I have rarely met with in business and never exactly found equalled within my own observation. After thirty years of continual service in banking, nominally the cashier, but really the chief manager of the bank of his connection, he withdrew for conscience' sake when new stockholders adopted a policy he could not endorse; retired without an adequate competency of means, but soon, almost miraculously, by a fortunate investment which he had reluctantly made found himself in affluence. With his advancing age and abreast of modern theologic thought, he espoused the "Brotherhood" movement at Rochester, under the leadership of Mr. Algernon S. Crapsey, the Episcopal clergyman deposed from the Saint Andrews rectorate for his alleged heretical opinions. Here Mr. Seward's liberality, cordiality, and great-heartedness give strong support to the Brotherhood movement. To myself, in times of discouragement and under trials, the consciousness of his firm friendship has proved a solace and strong support for which, with the other benefits received, I here attest my sense of deep obligation.

At the point in the Rochester experience now in mind — the time of special emotional awakening — the importance of the welfare of the prisoners assumed enlarged proportions; not less regard for the material objects of management, but increased interest in the essential immaterial, spiritual things and relations. This different mental attitude induced close contemplation of the prisoners there as viewed en masse, in classified groups, and studied individually. This different attitude incited, also, scrutiny of the means employed for their betterment. Belief was prevalent that every good must come mysteriously and directly from the supernatural source. More and more the chaplain preached and prayed and redoubled his persuasiveness; yet no miraculous moral changes were manifested. Everything remained substantially the same. The prisoners made no opposition; they were simply indifferent, and apparently their indifference was from want of comprehension. They were men and women, mostly adults of full age, habitually dissolute, generally dishonest, gathered in by the police and committed by the police court out of the city slums, sentenced for short terms of days or weeks or a few months at most, — police court and penitentiary rounders, an unpromising company of fellow beings to be benefited by cultural endeavor; and it seemed the invoked miraculous agency could but tarry. I seemed powerless either to originate or support measures for their reclamation or restraint from fresh crimes when soon again they must be released. Seriously I questioned my obligation at my time of life and with due regard to my family interests, to remain longer in the prison service. If then an opportunity had opened I should no doubt have turned aside to some other occupation. But no open avenue appeared and just then, in my sore dilemma, commissioners from Detroit came and offered me the superintendency of their new house of correction just finished and ready for occupancy. The commissioners explained that by legislation already enacted the house of correction was to receive and treat for reformation the usual municipal offenders, such as we had at Rochester and Albany, together with the more youthful criminals from the state prison at Jackson. In the exalted mental state of that period the offer seemed an illumined pathway, a providential leading, and it was gladly accepted.

CHAPTER V

THE DETROIT HOUSE OF CORRECTION

1861–1872

THE strongest inducement which moved me to accept the superintendency of the Detroit House of Correction, a service upon which I entered in April, 1861, was the reasonable hope for a better opportunity there to accomplish useful reformation of the prisoners to be confined in that new institution. Such expectation was quite justified by the favorable attitude of the influential men who were promoting the scheme of the house of correction then in process of construction; by the existing bad conditions in Detroit, as to frequency of crimes, pernicious police practice, insufficient jail accommodations, and pestilential influence of jail imprisonments. The situation was particularly promising of usefulness because of the statute enacted that year, which allowed conditional confinement of young felons in the house of correction instead of in the state prison at Jackson under such long terms of sentence as under existing statutes would necessarily have been imposed for felony. It is believed that this Michigan law (1861) is the first legislation in America which discriminates, for the purpose of prison treatment, between felons of sixteen to twenty-one years of age and older criminals. Thus was

68

presented to hand the very opportunity so earnestly desired. The act of 1861 is as follows:

"Upon completion of a contract between the inspectors of the state prison and the city of Detroit for the keeping of prisoners in the Detroit House of Correction, any male under the age of twenty-one years and over sixteen years of age who shall be convicted of any offense, murder and treason excepted, punishable by imprisonment in the state prison, may in the discretion of the court be sentenced to imprisonment in the said house of correction.

"And every male between the ages of sixteen and twenty-one who shall for the first time be convicted of any offense, murder and treason excepted, punishable by imprisonment in the state prison, shall be sentenced to imprisonment therein. Also *every female* who shall be convicted of any offense, murder and treason excepted, punishable by imprisonment in the state prison, shall be sentenced to imprisonment therein."

Although this act proved abortive, considerable historical interest should attach to the fact that the state of Michigan more than fifty years ago was the first state to establish institutions and methods for state care of the dependent, defective, and dangerous classes. In this connection it should be explained that the tardiness of Michigan in adopting the indeterminate sentence system is not fairly attributable to inert and sluggish popular sentiment, but rather to the technical conservatism of her supreme court at the time when the constitutionality of such a law was first referred for the court's decision.

As early as the year 1857 there were leading men in Detroit and elsewhere in Michigan alive to the unsatisfactory state of the jails and crime conditions in the community, although the conditions were similar to those of other states and cities where no particular interest was manifested. The *Advertiser and Tribune*, edited by J. F. Connor, had agitated the topic of a house of correction a year previously, in 1856, and Mayor Hyde communicated to the common council his recommendation, the reports of the Monroe County Penitentiary at Rochester, New York, being cited to show that such an institution could be made to be self-sustaining by the labor of prisoners. In 1857 I visited Detroit on invitation of the common council for the purpose of consultation as to an eligible location for the proposed house of correction. The project which then seemed ripe was delayed in execution, however, mainly by reason of the general financial depression which occurred in the autumn of 1857; and further delay was occasioned by competition of land owners to sell their outlying property to the city for a site, so that it was not until 1861 that the house of correction, even then but partly completed, was actually put into commission.

While the public motive in its establishment was protection from crime and the anticipated financial benefits, these did not exclude the moral consideration so honorable to the sentiment of that time. This is evident by the report of a committee to the common council in 1857, which says:

"Still another class (other than the dangerous class) appeals to our consideration; namely, the young who are to be reformed and added to the ranks of good citizenship by the corrective and reformatory policy embraced in the legislative provisions cited. Who can calculate the irremediable injury that has ensued to thousands of tender youth of both sexes who from some trifling infraction of the laws, induced by want of preventive restraint and moral training, have necessarily been sent to confinement to the general receptacle of criminals of every age and sex, where the little of their better nature still left in them is speedily eradicated forever, and the seeds of vice and crime rooted more deeply in their place by the pernicious contact? Who can answer the question how many of the inmates of our state penitentiary might have been saved to become good and useful members of society, had the mild and humane system of corrective discipline shed its gentle influences around their pathway? And what friend of this most needed safeguard to the young generations of our city would prefer to see a narrow and illiberal policy pursued here? Let us see to it that we provide for this want upon a scale commensurate with its great importance. It must be borne in mind that this institution (the House of Correction) is to occupy the position of a home to the friendless, rather than as a place of punishment. The city is to stand for the time being in the parental relation to those unfortunates who, deprived of their natural guardianship, are tempted on the threshold of crime. . . . Its object is to reform and restore the young, who have been tempted, before it is too late."

This quotation from a public document shows the lofty sentiment in the public advocacy of the enterprise, and suggests the high expectations that were then formed. Another brief quotation from a special committee of the common council, whose chairman was John J. Bagley, afterwards governor of Michigan, and a member of the first board of inspectors of the house of correction, will show how well the immediate projectors in those early days of prison reform had grasped not only the benevolent purpose but also the principles of organization and means of reformation required. He mentions as the objects to be sought:

71

"First, the moral influence to be thrown around those who are to be imprisoned; second, the physical improvement of the prisoners; and third, the pecuniary gain to the taxpayers, arising from the labor of the prisoners as contributing to their own subsistence.

"The moral benefits will be derived from the separation of the sexes from each other, and of the youth from hardened criminals, — indeed, from the isolation and separation of each prisoner from the moment of his entrance to the institution; from the habit of industry to come from compulsory labor at first; from the strict discipline to be enforced; from the instructions in the Sabbath school and chapel services, and from the important fact that prisoners on their release from the House of Correction will be in great degree free from that prison stigma that so attaches to the jail bird and state prison convict ordinarily."

The report goes on to speak of the physical benefits to be derived by the diseased and dissipated persons to be confined there; enters in detail into statistics and arguments to show the economical advantages to be expected; and concludes with the recommendation, followed by the formal motion of the chairman, to appoint me as the superintendent. This final report, of which the above is only a fragment, was at once adopted, the superintendent duly appointed, and the Detroit House of Correction was then and there launched on what was at that time in Michigan considered a somewhat novel career as a place for treating common jail prisoners for their industrial, educational, and moral good.

Mr. Bagley, by his activity and influence as a member of the city council and a public spirited citizen, probably contributed more to the establishment of the house of correction than any other single individual.

He gave a cordial and important support to its superintendent and to the measures adopted at the house of correction, not only during his brief term as inspector, which terminated with the first year of its activities, but officially and unofficially he remained my personal friend until his death which, too early, occurred July 27, 1881, when he was but forty-nine years old.

In personal appearance Governor Bagley was tall, large, swarthy, with a long, full beard, and an open, benevolent countenance. He was a large-minded man with penetrating, clear, quick perceptions, unusually strong domestic affections, and responsive humanitarian impulses. With tender religious susceptibilities he made no formal religious profession nor expressed regard for religious institutions and observances except for their social and civilizing use. His excellent personal qualities, together with his affability and generosity, insured his popularity; his unfailing common sense, instructive philosophic insight, and unquestioned moral integrity, together constituted him a remarkably safe guide in important public affairs; and his broad philanthropy, thus based, affected favorbly general public sentiment, and led him to attempt and achieve valuable improvements in the penal, reformatory, and charitable institutions of the state. Governor Bagley's special message to the Michigan state legislature, February 12, 1873 (twelve years after the opening of the Detroit House of Correction), shows the enterprise, wisdom, and grasp of his mind in such relations. He said:

"The prevention, cure, and punishment of crime demand most careful attention not only of legislatures but of the whole people. . . . There is being evolved a better knowledge of improved treatment of crime; kindness is taking the place of brutality . . . reformation of punishment. . . . We ought to classify and grade the inmates of the institutions of the state and thus prevent the demonstration that prison life spreads like a pall over all who suffer crime. . . . We would not treat the cattle on our farms in the present manner. . . . The 'House of Shelter' at Detroit, now in connection with the House of Correction, is my ideal of what all prisons might be; not only for women and girls, but for men and boys — or rather it is my ideal of the plan upon which prisons should be erected and administered. . . . I earnestly hope that the confinement of any person in jail *after conviction* will be absolutely prohibited. . . . The striped prison dress should be abolished. . . . Give the prisoner a portion of his earnings as a reward and incentive. . . . They should have opportunity to learn trades by which they could earn their living when they are discharged."

Governor Bagley favored the "indeterminate sentence" plan, which was brought to his and to public attention in 1870. He also recommended a visiting agency for the care of children sent out to families by public institutions, a recommendation which was adopted. He urged the legislature to appoint a commission to examine thoroughly all the criminal laws of the state and to report a revision of the same, which was done. The Coldwater State School for dependent children largely owes its existence to Governor Bagley's influence; the Adrian Reform School for Girls would not have existed if Governor Bagley had not lived; the Reform School at Lansing became a truer type under his administration as governor of the state. He was instrumental in enlarging and greatly improving the

The Detroit House of Correction

state prison at Jackson—providing a new chapel and an admirable school building, facilities and improvements which toned up the whole prison establishment. His total life, as a citizen and business man, in his official relations as a member of the municipal government and during his administration as governor of the state, was successful, noble, and always characterized by a genuine regard for the less fortunate of his fellow creatures.

To resume the account of the development of the house of correction: The date (August 1, 1861) when it was first opened for the reception of prisoners, was most inauspicious for launching such a public enterprise. It was near the commencement of our great civil war. The disheartening effect of the defeat of northern troops in the month of July was at its height. All branches of manufacture were at a standstill; the general business of the country was deranged. Able-bodied men of the class from which prisoners usually come had quite generally enlisted as volunteers in the army, so that it was with a small number of miserable women and broken-down men transferred from the county jail that the house of correction was opened. The people of Detroit were looking with much hope for some salutary influence on the city, so long and urgently needed, from the opening and administration of the new institution, whose success seemed so dependent upon the normal conditions which govern success in right enterprises generally, just then so greatly disturbed.

The buildings had been provided at a cost of $80,000 exclusive of the cost of the site. They were well arranged for economical supervision and use, supplied with good sanitary and other conveniences, and flooded with light from the large corridor windows. The walls were white and there was a grassy interior court. Outside and inside it presented a cheerful aspect not usual in prisons of that day. The general objects of the institution were well and clearly defined with special reference to the treatment of the offenders in whom I had already become greatly interested, — the disorderly and criminal element of cities, — a class which, in times of national peace, is mostly composed of persons of both sexes who are between sixteen and thirty years of age. How well the board of inspectors had become imbued with a true theory of methods and how comprehensive was their benevolence appears from the earlier of their reports.

It was intended that the house of correction should accomplish much for the hitherto neglected class of common jail prisoners. Mental and moral isolation, under our "social-silent" or "Auburn system," thorough supervision, strict discipline, with complete occupation of all their waking hours, — this was the system designed for improvement of the prisoners, who were to be vigorously engaged in instructive and remunerative mechanical work, with opportunity to earn something for themselves while imprisoned, either by allowance for overwork or by a co-operative system, or both together. They were to be supplied with employment on their release and supervised for a period — substantially the same methods that have since been here and there established under the indeterminate sentence system. A complete educational plan was early outlined in the mind of the management, which should include some effort at education for all the prisoners, old and young, men and women, short and long sentenced prisoners. Special efforts for the religious impression of the prisoners by public, private, and carefully arranged ministrations were also included in these early plans. And, beyond the immediate conduct of the house of correction, the management contemplated establishing, in connection therewith, a reform school for girls and an industrial home or lodge for the temporary care of discharged worthy prisoners awaiting employment.

With the exception of the co-operative industrial home or refuge for discharged prisoners and only partial realization of the girls' reform school in the form of the "house of shelter" to be hereafter mentioned, the forecast of theory and practice just mentioned was remarkably fulfilled and almost to complete demonstration during the years of my superintendency. While an institution such as was contemplated but never realized, for the temporary care of discharged prisoners and to provide transient employment for indigent persons not criminals, might have proved useful as connected with the house of correction and supported, as it would then have been supported, by the exceptionally intelligent and benevolent prevailing sentiment, it could not, probably, have long endured the changes that subsequently took place in the government of this institution. That this part of the original scheme was not carried out is not now, in retrospect, at all disappointing; not alone for the reason stated, but also because it is questionable whether such institutions for discharged prisoners can be made more helpful than harmful. If, under the determinate sentence system, there is apparent need of such establishments (and granting their usefulness in some individual instances), it is nevertheless evident that under the indeterminate sentence system they are unnecessary, wrong in principle, and as such existing resorts for ex-convicts are administered, they are often damaging and a public menace.

Reformation of prisoners which affords adequate measure of public protection from their further crimes must include rehabilitation, by which is meant reabsorption of reformed individuals into the mass of industrious orderly inhabitants, putting out of sight completely, if gradually, from the common recollection and from any degrading self-consciousness, the former fault and imprisonment. As a gunshot imbedded in the flesh may become encysted, the wound healed, the injury be unobserved and unconsciously borne, so the injury of a criminal act and conviction may be covered with the cloak of constant good behavior and fade from the discharged prisoners' habitual remembrance, in its cyst of conscious social rectitude. Due preparation for such rehabilitation must be had during prison treatment, as in modern reformatory prisons, and tested by conditional release. Any interval between departure from prison and entrance upon the intended legitimate career is unnecessary and should be avoided. Especially should there be no interval of idleness or fugitive, divertive engagements, nor association with discharged convicts such as is inevitable in existing "convict homes."

I believe the good intended by the benevolent projectors of such homes is often counterbalanced by unintended and unavoidable evils. The evil is included in the institutional inheritance — the gathering together, in one home and habitation, of a number of persons of similar regrettable history, devoid, by their circumstances, of the normal counteracting social influences of ordinary free society, and unable to at once pursue their trade or permanent occupation. The utmost care on the part of attendants and the extremest religious effort by the supervisors cannot in the freedom of such houses obviate the evil. It is also possible, as experience has shown, for them to become centers of criminousness from which, covertly, thieves make incursions to other places, returning there for safety, and even carrying and secreting there the stolen goods. Good and evil are always closely associated with each other — inextricably interwoven, a fact very apparent to those who are closely acquainted with institutions having the care of the defective, dependent, and delinquent. The intended good is uncertain, the associated evil is sure, for which reasons it is often the part of prudence to withhold the good endeavor for the sake of avoiding the certain evil.

The financial results at this municipal prison in Detroit were deemed phenomenal. The prisons throughout the country were generally reporting greater deficits of earnings to meet expenses than in previous years, occasioned by the increased cost of necessaries for subsistence and a reduced number of prisoners as laborers, attributable to enlistments for the war. Yet at the house of correction at the close of the second full year of operation, when the number of prisoners had averaged only 58 males and 68 females, all serving but brief periods, the deficit was very small — exactly $2,237.83. The third year, with the average of prisoners only sixteen more, the income exceeded the expenses by $2,011.80. From this time on an annual profit was derived to the city from this prison establishment: the fourth year, $10,097.27; fifth year, $20,108.32; and, when ten years had passed, the tenth year showed a profit of $34,303.90, and the whole period from the very beginning a balance profit of $103,004.50. This profit to the public treasury was derived from the labor of prisoners and for the support of prisoners sent from other counties, over and above all maintenance expenses (among which is an expenditure of $74,497.65 for items not usually included in current institutional expenses, such as repairs and alterations), interest on borrowed capital, gratuities to prisoners on their discharge, the house of shelter experiment, etc. — and with an average prison population of 269.6, of which 96.7 were females, whose period of detention averaged for the five years immediately preceding the decennial statement only about ninety-five days.

It cannot be inappropriate to add, since it suggests the soundness of the industrial system then introduced, that excellent financial results have since been attained at this institution. The published reports — the fortieth (1901) and the forty-first (1902) — show that prisoners were still detained for about the same short average time — ninety-two days — but the gain over cost for 1901 was $36,478.77, for 1902, $26,179.57. The number of prisoners confined and employed was, however, greatly increased. These late reports also contain the gratifying intelligence that the evening school which was organized at the very beginning — more than forty years before — was still maintained.

Co-eval and correlative with the economic management and results were the efforts introduced for improving the prisoners themselves, more comprehensive, forceful, and effectual than had ever hitherto been known for American prisons and prisoners of this class. Any just appreciation of this reformative painstaking at the house of correction which, at this writing, appears but a rough-hewn model for the better perfected system afterward built up at Elmira, requires further reference to the forbidding character of the class of prisoners.

It should be recalled that the prisoners were chiefly misdemeanants, adults of the common jail class who were imprisoned for short terms averaging less than one hundred days. The total number of prisoners received in the ten years was 8744, or 6339 men and 2405 women; 8305 were released, leaving in confinement 439 prisoners at the close of our decennial period, December 31, 1871. Of the prisoners received, 6600 were from the city and county where the house of correction is located, out of the slums of a considerable city and populous community; 2045 were from rural communities — the 36 contracting counties in Michigan; and only 99 were federal prisoners convicted and sentenced for longer terms in the United States courts in far western territories.

One of the seriously interposing obstacles to any systematic improving efforts for such prisoners was their early and often premature release: 6077 were discharged at the expiration of their brief terms of sentence, while 2228 did not complete their sentence, being prematurely released — not infrequently through the influence of petty politicians, procurers, former convivial associates, and mistaken alleged philanthropists — by means of the bail process, payment or remission of fines, habeas corpus proceedings, pardon, and peremptory order of court.

On their reception at the prison these prisoners, almost without exception, were penniless, and for one reason or another generally incapable of exercising common human providence in their own affairs: 50 per cent of them were above thirty years of age and the remainder were not juveniles but adults; 43 per cent could not read or write, while those certified as capable in this regard were usually not proficient enough to derive pleasure or profit from books and correspondence. Nor were the more promising susceptible class of prisoners received those intended, by the before mentioned act of 1861, to be confined and treated in the house of correction instead of the state prison, and whose prospective custody and care under my supervision constituted the chief motive for my change of field from Rochester to Detroit. That class never formed any part of the prison population at the house of correction. This failure of the law and plan was an overwhelming disappointment that nearly wrecked my hopeful ambition and too definitely assumptive faith. The law was plain enough upon its face, only conditioned upon the action of the state prison inspectors and managing board of the house of correction as to when these youthful prisoners could be transferred. Apparently there existed no obstacle to this mere formal procedure. When that was done then my heart's desire would be met and another step be taken in the line of providential leading! Naturally some delay must occur, but only a few weeks passed for conferences over the written rough outline of points to be considered, when one day — how well I remember the occasion — the last conference was held at the office of the house of correction, the points one by one were finally considered and modified, differences removed and an agreement reached, and the way made clear. So strong had been my hope, so apparent the mystic guidance, that the completion of the agreement with its opening vista of coveted opportunities produced an overpowering spiritual exaltation never since perhaps quite equalled in my experience, but it was doomed to an early and most depressing disappointment. The memory of it now gives realistic interpretation to Longfellow's lines:

> "Keen is the most exalted state,
> Relentless sweeps the stroke of fate."

The very day the mutual understanding was concluded, the whole matter was submitted, for the draft of a formal contract, to United States Senator Jacob Howard, our attorney present then in Detroit, when, to the amazement of all parties and to my own consternation, we were advised that the act under which we were proceeding was clearly in contravention of the state constitution; that any contract intended to carry out the provisions of that law would be void; and that any prisoners transferred from the state prison to the house of correction, as contemplated, could easily gain their release by habeas corpus proceedings and have good claim for damages on suit for false imprisonment.

The disappointment produced at first within myself a violent and painful revulsion of feeling from exaltation to depression, with chagrin at the foolish faith I had reposed in a supposedly traceable providential leading. It was a trying crisis of my inner moral life and would have proved disastrous but for unplanned favoring circumstances. A rash over-expression of my inward tumult was somewhat restrained by the immediate social environment. The dictates of common prudence induced deliberation. The previously mentioned schoolday incident of surrender to necessity assisted. My native caution aided, and withal a law of human nature that no mood is long sustained without a change, served to hold in harmless leash the turbulence of my feelings until in time reflection wrought a restoration of belief in the existence of universal ruling moral order. But never since that convulsive inward agitation have I again so presumptuously assumed to know, forecast, and follow any apparently particular providential indication.

The change of view as to the functioning of the inscrutable universal influence in the affairs of men, and the consequent changes of means and methods used for reformation, might not inappropriately, so far as my own agency is concerned, be reckoned the birth of more scientific methods of reformatory treatment of prisoners in America, which as developed in Elmira has become recognized the world over as one of the three distinctive theories of penological science.

In place of previous assent to the inconsistent doctrine of an exclusive anthropomorphic Infinite Being corralled in edifices — temples, cathedrals, churches, cloisters — governing from the outside at the instance of apostolical agents, or adherents of specific dogmas, the Infinite was now conceived of as the highest ultimate principle of all existences, absolutely immaterial, the basis of the order of the universe, operating always, everywhere; the divinely purposeful immanence whose ways are to us incomprehensible. Religiousness, which had been accredited only to declared believers, church communicants, observers of ceremonials and those following a certain standard of behavior, now seemed to be the native quality of all humanity, of all who, however dimly, see or feel in reverence or in awe a Power beyond the human ken — and who does not so see or feel?

The ancient doctrine of the independent freedom of the human will and the correlative belief in unconditioned retributive moral accountabilty was also put aside as an incomprehensible theory for any human administration. We must invade the will of those committed to our charge and determine their behavior quite outside their own election. The dismissal thus of these old doctrines — of an outside governing passionate God; of free will and responsibility as measured out by human hands — cleared the field of our endeavor and opened wide to science that which had been dominated by sentiment alone.

CHAPTER VI

FEDERAL PRISONERS IN DETROIT

PREVIOUS to relating the unusual cultural means introduced and used in connection with sustained religious endeavor for all the prisoners, I venture to give an account of the contingent composed of the before mentioned ninety-nine federal long-term prisoners. They did not constitute an element compensative for the youthful long-term prisoners whom we had expected to have transferred to us from the state prison, nor did their presence require any considerable change of régime; but, taken together, they were an interesting contingent possessed of positive characteristics in marked contrast with the characterlessness of the misdemeanor prisoners. I have chosen typical men of the group.

Stewart, one of the far western prisoners near forty years of age, was a large man, not stout but rugged, shapely not handsome, with brown hair, gray eyes, strong masculine countenance, muscular and iron nerved. Of sanguine temperament he was yet of quiet mien, with a smooth low voice. He was a deliberate, determined character, and a natural leader of men. Being sensible and self-controlled he did not come into conflict with the prison routine. He was never disturbed by trivial annoyances, and was too wary to engage in forlorn schemes, but with a fair show for success he was ready to face any danger. He neither sought nor desired any special consideration, and for favors voluntarily bestowed seemed not unmindful though scarceful grateful. He could suffer injustice without show of retaliating or weakly forgiving. The pitiful moved no tenderness in him, but he did not gloat at cruelty. Religious ministrations were neither despised nor respected. Apparently capable of strong attachments, lack of friendship gave no pain of deprivation. Neither cheerful nor sad, he sat broodingly in his cell or elsewhere adjusted himself to the prison routine as one who is philosophically reconciled to the inevitable, but at the same time portentously biding his time and opportunity. Had Stewart been well-educated and his lot appropriately cast, he would have inclined to materialism in metaphysics, to stoicism in philosophy, and to militarism for a profession and vocation. This strong, interesting character was inaccessible to any ordinary familiar approach and quite immune to a chaplain's direct appeal — the "personal touch." Strange that such a man should be a criminal! He was not natively, professionally, or habitually a criminal, though he was in prison for felony and after his release did further crime. He was the product of environment such as prevails in rude society where each inhabitant is a law unto himself, the creature of circumstances.

The following prison incident with which Stewart was connected is illustrative of a phase of his character. On a bleak night fourteen prisoners gained access from their cells to the corridor. This was accomplished by means of a false key and an ingenious mechanism invented, made, and used by one of the fourteen, who first released himself and then the others with intent to escape. Stewart refused to leave his cell until a breach in the outer wall should be completed, but he counseled them as back and forth from breachwork to Stewart's cell the escaping prisoners sought advice. This was the extent of his proven participation. The night watchman was captured, bound, gagged, and confined in a cell with a prisoner placed over him as guard. So restless was the captured watchman that it was thought to kill him and Stewart's advice was sought. He hesitated, then in his quiet way said, "No, not now, for if you are surprised and the escape prevented it would be an awkward situation to find the watchman dead; and, if you do escape, his death would stimulate pursuit and detection. Wait a little and see how things go." Neither hunger for tragedy nor sense of pity influenced his decision, nor was he restrained by fear of final consequences. He was governed in this advice by his judgment of good immediate policy, simply that.

Since, as relates to this affair, inhibition to murder was the product of judgment apparently uninfluenced by moral principle or compassion, the inquiry at once arose whether the subjective safety from crime might not be a reasonableness, a matter of judgment, rather than of maxims and sentiment. The inquiry stimulated a permanent leaning to rationalism, and — not immediately — to complete substitution of rational culture in place of the usual procedure to accomplish reformations. The attempted escape was frustrated. Stewart was released at the expiration of his sentence and quickly passed beyond our observation, but strange to say, after the lapse of forty years he came to view again. His judgment must have failed him, for in 1904 my brother, visiting the state prison in Rhode Island, saw Stewart there, grown stout and crowned with thick snow-white hair. He was near finishing a five years' sentence for the crime of forgery.

Another prisoner, Cameron, a variant specimen of the border human species, sentenced for a term of years, convicted of stealing a government mule, proved to be an unusual character. Tall, athletic, tawny, his age between twenty-five and thirty years, bold, demonstrative, with paroxysmal passions, alert of mind, capable but unpracticed in sound reasoning, with little power of self-control, he was at first a troublesome and always a somewhat vexatious prisoner. Homeless, a transcontinental tramp, traveling with a caravan across the western plains, he strayed away from the procession, found afield, grazing, a mule branded on the shoulder with the letters U. S. designating ownership — strayed or left behind perhaps by some traveling troop of army soldiers. He appropriated the mule and rode away to a far off ranch where he sold the animal and with the proceeds of the sale finally reached a settlement where, riotously behaving, he was apprehended. The theft was discovered and on conviction thereof he was by the territorial court committed to the prison under my charge at Detroit. After some months of imprisonment, the following conversation occurred between us, which shows on his part acumen if insincerity, and indicates that more of orderliness in his mental processes had already supervened. He asked with every appearance of sincere and earnest inquiry,

Q. Is not a government under moral obligations to individuals in some such way as all must recognize there is a moral obligation between individuals themselves with equals or inferiors?

A. Suppose I give an affirmative reply, what next?

Q. Is there not a moral obligation which rests alike on governments and individuals, to deliver, when it can be done, a human being from threatening death or great distress?

A. Generally speaking, it must be so.

Q. If circumstances are exceptional and such that the rescue must needs be accompanied with some technical but not very harmful infraction of statutory law which is enacted for general application, might not the moral obligation in such an exceptional instance rightly rule the conduct?

A. Yes, such a situation might exist when moral obligation, or humanity, would annul, in conscience and before mankind, the common moral duty to observe the law.

Q. Recognizing that self preservation is the first law of nature and always rightly dominant, might not a man, to save his life, *himself* appropriate relief not else available, but which relief according to the higher law of duty you yourself concede is, in justice and morality, very clearly his due?

A. Well, let us have the concrete case to which you would apply your principle; then answer may be made.

Here followed the recital of his own case substantially as follows:

"The government was morally obligated but inaccessible. I took the mule by which means I saved my life. Thus I myself obeyed the highest law of obligation and, at the same time, enabled the government to discharge its moral duty: that's all. For this truly meritorious deed I am now a criminal to be confined for many years — too many for justice, had my offense been verily crime. Is not this a case of gross injustice? In truth, I should be *rewarded* by the government instead of punished."

The insincerity of the man was evinced when under cross-examination he could not satisfactorily explain his own straying from the caravan, with the strayed mule, his sale of it, and subsequent disorderly conduct and reckless expenditure of the proceeds. When thus confronted with the damaging aspects of the facts he surrendered with a shoulder shrug and elevated palms. Yet his argument, however inconsistent it might be, revealed enough sagacity to warrant a new appeal to his reason, for governance of his conduct in prison, since neither moral and religious appeals nor prison punishments had availed for improvement. Therefore when another of his recurrent outbreaks of insubordination took place the experiment of such an appeal was tried and with a fair measure of success.

Of the unreasonableness of misconduct he was easily convinced, indeed needed no convincing for he was already aware of it; but he recognized no obligation to the state and prison government, believed he had received injustice although his argument to prove it had failed, and the adjudged severity of the sentence term, the loss of time and restraints of imprisonment, operated to rasp his native irritability of disposition. It was now suggested to him that in our human relations there is no uniform standard of absolute justice; that the nearest approach to justice is a mean or compromise between extremes; that such a mean can never be exactly reached — can only be approximated; and that abandoning thus all hope of pure justice we must logically concede that there can not be complete injustice, as imperfection of justice involves an element of injustice so that incomplete injustice savors of the just; that different times, tribes, and men hold different notions of the right and wrong in all concrete affairs as in all appearances. He was reminded that our pains and pleasures depend not so much on circumstances as on our opinions; that circumstances often are beyond our control, but our opinion we can considerably regulate; that a man of good intelligence would only strive for that which is within the regulation of his will, and not be worried over that which he cannot change or influence; that the mass of men — normal social beings — adjust themselves to the inevitable, adjust opinion to condition; that not to want is the same as to possess; that things are as we find them day by day; and he was urged to dismiss protest, accept what is and must be, and thus gain happiness.

Explanation was renewed: that the disciplinary measures to which he was subjected from time to time as he rebelled were not retributive but remedial, needful for the preservation of the general order of the prison community of which he was of necessity a member, but that such measures were mainly intended to aid him to overcome himself; that as a sick man seeks the doctor so he, Cameron, if unable to adjust himself should seek the aid we had provided but which he mistakenly esteemed punishment. He was asked to consider the question whether all his troubles were not attributable to his own abnormality and to undertake to cure himself by use of disciplinary means, to be thereafter self-imposed. And it was promised him that should he take that attitude no further authoritative disciplinary measures would be applied except on his request and with our advice. This appeal was so far successful that from time to time whenever he felt within himself a premonition of a passionate explosion he did voluntarily seclude himself in what was known as the "solitary punishment cell" and there remain until he gained a victory and asked to be released. His general conduct, much improved, was not completely changed; his natural disposition remained the same, — even when held in check by some increase of self-control. It was a novel prison incident to see a prisoner, while maintaining fairly good behavior, take the "dungeon treatment" at his own request, quietly endure it, and come forth whenever he should choose to do so.

Finally, when his court sentence had expired, Cameron went his way, released beyond our care and ken. It is however pleasant to note that two years or more after the date of his discharge from prison we casually met upon the street in the city of Detroit. He was well dressed and groomed, in buoyant spirits, and in his hand held a roll of banknotes with which, he said, he was paying off, about town, the expenses of a recent steamboat excursion of the guild of which he was the treasurer — a society of the "Sons of Temperance."

Out of this experience with prisoner Cameron came anew three impressive suggestions which have never since been effaced: that exercise of governing authority for the purpose of its own vindication is of doubtful use and very often harmful; that the assumption of individual moral accountability based on the doctrine of free volition is not always a justifiable assumption, but is often a fallacious view; and that for a reasoning intelligence, that which is reasonable may influence conduct more for moral rectitude than that which transcends the human reason, dwelling alone in imagination.

More interesting than the common run of prisoners was Brooks, a western federal prisoner, a young man of twenty-five years, without relatives, committed for the crime of murder in the second degree and serving a sentence for life. A law student in Chicago, impecunious, under special mental strain, he overworked and broke down with nervous prostration. In order to recover health he went to herding cattle on the western plains. One morning, when the others went to the pasturage with the herd, he with one of his fellow herdsmen, both ill or feigning illness, remained in camp bunked within the cabin. Brooks shot and killed his cabin mate, then joined the herdsmen at the pasturage and there surrendered himself to their custody. He gave no motive for his deed, nor did a motive appear upon his trial, except the doubtful theory of the prosecution that he intended to kill all the herdsmen and then stampede the herd. Later Brooks declared and always afterwards maintained, that until the explosion of the gun he had no consciousness of his movements in the cabin, but awoke to partial consciousness when the pistol was discharged and even then but dimly realized the murderous act and the dreadful consequences. His claim received some confirmation from the fact and manner of his self-surrender and his ultimate complete derangement; and this view, no doubt, had influence in the court proceedings in the leniency shown, by which he was allowed to plead guilty to murder in the second degree with penalty of imprisonment instead of hanging.

Glad to have come out of the trial with his life saved, and not yet despairing of future relief by pardon or otherwise from the full rigor of his life sentence, Brooks was at first comparatively cheerful; but as time wore on bringing no release or sign of movement for it, hope waned and was succeeded by despondency only mitigated by occasional gleams of faint hopefulness. His youthful active mind built castles in the air. He knew they were of air and sought solace in arguments, useless, as he very well knew. In one of our conversations he presented the following argument and seemed to find some comfort in it. He said: "My act was the crime of murder in the first degree or it was not a crime at all. It is wrong that for murder in the second degree I should be imprisoned as I am with a life sentence over me, or indeed any sentence. The verdict of the jury was, evidently, influenced by doubt of sanity and, by right, the doubt should have operated to consign me to some lunacy hospital or should have effected my discharge. I now demand as my legal right and as moral justice that I be hanged for my crime, sent to the hospital as a man insane, or that I be set at liberty." Law student as he was, he knew — of course he knew — that he could not be twice tried for the same offense, so he could not now be hanged. He could not be proved insane and so could not now be transferred to a hospital as he demanded. And he should have known, if he did not, that society is quite justified in restraining

95

for his natural life the liberty of one so unsafe to go at large as his crime showed him to be.

Now to relieve his despondency and unrest, also to extend an experiment in prison administration then afoot to utilize intelligent prisoners for their mutual custodial and monitorial control, Brooks was assigned to some duties usually performed by civilian officers. He was entrusted with some inside prison keys and given our general confidence. He was entirely faithful and remarkably efficient. He seemed to recover his normal mental tone and cheerfulness and he was so engaged when I resigned my office and left the institution. Later he relapsed into melancholia, became a permanent hospital patient, and died.

The experiment of engaging prisoners in monitorial and mechanical supervision and in educating their fellow prisoners, as it was conducted at the Detroit House of Correction during my superintendency, was ennobling to the prisoners who were so assigned, and at one stage of the experiment it seemed feasible to establish in such a municipal prison (at least in the details of its administration) a system of almost complete self-government. So much confidence did this measure evoke that on an occasion when a majority of all the citizen officers conspired to force my compliance with an unreasonable demand by refusing further service, with the intent of closing the manufacturing activities of the establishment as the alternative, at the usual turnout noon hour I ordered that the six hundred prisoners be sent from their cells to the factories in the enclosure, there to be guarded and directed by the fellow prisoner monitors selected and designated for such service. But this was not put to the test because the striking officers relented and returned to their duty.

The promotion of prisoners to semi-official relations and duties, a practice that worked so well at Detroit and afterwards at the Elmira Reformatory, was very different from the use of "trusties" in common jails and prisons. The duties were less servile and the institutional social status of the prisoners thus engaged was much more elevated. It is an important and sound principle of reformatory prison science, as was attested by Maconochie at Norfolk Island, although it is disesteemed by many wardens. The inception of the practice in my prison experience is closely associated in memory with the service of Brooks, Stewart, McKay, and others of the longer sentenced United States prisoners who were confined with the common class of misdemeanants in the Detroit House of Correction, but who were more intelligent.

Burley, "Lake Erie Pirate" as he was named in the newspapers of the time, was committed to the Detroit House of Correction by the federal authorities not on a final sentence but for safe keeping. He was a young Scotchman of excellent family and education whose sympathies were with the southerners in our civil war and who had united with a number of southerners and foreign sympathizers at Windsor, Canada, just across the river from Detroit, — neutral territory. From there they observed and reported to the south the progress of the war sentiment and the preparations in the north. An adventurous and dangerous company of men they were to be on the border. It was alleged then that they were agents of the plan for burning Detroit and several other northern border cities, and that they were also agents for distributing epidemic disease by means of infected clothing and rags. So solicitous were the inhabitants of Detroit, many of whom could remember the destruction of the city in 1805, lest it should be again devastated by these alleged incendiaries, that a volunteer police force was recruited and organized to patrol the river front night and day and a tocsin signal was designated to summon in a moment of danger the whole population to the public defense against a conflagration. It was at this exciting period that Burley, together with a few of his Windsor conspirators, took passage on the steamer "Philo Parsons" which plied from port to port on Lake Erie. On Burley's signal they held up the officers, crew, and passengers at the pistol's point and took charge of the steamer as their captured prize. Soon overcome, the mutineers were arrested and Burley committed to the county jail; but so insecure was the jail for the safe confinement of such a desperate prisoner, and so near were his confederates across the river, that he was soon transferred from the jail to the house of correction for better custody.

The presence of Burley was the cause of much anxiety and so disturbing, that I awakened in the small hours of every night to inspect personally the corridor where he was confined and to note the vigilance of the patrolling guard. That the utmost watchfulness of this prisoner was needful is evident from the following recital of a coincidence of prevision and event.

Once at the usual midnight or early morning hour of wakefulness — whether dreaming I know not — there came suddenly and plainly into my mental view as through a wicket in the wall, a scene in which the prisoner Burley, surrounded by guards, was in process of being manacled. The vividness of the vision together with my habitual anxiety about Burley's safe custody made it very impressive at the time, but my disregard of dreams coupled with engrossing cares soon drove the recollection quite out of mind. Not many days had passed, however, when business called me to the street fronting the river quay, where, apparently avoiding recognition, I saw among the pedestrians a Scotch clergyman of Detroit who had been admitted to visit Burley for friendly spiritual ministrations. Without a shade of any suspicion, from our familiarity of acquaintance I urged myself upon his attention until he could no longer avoid a recognition, when, to my surprise and subsequent indignation, he suddenly turned and approached and unbosomed his troubled mind by making a confession. He said that in his interviews with Burley he had betrayed our confidence and disgraced his office of a religious leader and now felt himself to be degraded. He had been the medium of secret communications between Burley and his confederates on the Canada shore, and was himself cognizant of a plot to rescue Burley by force and, if necessary for the rescue, to make a general jail delivery from the house of correction.

On returning to the prison I directed that Burley should be placed in irons. An hour or two afterwards on casually passing the wicket windows in the guard-room door, with no thought of my midnight vision, I saw exactly what the vision had forecast, — the prisoner Burley surrounded with guards and having fetters riveted on his ankles.

For the sake of further security against a possible rescue, United States soldiers detailed from the garrison at Detroit patrolled the outside premises day and night during the remainder of Burley's incarceration there. He was finally released and went home to Scotland where he wrote a book on his American experiences during our war in which he included an abusive account of his alleged unnecessary severity of treatment by myself at the house of correction. This account of prisoner Burley is I suppose a hitherto unwritten incident of the war. It reveals the real cause of much opprobrium heaped upon police and prison officers by dissatisfied discharged culprits. This mention of individuals of the class of United States prisoners—numbering not more than a hundred at any one time — introduced among the mass of misdemeanants, may serve to conclude this general description of the prison population for whose tutelage and treatment with the object of their reformation, — measures then so novel and interesting, — presaged the more complete modern reformatory system.

CHAPTER VII

EDUCATIONAL WORK AND CO-WORKERS
IN DETROIT

THE educational work at the Detroit House of Correction for such unpromising pupils was at the time quite unique. The thoroughness of the experiment, the exceptional qualifications of the pedagogues in charge, and the progress of the adult prison pupils in primary education were extraordinary features of a prison school and revealed new possibilities and advantages, indeed the indispensableness, of a school of letters in any rational system of prison reformation. Out of an average prison population of 385 for the year 1871 the average attendance in the evening school was 291, or more than 75 per cent of all the prisoners. The absentees were chiefly those discharged from prison almost immediately after their admission by giving bail or payment of fines. They were discharged too soon for school enrollment and attendance. The infirm prisoners and those temporarily assigned to cellular confinement for a disciplinary purpose, and a small number who were necessarily occupied with prison duties during the school hours, accounted for the remaining absentees.

The regular school sessions were held two evenings each week but on two other evenings opportunity was

CARL A. RUDISILL LIBRARY
LENOIR RHYNE COLLEGE

given for writing lessons for some of the pupils. Owing to the short sentences under which most of the prisoners were held the average period of school attendance was only 70 hours. Virtually there were four sets of pupils per year, but the amount of school instruction for a prisoner who remained a full calendar year was only 210 hours. The actual educational progress of these pupils, when compared with the progress of pupils in the public schools of the city of Detroit pursuing the same studies, whose school year includes 975 hours, is so astonishing as to be scarcely credible. In the prison school for male prisoners progress was two and a quarter times, and, in the women's school, two and three-eighths times that of the public school pupils. This estimate is attested by two of the most competent and conscientious instructors it has ever been my privilege to know: Professor H. S. Tarbell, at that time superintendent of a large union school in Detroit and since then for twenty years or more the superintendent of public instruction in Providence, Rhode Island; and Miss Emma A. Hall, who came to our assistance from Professor Sill's high class Ladies' Seminary. This almost phenomenal progress of such pupils is worthy of careful study for its value to pedagogics, but allusion here must be limited to the mere mention of some apparent agencies that served to arouse the dull minds and stimulate hunger for knowledge.

The instructors in charge, Professor Tarbell and Miss Hall, were both of superior personality, thoroughly trained teachers, intensely interested in this educational experiment, and they communicated their own tranquil but profound enthusiasm. It was an attractive scene, the considerable company assembled in the evening in the well-lighted auditorium. The infrequency of these sessions heightened their attractiveness, and the contrast between the daily prison routine — the workshop and the cell life with its necessarily somewhat repressive disciplinary régime — afforded variety and relaxation that were altogether helpful.

The opening school exercises were stimulating. Singing led by Miss Hall and a short address by Professor Tarbell on some educational topic, put the whole company of pupils in an excellent frame of mind for the instruction which immediately followed, conducted in the several classes by prisoners selected and assigned for teaching. Of special service were the frequent lectures delivered before the prisoners on other than school evenings by very capable public men and often by eminent specialists who generously gave their services. A schedule of the lecturers and lectures of a single year is as surprising as the school progress of the prisoners. Thirty lectures in 1870 covered such topics as The Nobility of Work, The Labor Question, How to do Business, Money and Banking, The Restraints of Law are Good, Self-Conquest, Courage, Individual Influence, Ancient Architecture, Chemical Combinations of Bread, History of the Alphabet, The Ocean and its Inhabitants, The Amazon and its Valley, Heat, Beauty, Flowers, Humorous Poetry, Vocal Power Illustrated, An Evening with Charles Dickens, etc. Professor Kent of the Michigan University gave us an evening on the topic, The Emotions and the Will. Perhaps the most remarkable and useful of these lectures were a course of twenty by Professor Mayhew on psychological topics. These lectures occupied each an hour or an hour and a half, holding to the end the attention of the audience. One incident connected with Professor Mayhew's psychological lectures to the prisoners shows the interest awakened in what is ordinarily esteemed an abstruse subject, and suggests the great possible value of the lecture feature in a reformatory system with even the uneducated and low social grade of men and women such as were here confined for gross vices and minor offenses. This is the incident:

On a duly appointed lecture evening, owing to delayed trains, because of the dreadful storm raging and the obstruction of railway tracks and progress by driving snow, the arrival of the lecturer was delayed and was indeed given up as impossible, when unexpectedly he reached the prison at nine o'clock. The prison was closed for the night and all the prisoners were in bed as was required by the rules. However, in view of their interest in lectures, as an experiment I aroused the men from their beds, summoned the officers, illuminated the auditorium, and gathered the whole prison population there at that unseasonable hour. When Professor Mayhew advanced upon the platform to commence his address he was received with round after round of the heartiest applause and for a full hour the prisoners listened with hushed and closest attention to that late night discourse upon the philosophy of our conscious and unconscious mental processes. At the conclusion renewed applause expressed the enjoyment and great satisfaction of the men.

The most valuable moral precepts were inculcated and lasting impressions were made. A wide field of striking illustrations was used from the exhaustless

Michael Mahoney

Miss Emma A. Hall

storehouse of Professor Mayhew's mind. These lectures abundantly demonstrated the important truth that the successful public address to such uneducated, and supposedly exceptionally obtuse minds, should be on topics from an elevated plane clothed in simple language and well illustrated. The lecture scheme carried out at the house of correction quickened and ennobled the minds of prisoners and officers. It elevated and improved the general tone of the whole institution and greatly contributed to the reformatory efficiency.

That such men at my request should gratuitously prepare and deliver such lectures to the prisoners of my charge excited my admiration and gratitude and greatly encouraged me to proceed with further educational effort for prisoners, and on a larger scale, after I was placed in charge at Elmira.

Accuracy, justice, and affection demand that any account of the impressionable and significant years of my life spent at Detroit shall include some mention of collateral agencies and of assistants in the educational and religious work of the house of correction. The rational procedure was influenced by the working of the house of shelter for women, which was established during those years, and the religious phase was heightened by contact with the large mission Sunday school near by. This blend of reason and religion was effective for the house of correction through Miss Emma A. Hall, whose remarkable character and ministrations ultimately united these elements of influence. Miss Hall was amply endowed with native intelligence and was also a cultivated and refined person. Her large-hearted, comprehensive benevolence, her firm faith and complete devotion, enabled her to render a personal service in the reformation of criminal and abandoned women which exceeds both in manner and extent that of any other individual I have ever known. Her faith and her work greatly sustained my own hopeful interest in the possible reformation of prisoners, and now after the passage of so many years there remains the hallowed memory of herself and her efforts.

The house of shelter was opened in October, 1868, as an adjunct to the house of correction. Mrs. A. A. R. Wiggin, an excellent woman imported from Massachusetts, was first placed in charge as matron, while Miss Hall was teacher. This interesting auxiliary, the only one of its kind attached to any prison maintained at the public cost, grew out of the manifest need to reform women prisoners committed to the house of correction. It sprang out of a suggestion after a casual visit which I made in 1867 to the reform school for girls at Lancaster, Massachusetts, and from the further fact that funds toward the first expenditures were already in hand from the surplus earnings of the house of correction prisoners. The Lancaster visit was most impressive. Out from the crowds and din of Boston streets one summer afternoon, transferred as by magic to the quiet charms of Lancaster with its wide loamy roads and ancient elms whose thick-leaved branches relieved the glare of the sun and sheltered many chirping birds, the mind and mood could but be favorable for the best impressions. On approaching the reformatory institution, composed of several attractive brick residences (instead of the rude cottages imagination had depicted), situated along the street in the shade of massive trees and with grassy lawns, there came through the open windows the glad song of children's voices which intensified the grateful thought that such provision could be made for these unfortunates. But the inspiring revelation came when, conducted by Dr. Ames, the superintendent, through the several homes for inmates, the comforts and the educational work appeared to be directed in each house by women of the New England cultured type, every one of whom seemed qualified to carry on a woman's college. So great a thing it seemed for these poor inmate girls to live and learn in intimate association with such ladies that pity and the grateful sense of charity were merged in the nobler aim and scientific process that everywhere appeared in use for their recovery. Then clearly came to view what could be done to save our women prisoners, and on my return to Detroit I asked and readily obtained permission to build what we named the "house of shelter." The board of inspectors of the house of correction in their report for 1868, dated immediately after the opening of the house of shelter, show both the practical intention and the spirit of the project. They say:

"It is intended to receive here as into *a home* women who on removal from the prison seem willing to adopt a reform of life. It is intended that they should be here (while yet under legal custody) received into a *family life* where they shall receive intellectual, moral, domestic, and industrial training, under the influence, example, and sympathy of refined and virtuous women. At the table, in the workroom, and in the room for social intercourse and conversation, it is intended that the features and atmosphere of a family, of which the matron and teacher are the head, shall as far as possible be preserved.   In this way it seems to us probable that some, and we hope many, may be reclaimed to a life of usefulness and honor.   . . .

"In announcing the opening of this house of shelter we wish earnestly to commend it to the countenance and sympathy of the mothers and daughters of every virtuous home in the city of Detroit.   . . .

"Let then the women of Detroit see that this house of shelter brings to the repentant woman the heartfelt assurance that however her vices had estranged her she was not lost to the tender care and sympathies of the virtuous of her own sex."

This high purpose was well executed for two years under the joint incumbency of Mrs. Wiggin and Miss Hall, when, for the reason that there were so few suitable subjects among the greatly reduced number of women prisoners at the house of correction — indeed none that could be safely transferred to the house of shelter without authority of law for more extended custodial control; that Mrs. Wiggin, the matron, was about to resign her position and take up different duties elsewhere; and because of the necessity for alterations and repairs on the buildings and appurtenances, the house of shelter was temporarily closed.   After six months, during which period the "three years law"* was enacted and became effective, conferring the desired additional custodial authority, new recruits were selected and the house, completely renovated and in every way much improved, was opened again with Miss Hall alone in charge, both as matron and as teacher.   She was also teacher at the house of correction.

Let us look more in detail at the kind of life Miss Hall lived at the house of shelter.   She had not, nor under

---

* For explanation of this law, see page 126.

the circumstances could she have, any social life outside the institution where she lived; no outside entertaining occasions either private or public, not even the social contact of an ordinary church attendant; yet she felt no deprivation of social privileges for which by her native and acquired endowments she was so eminently fitted. Sole head of the house of shelter, without assistance beyond the service of prisoner women of her charge, she must herself be always present early and late, attending to all the details of the family life — its domestic work, industrial and earning efforts, and the school. In addition, the disciplinary management and the social features of the family life devolved on her. Besides the long hours and close application at the house of shelter, Miss Hall found time for frequent visits to the women prisoners at the house of correction at hours when they were locked in the cells, — visits at the cell door for comforting, persuasive, and religious ministrations. Her strength and enthusiasm were self-communicative and affected others as by magic.

Because Miss Hall was the pioneer of educators and comprehensive effective educational effort among adult prisoners in America, her brief statement reviewing its beginning should be quoted:

"In January, 1869, five years ago, and two months after the opening of the house of shelter, I organized the school among the female prisoners in the house of correction by giving to a few who were unable to read or write an opportunity to acquire such useful accomplishments. The utterly aimless, care-for-nothing, dejected and hopeless condition of mind of the prisoners in both the male and female departments of the prison at that time made the educational effort exceedingly difficult. Various other incentives brought to bear upon the prisoners — rewards of overwork, etc. — had failed to awaken their dormant faculties to any good and permanent degree. It was prophesied that the prison school, too, would prove to be a delusion of enthusiasm. Now, by the following November, the number in regular attendance had become so increased, the progress was so surprising, and the school so decidedly beneficial to the inmates and institution, — as indicated by the prisoner's attention to his own tidy and good appearance, by more and better work in the factories, improved general behavior and accelerated general cheerfulness, that the school of the male department of the prison was then organized and soon with similar beneficial results."

A year or so after my own retirement from the management of the house of correction (early in 1873) Miss Hall withdrew herself from service there, the house of shelter adjunct was closed, and her extraordinary influence for reformation of the women prisoners was lost to them, to the institution, and to the public.*

For historical accuracy it should be stated here that the reason for closing the house of shelter in no way reflected upon the usefulness of the institution. A decision of the supreme court had limited the operation of the "three years law" to Wayne County alone. A large increase in the number of prisoners in the house of correction, attributable to the growth of the city and state population, made demand for more room there, so that the house of shelter buildings were required for officers' quarters and offices. There was, too, on the part of my successor as superintendent of

---

* For further reference to Miss Hall's life and work see Appendix II, p. 409.

the house of correction, less appreciation of the importance and practicability of accomplishing reformation with prisoners, notwithstanding the facts and results so clearly manifest.

A QUARREL AND A TRAGEDY

An interesting member of my staff at the house of correction was Michael Mahoney, the bookkeeper. He was just past twenty years of age, physically full grown and of good appearance. He possessed excellent native mental ability and was amiable and affectionate in disposition. An academy course was the extent of his education. He was of pure moral habits and a devoutly religious young man of the Roman Catholic faith. In addition to his work as chief accountant he voluntarily assisted as teacher in the evening school, where both by his aptitude and personality he was of valuable assistance and exerted a most excellent influence.

As illustrative of his broad catholicity and disinterested benevolence, qualities of character whose diffusive influence made Mahoney so morally useful among the men pupils of the evening school, Roman Catholic though he was, he assisted me on Sundays at my great undenominational Union Mission Sunday school, situated near the house of correction, — not a part of it nor in any important way connected with it. He took charge of and taught the infant class, which was composed of one hundred or more young children gathered in from families in the neighborhood of the school, families of different nationalities and very different religious proclivities or of none at all. Here, too, his lovable character impressed itself upon the children and his large store of religious and ethical traditions and axioms derived from his special religious education, his reading, and his active, healthy imagination, afforded abundance of most entertaining material for instruction. Most earnestly and conscientiously did Mahoney prepare for and execute these voluntary educational and religious ministrations both at the evening school and at the house of correction and the mission Sunday school. They were always accompanied by his salutary moral influence. It was his custom to go often to the unoccupied prison auditorium — the chapel — alone, where with closed doors, not liable to interruption, he put himself into a devotional frame of mind and rehearsed to an imaginary class his intended lesson.

Mahoney's good service with us was suddenly terminated by a lamentable tragic incident. On a winter morning soon after the prison was opened for the day he went to the shipping office which was in charge of a fellow clerk, his subordinate in rank, a hot-tempered young man of Spanish antecedents. A controversy arose between these two clerks over a trifling matter of accounting, the Spaniard violently assaulting Mahoney, who, after receiving in the face repeated blows from which he did not even attempt to shield himself, struck out blindly with the open penknife with which at the commencement of the affray he was trimming his fingernails. The blade of the small knife penetrated the intestines of his opponent resulting in his death a few hours afterwards. Mahoney surrendered himself immediately and was committed to the county jail, but was soon released on bail furnished by Captain

Owen, a large-hearted man who to release Mahoney from jail pledged an amount equal to his small total fortune and without any guarantee of security except his confidence in the integrity and honor of the young man. Mr. G. V. N. Lothrop, afterwards United States minister to Russia, a distinguished man of the highest standing in the legal profession, at that time long retired from criminal practice, consented to defend Mahoney, out of his desire to see justice done to one who, altogether worthy, had been accidentally brought into this unfortunate predicament. The trial of the case in court was commenced and concluded in a single day. The killing was admitted, the circumstances of the occurrence carefully explained, and testimony adduced to show that it was not intentional but accidental and in self-defense; but the main reliance for the acquittal of the defendant was made to rest on his good character and therefore the absence of any probable criminal intention. In a quarter of an hour the jury returned with a verdict of acquittal and Mahoney was freed. The verdict was greeted with applause that could not be immediately repressed. The court adjourned and friends gathered around Mahoney offering him congratulations. Very favorable employment was then secured for him, but he never recovered his previous tone of mind. The jail confinement pending the trial and until released on bail, the criminal trial to which he was subjected, his constant remembrance of the tragedy, intensified by irritating missives frequently received from living relatives of his victim, produced deep and habitual depression. One of these missives received through the mail at Christmas time every year was a note containing a sprig of cassia from the grave of the deceased clerk fallen by his hand, with the words "curse you" and signed "from the murdered to his murderer." After a year or two a disease developed under which he suffered dreadfully, lingering about three years, when he died.

The memory of Mahoney is cherished for the admirable discharge of his duties at the house of correction and at the misson Sunday school, but still more for his inward excellencies, the virtue of his incorporeal selfhood. It is plain now, viewed in retrospect, that his presence among us produced a good influence, all the more effective because he was so unconscious of exerting it. His morality, goodness, and quick spiritual apprehension, were native rather than cultivated qualities of character. His influence extends beyond the period of his natural life, whose tragedy of suffering and untimely termination is indeed a sorrowful remembrance.

There were others of the assistants at the house of correction whose zeal and faithfulness contributed greatly to the common aim and bred enduring friendship. Recalling them now, feelings of warm regard spring up; an attachment incident to our community of interest and co-operative effort for the benefit of the objects of our charge. Many of these faithful helpers are dead; others absorbed in other occupations are lost to sight; but the abiding affectionate remembrance of them is a happiness that helps to dim much of the disagreeable part of that period. Withholding individual mention of these assistants, some allusion must be made to the board of inspectors.

The supervising authority of the house of correction

James McMillan

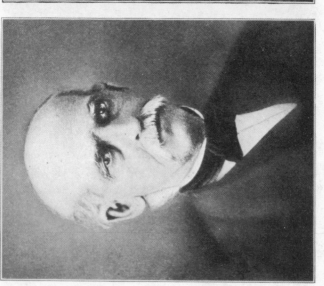

L. M. Mason

was vested in a board of inspectors composed of three members appointed by the common council on nomination of the mayor. The appointments were for three years, so arranged that the term of one member should expire every year and a new appointment be made, which was usually a reappointment of the same individual. The members were always selected from the highest class of citizens, who were able and willing to serve without pay; men too noble and devoted to give attention to patronage or any personal or partisan advantage in the conduct of the institution; men large enough and wise enough to confine their work to inspection and aid, without too meddlesome direction of details of management. Such was the character of the board in the discharge of its functions, and so scrupulously did I myself avoid participation in municipal affairs and intimacy with local politicians that throughout my whole term of service no taint of political partisanship ever affected the management. Vain attempts were made by individual politicians to bring the management of the house of correction into the political arena, — indirect skirmish assaults which further on in this narrative shall be more particularly mentioned. The board of inspectors and every individual member of it gave ever to myself as superintendent the utmost confidence and cordial support.

Most notable of the inspectors, after Mr. Bagley's efficient agency in establishing and launching the house of correction, was L. M. Mason, who continued as a member of the board from the very beginning, 1861, to the close of my own service there in 1871. The public is more indebted than it knows to this noble man for his large financial aid and wise coun-

sel in connection with that institution; and personally, I can never forget nor be sufficiently grateful
for the unreserved confidence he gave me, the support of his manly espousal of my cause when that
was serviceable, and for his cordial personal friendship throughout that ten years' stressful period.

Mr. Mason possessed a rare combination of qualities
which specially fitted him to aid in building up this
early municipal prison with its advanced methods
which, in the sequel, has exercised a far-reaching influence upon the penitentiary system generally. He
was, in business, a bank president, dealer in pine lands
and lumber, and he possessed ample means. He was not
a politician but was sufficiently interested in politics
to consent once to represent his district in the state
legislature. Energetic, bold, and disregardful of tech-
nicalities in law or ethics when such restrictions interfered with worthy objects, too large minded to be
tied to mere routine, he was a safe man to be given
the rein — a man honest to the core, of unquestioned
moral probity in every way, genuine, tenderly sympathetic, always brimming with wit and humor.

Detroit, with a population at that time of a little
more than 40,000, was so small a city that any increase
of annual taxation was quickly noted and keenly felt
by the tax-payer; the aldermen and local politicians
were avid of every item of patronage to be had from
public expenditures and appointments, so that to increase the annual budget for any purpose was deemed
bad politics for the dominant party, and stirred up
disturbing strife among the party leaders. The city
had already expended $80,000 to provide the house of
correction plant, and it seemed imperative, if the in-

116

stitution was to be kept out of politics and made serviceable for its good purpose as planned by its projectors, that the current cost of maintenance should be gleaned from the labor of the prisoners and other possible inherent income. The circumstances and the apparent necessity pointed to the contract system of employment as simplest, most profitable, and obviating need of application to the common council for funds for an operating capital, as would be required under the state account system. Mr. Mason and the other inspectors readily saw the advantages of the state account plan and approved my proposition to proceed to install it without consultation with the city authorities and without a working capital except such as could be indirectly obtained by time purchases, and by borrowing —for which there was no direct authority and which was, indeed, of very doubtful legality. Mason endorsed my notes and discounted them at his bank, and other banks followed suit. Thus the working capital was had until the surplus income over cost of maintenance itself supplied it. It was indeed good fortune that this man of wealth, of so much genuine worth and ready wit, could be induced for the first ten years of its existence to develop and defend this house of correction enterprise.

THE FRIEND AND THE MISSION

A seemingly trifling circumstance, but really one of far-reaching influence, suggests the reflection that rightly considered no circumstance is trivial, but each is serious when seen in its remoter relations. I refer to the casual commencement of an invaluable personal friendship of precious remembrance. It happened — if truly there is ever a happening — that on the train from Rochester to Detroit, when in 1861 my family and myself were removing thence, James McMillan of Detroit was a passenger in the same Pullman car. His attention was attracted to us frequently during the day by the sobriquet "Mac" overheard when addressed to McConnell, our traveling companion. He quickly divined who we were, and resolved to make our acquaintance after our settlement in his city. We soon were fast friends and united our efforts in establishing an undenominational mission Sunday school in the outlying district near the house of correction, intended for the benefit of children of the foreign and native families in that vicinity. Such unity of effort increased our intimacy and cemented the friendship which, notwithstanding the subsequent divergence of our lines of life, endured until his death on August 10, 1902.

On an appointed day each week Mr. McMillan and myself visited this sixth ward district to observe the social conditions and make acquaintance with the inhabitants and the children. The school was opened in 1863 in a building provided and supported chiefly by Messrs. McMillan and Newberry, both of whom became active workers at the mission, the former as teacher and manager of a class of untutored youths, the latter directing and leading the remarkable musical feature of the school sessions. Every Sunday afternoon the spacious platform was filled with interested spectators attracted by the novelty of this nondenominational school, by the large habitual attendance, and mainly it is believed by the remarkable volume and quality of song under the influence of Mr. Newberry's magnetic personality and his melodious, penetrating tenor voice. This Union Mission Sunday school was one of the earliest of such missions in our large American cities, and the first of its kind in Detroit. So impressive is the recollection of my connection with the organizing and carrying on of the mission and association with the array of unusual participants that rather full mention of the enterprise is requisite.

The actual average attendance of pupils throughout one of the years of its existence numbered by actual count 1192. The attendance sometimes greatly exceeded this of course. There were present on the day the new building was dedicated (1868) over 2200 persons. So great was the capacity of the new building and so considerable was the general public interest in the mission enterprise that there was handed in, on that occasion, a total amount of monetary gifts of $4400. The enterprise enlisted as volunteer teachers and helpers a hundred or more men and women prominent in business and in the social life of the city, and among these quite a number of such persons as do not commonly engage actively in Sunday schools. For instance, there were among our helpers John J. Bagley, business man, city councilman, afterwards governor of the state; Mr. Trowbridge, president of the Tug Association of the river and lakes, and a shipping merchant; the brother of the latter, a practicing attorney and United States collector of the internal revenue; Mr. Clark, president of the board of trade, and grain dealer. Major General Pelieuse of the United States Army, then stationed at Detroit, took charge of a Sunday school class composed of rather "tough" boys, and this class proved to be the nucleus of a regiment of a thousand lads of the same sort in the city, which, organized by General Pelieuse's direction, under the immediate control of Captain Rogers also of the Detroit garrison of U. S. troops, accomplished much good for the boys of the city of Detroit. The regiment went in force to the centennial exposition at Philadelphia, and formed the basis of the present military academy at Orchard Lake, Michigan. Professor Sill of the Seminary, Mr. Backus, editor of the leading daily journal of the city, with other professional men, merchants, and cultured influential women co-operated as teachers and in various ways. Mr. Newberry, who was then a prominent admiralty lawyer, the representative of much wealth, was afterwards elected to the national Congress.

Mr. McMillan had a class of boys quite similar to the lads of General Pelieuse's class. He brought to bear upon them, individually, the ennobling influence of his strong and charming personality; fastened himself upon them and followed each of them into their subsequent life, providing employment, advising and inducting them into business for themselves, and often providing them with their early invested capital. Such thoroughness was always characteristic of McMillan in all his relations to people and to affairs. He was then at the head of various important heavy manufacturing concerns; interested and active in the material advancement of his city and state; and, naturally, quite unavoidably became in time prominent in politics. He was a member and contributor to the Detroit Museum of Art; member of the board of park commissioners which produced Belle Isle Park; member of the board of estimate of the city; member and for many years the chairman of the republican state central committee. In 1889 he was elected to the United States Senate, served his six years' term, and was in 1895 re-elected, receiving every vote of both republicans and democrats in the joint convention of the legislature.

The broad catholicity of our Sunday school is sufficiently indicated by the fact that one of the classes was made up of thirty and more inmates of the house of shelter connected with the house of correction, of which class Miss Hall was the teacher. The class was fellowshipped without ever a shade of objection or ostracism. The infant class, of more than a hundred children from families of several denominations, was under charge and instruction of Mahoney who, as I have already stated, was large-minded enough to put aside for the time any purpose of denominational propagandism and devote himself in co-operation with the rest of us to catholic rather than Roman Catholic effort for the moral uplift of the pupils. This infant class, under such direction, existed in the school without any friction from patrons and teachers, or any opposition from the priests of Mahoney's denomination.

It is the recent testimony of those who best know, that the influence of that mission Sunday school enterprise and of the church into which it has grown has operated greatly to change for the better the social and so the moral tone of the neighborhood, an improvement which in its effects cannot be accurately estimated nor be overestimated.

The Detroit *News Tribune* of January 27, 1895, sums up the outcome in the following language:

"The Church of the Covenant is the outcome of an unde-nominational mission Sunday school established in 1863. This school met with phenomenal success from the first. In 1864 a small frame chapel was built on the northwest corner of Napoleon and Russell Streets by contributions of persons of every denomination. In 1866 the house was enlarged by an addition 26 x 30 feet, and in 1868 this house was removed and a brick structure 75 x 90 feet erected in its place at a cost of $16,000. It was capable of accommodating 1500 to 2000 children and during its days of greatest prosperity was kept well filled. As long as Mr. Brockway had control of this mission school it continued to flourish wholly distinct from any religious denomination. The school achieved a wide notoriety throughout the state for its numbers and efficiency. Many church-going people had pride in taking their visiting friends and strangers to visit 'Our big City Mission Sunday School.' But in 1872 Mr. Brockway re-moved from the city and the school at once began to go down, until it was entirely closed within a few months. In 1874 the Presbyterian Alliance secured the property and on the 18th of February, 1875, organized the Union Presbyterian Church with sixteen members. . . . In 1899 the present fine structure was erected and the name changed to Church of the Covenant. . . . The church proper can accommo-date from 700 to 800 persons. . . . The chapel . . . has room enough to take care of 1500 children. The whole property represents about $50,000. . . . The Church of the Covenant is said to be the only English speaking church in a population of 30,000 people. . . . Fully one-half of the members, it is said, speak German as fluently as Eng-lish. The pastor says of his four elders that one is a German, one a Dutchman, one a Scotchman, and the pastor himself is of French descent."

Such is the outcome of the Union Mission Sunday school established in 1863.

Mr. McMillan was noted for doing rather than merely saying things, and it is in no small measure due to this quality of his character that the mission was established and maintained. The same quality brought him into very unusual favor with his political party and with the people of his state. He was a loyal republican partisan but in all his political contests as in his business ventures he could be relied upon to accord his opponents a "square deal." Once, in municipal politics, he was approached by the leader of the opposition with the proffer to turn over to him the support of the democrats on very simple and honorable conditions, a proposition that he promptly rejected with the response to the leader: "You had better adhere faithfully to your own party." He could not stoop to benefit by concessions of his opponents, preferring as he always did in all relations, an open, fair contest with whatever of risks it might involve. As a political leader in his state he held his party in complete ascendency, and in his senatorial career he was noiselessly influential in large and most important legislative affairs. He drew to himself the warm attachment of his fellow senators by his recognized native ability, his honorable character, and by his pleasing personality and address.

He was the best balanced business man I ever knew, and his grand business success can only be properly attributed to the qualities of the man. He presents the rare example, in these days, of a multi-millionaire made so by his own abilities exercised in legitimate pursuits; a business man who accumulated by expending rather than by withholding, — accumulating great wealth without taking undue advantage of another's ignorance or misfortunes. While not given to excessive pleasure in any direction, he nevertheless lived a full life of enjoyment in all rational pleasures; fond of manly sports and participating in them he was above their frequent gambling feature; and when traveling luxuriously in his private car or yacht his invited guests and companions generally included, with his family, agreeable ladies and gentlemen of limited private means and restricted opportunities. His generosity was a native quality — a birth-right; it was bred by practice from earliest manhood and continued throughout his whole career. With his increased income he increased the pay of household servants and of others in his service. The thousands afterwards employed in his foundries, mills, car works, steamboat and railway transportation lines, were so well paid and satisfied that, within control of his own management, there was never a strike of operators for wages or conditions; and to my knowledge, men in his employ have risen, by opportunities he has afforded them, from positions of salaried income to independent and ample fortunes.

Always cheerfully serene, with a mind capable and well balanced; possessing the courage of his convictions; generous and considerate, honorable and upright in all his private and social life, in his business relations and in his political career, and withal, so eminently successful, I estimate that McMillan of right belonged to the very elect of the noblest men.

I cannot conclude my reference to this noble man without recording that he was very much to me. In the retrospect I appreciate more even than in the days of our familiar intercourse, my indebtedness to Mr. McMillan for important practical aid in many ways; and particularly for the inspiration derived from him. His calm, brave, strong character was self-communicating, and heartened whoever was privileged to form close relations with him. His resolution and constancy buoyed and saved many men who were discouraged and failing. I count this friendship to be the greatest happiness and most helpful fact of the years spent at Detroit.

CHAPTER VIII

BIRTH OF THE INDETERMINATE
SENTENCE LAW

IN THE year 1869 I drafted a bill which received the approval of our board of inspectors and was enacted by the Michigan legislature, the so-called "three years law," mentioned already in connection with the work in the house of shelter. While this act conferred discretionary powers upon police magistrates and justices of the peace throughout the state to commit female offenders not more than fifteen years old to the house of correction until they should reach the age of twenty-one years, the important initiative feature of the law was the *mandatory* section relating to the courts of record and the police court and justice courts of Wayne County — the county where the house of correction was located — to so commit such young offenders, and also the mandatory requirement upon all courts to commit every woman more than fifteen years of age who was a common prostitute to the house of correction on a sentence of *three years*. The act contained provision for the conditional release and re-arrest, should need be, of both the juvenile and the adult female offenders, by the managing authorities of the house of correction.

This "three years law" was, as has been mentioned, practically nullified after two or three years, by the action of the courts construing it as applicable only to Wayne County, and by reason of my own retirement from the house of correction and the temporary closing of the house of shelter; but the effect upon the disorderly women at large, while it was intact, the reformatory effect on such as were committed, and the stimulus to further similar effort, were interesting enough to note.

Immediately upon the enactment of the law and its publication in the newspapers there was an exodus of disorderly women from Detroit and the populous cities of the state. Mr. Moody, the evangelist, traveling eastward on the Grand Trunk Railroad at that time said that he was greatly surprised to see on the train a hundred or more women whose conversation and conduct revealed their bad character. On inquiry he learned that they were fleeing the state to Buffalo and points east in order to avoid their liabilities under the newly enacted "three years law."

The following extract from an interesting paragraph of the report of 1871, relating to the operation of the law upon imprisoned offenders, is certainly worth preserving for its historical value:

"Seventeen women and girls have been received during the year, who were committed under this law; ten of them are sentenced for three years each, and seven until the age of twenty-one years. (It will be understood that these sentences are not unalterable, but may be modified or annulled by the board of inspectors at will.) . . . Their ages, are respectively, 15, 16, 17, 19, 21, 22, 23, 24, and 32 years. They all remain at this date, save one, who, admitted March 9, her eighth committal to the house of correction, was nevertheless released November 22. Her husband, with whom she had not lived for years, came, and on her promise to return to his home she was allowed to go, with full knowledge that if she returned to Detroit during that time she would be arrested and recommitted. Six of the ten had each previously served sentence here and were at the time of their admission exceedingly abandoned in character. With one exception, they are all now improved so much that they are regular guests at the Thursday evening entertainments at the shelter. One of the ten was transferred to the shelter to reside, within two months of her admission here, but has since been returned to the house of correction for training. Two of the others are best as they are (at the house of correction) for some time to come. Of the seven children, two have been tried at the shelter, and since returned here for correction. One, committed in September last, had been at the shelter voluntarily previous to her arrest, was found incorrigible for the time, and is receiving suitable training here now. The remaining four of the children are at the house of shelter. . . . Two of them are remarkably interesting cases of criminal treatment by the courts. One, fourteen years of age, of good parentage, sent to service by her widowed mother, was abused by the master and mistress and ran back to her mother for protection, wearing a shawl which she had worn two years but which was claimed by the mistress as her property. For this so-called larceny she was arrested and committed to the house of correction. The ladies of the shelter say they find no fault in her. Thanks to the existence of the house of correction and its shelter department, she has found friends and is saved from the degradation that must otherwise have followed. The other, eleven years of age, taken from the almshouse by half-breeds to their hut in the woods to aid them in gathering nuts and berries, motherless and friendless, was outraged by brutish boys and then sentenced to imprisonment. She now has a home, a friend and is regularly at school in the public school of the ward in which the shelter is situated. These two cases are in and of themselves a strong argument in favor of the 'three years law' not only, but teach the importance of such change in the law for committing all classes of offenders as shall confer upon properly constituted authority the discretion asked for in the reformatory sentence bill presented to the legislature at the last session."

The draft of the law for Michigan referred to in the last clause, presented to the legislature of 1870, discussed there and defeated for the time, is a concrete expression of the most advanced ideas of that period about such legislation. It was substantially as follows:

"Section 1 . . . Any person who shall be convicted of any offense punishable by imprisonment in the Detroit House of Correction, and who may be sentenced to imprisonment therein under any law now in force or hereafter to be enacted, shall be and hereby are constituted wards of the state and subject to the custody and control of the Board of Guardians as hereinafter provided by this act.

"The circuit judge of the county of Wayne for the time being, together with the inspectors of the Detroit House of Correction, shall constitute and be denominated the Board of Guardians, whose powers and duties shall be as further provided by this act, and said circuit judge shall *ex officio* be chairman of said Board.

"Section 2. All courts of record having criminal jurisdiction, in the state of Michigan, and all police justices and justices of the peace in said state, who, under the provisions of law, may sentence offenders . . . to confinement in the House of Correction . . . shall sentence all offenders convicted before them of any offense now or hereafter made punishable by imprisonment in the Detroit House of Correction, to the custody of the Board of Guardians aforesaid, but shall not fix upon, state, or determine any definite period

129

of time for the continuance of such custody; provided that in cases of assault and battery of which the justices of the peace have jurisdiction, fines may be imposed in accordance with existing laws; and provided further that this section shall not be construed to take away any power to suspend sentence, that said courts and justices may have; and in case of such suspended sentence the courts or justice before whom such offenders may have been convicted, may at any time cause the re-arrest of such offenders for the purpose of having such suspended sentence pronounced and executed."

This section further contains certain details of direction of procedure as to witnesses, evidence, delivery and receiving of prisoners at the house of correction, and the form of commitment to be used. The third section confers upon the board of guardians their powers to receive, detain, conditionally release, re-arrest, re-commit, etc. The essential features of the fourth section are as follows:

"Section 4. It shall be the duty of the Board of Guardians to maintain such minimum of control over all wards committed to their custody under this act as shall prevent them from committing crime, best secure their self-support, and accomplish their reformation.

"The said Board shall actively undertake the reformation of the wards aforesaid by means of culture calculated to develop right purposes and self-control, and by granting them social privileges under such social and legal restraints and influences as will best cultivate right purposes and promote correct conduct, when this may be done with safety.

"When any ward shall be received into the said Detroit House of Correction, the said Board of Guardians shall cause to be entered in a special register the name, age, nativity, nationality and parentage of such ward, with such other facts as can be ascertained, indicating the constitutional tendencies and propensities, the social influences connected with the early life, and based upon these an estimate of the present condition of such ward and the best probable plan of treatment.

"Upon such register shall be entered quarter-yearly or oftener minutes of observed imprisonment or deterioration of character, and notes as to the method and treatment employed; also all orders and alterations affecting the standing or situation of such ward, the circumstances of final release, and any subsequent facts of the personal history which may be brought to their knowledge. An abstract of the record in each case remaining under their control shall be made semi-annually, submitted to the Board at a regular meeting thereof, and filed with the county clerk of Wayne County, which abstract shall show the date of admission, the age, the then present situation, whether in said House of Correction or elsewhere, whether and how much imprisonment has been made, and the particular reason for release or continued custody as the case may be.

"The Board of Guardians shall establish rules and regulations by which any ward may have the privilege to see and converse with the said Board of Guardians quarter-yearly at least.

"When it appears to the said Board that there is a reasonable probability that any ward possesses a sincere purpose to become a good citizen, and the requisite moral power and self-control to live at liberty without violating the law, and that such ward will become a fair member of society, then they shall issue to such ward an absolute release, but no petition or other power of application for the release of any ward made by any person whatever, and based upon any ground save that herein stated, shall be entertained and considered by the said Board.

"Section 5. If any person through oversight or otherwise be sentenced to confinement in said House of Correction for a definite period, said sentence shall not for that reason be void, but the person sentenced shall be entitled to the benefit and subject to the liabilities of this Act, in the same manner and in the same extent as if the sentence had been in the terms required by Section two of this Act, and in such cases said Board of Guardians shall serve upon such ward, a copy of this act, and written information of their said relations to the said Board.

Following the publication of this, the original in-determinate sentence form of law, there appear in the report some brief answers to such objections as it was foreseen would be raised to any radical legislation, and some arguments in its favor; but in a paper which I read in Cincinnati in 1870, before the National Prison Congress, entitled The Ideal Prison System for a State, the entire scheme of a reformatory (state) prison system based upon the full idea of the indeterminate sentence was more definitely sketched.*

The phraseology of the form of law referred to has been adopted for all the so-called indeterminate sentence laws since enacted in the several states, and, although marred by the limitations of such laws, has been generally accepted as the basis of the reformatory prison system which came into existence during the last quarter of the last century, and which, in the language of the late Charlton T. Lewis, the distinguished scholar and jurist, "is destined to radically change men's habits of thought concerning crime and the attitude of society towards criminals, to rewrite from end to end every penal code in Christendom and modify and ennoble the fundamental law of every state."

In 1875 the legislature of Michigan appointed a commission composed of Governor Bagley, Mr. Croswell, who was afterwards the governor of the state, and myself, to revise the criminal laws of the state. The commissioners unanimously reported to the legislature as follows:

"After much and careful investigation we are opposed to the system of time sentences as it now stands

---

*An abstract of The Ideal Prison System for a State will be found in Appendix I, p. 389.

and recommend a change in that system, and the introduction of reformatory sentences applicable to all crimes punishable with imprisonment in the state prison, with exception of some of the most aggravated crimes."

The "three year law" was thus the beginning; the paper, The Ideal Prison System for a State, presented at the congress of the National Prison Association in Cincinnati in 1870, contained the argument; and the bill before the Michigan legislature of 1870-1871 was the first attempted practical application in America of the profound principle of the indeterminate sentence system, which substitutes both in the laws and in prison practice reformatory in place of the usual punitive régime. It has been said by those in a position to know, that these measures and their advocacy put in motion the reforms and directed the progress that have since taken place in this department of administrative affairs.

As to the influence of the Cincinnati paper (1870) I may be indulged in quoting the estimate placed upon it twenty years afterwards, at the National Prison Congress held in the same city in 1890, by Dr. F. H. Wines in his paper entitled, Twenty Years' Growth of the American Prison System. He said, "But the most remarkable paper read at the Congress (1870) was that entitled The Ideal Prison System for a State, in which is elaborated a complete system of penal and reformatory institutions for a state, which presented in germ all the theories as to the nature and the needs of the criminal, the practical exemplification of which is seen at the New York State Reformatory at Elmira."

At the annual conventions of the American Prison

Association I was a very regular attendant and contributor. Agitation of the question was kept alive from year to year, and ere long the system was heartily endorsed. Elsewhere on invitation I made addresses on the topic, notably soon after the Cincinnati Congress, before the legislatures of Indiana, Illinois, and Michigan; and I continued the advocacy as occasion arose before clubs and churches. I was credited with originating the idea of the indeterminate sentence and for a long time innocently accepted the credit supposing that the suggestion came to me from my observation of the folly of short term imprisonments, not knowing until years afterward how the plan had been foreshadowed and attempted.

In 1832, Whateley, Bishop of Dublin, indicated it in his book on Secondary Punishments. In the forties, Maconochie suggested it in his pamphlets relating to his administration at Norfolk Island; and the charges to juries by Recorder Matthew Davenport Hill of Birmingham, England, from 1850 to 1878, openly declared for and advocated the indeterminate sentence. At the time I first wrote on this subject I had no information of Sir Walter Crofton's celebrated Irish Prison System, of the Western Australian System, or of the remarkable prison administration of Montesinos in Spain. It is true that the same underlying principle animates these European examples, but the American indeterminate sentence system as suggested by me differs somewhat in the characteristics of the prisoners to whom it is applied and differs considerably in the civic social environment; also in the scope and use of reformatory means as developed later at Elmira.

The Cincinnati Prison Congress of 1870 thus aroused much interest in prison management and in the criminal laws. In Europe that interest was quickened by Dr. E. C. Wines, who visited European governments with the result that a permanent official International Prison Commission was created. The first international meeting was held in London, 1872; and ever since, quinquennial international meetings have been held in the several countries. While I could not attend these international congresses held in foreign countries, it was my privilege to contribute papers for consideration and publication in the proceedings; and always the question of the "indeterminate sentence" formed a topic for discussions. But not until the meeting in the United States, at Washington, 1910, did the International Congress formally sanction the indeterminate sentence system.

CHAPTER IX

ACCUSATION AND EXONERATION

DURING my service as superintendent of the Detroit House of Correction two public attacks were made upon the institutional management; and one indirect malicious prosecution intended for my personal annoyance. The instigation of these attacks, the investigation of the charges, and the conclusions reached, are worthy of recital as showing again the liability of good prison management to misrepresentation and assault, the safety and satisfaction of thorough impartial investigations, and the spread of sound principles of prison administration with increase of individual influence and usefulness which are sure to be the final result of groundless persecution.

Early in the year 1865 there appeared in the morning issue of a local partisan newspaper — to my great surprise for I had had no inkling of it—a formal presentment against the management of the house of correction by the recently risen grand jury, accompanied with a full column, double headed, denunciatory editorial article. We were charged with furnishing insufficient and unsuitable food to the prisoners and with use of unduly severe disciplinary measures. This surprising and as the sequel showed baseless public assault originated with three discharged employes, one of whom was a connection of the district attorney, the legal adviser of the grand jury. The district attorney, supposedly offended at the discharge of his relative, did in this instance use the well intended institution of the grand jury apparently for a personal satisfaction rather than for a legitimate public benefit. Thus the grand jury, admirable contrivance as it is in principle for the security of innocence against unjust prosecutions, became then, and often becomes, by reason of its secrecy, absence of individual responsibility, its ex-party inquiries and its easy manipulation by the district attorney, a cumbrous and dangerous agency. Subsequently the legislature of Michigan abolished the grand jury as has been done in many other states. In our present state of civilization there is no need of the grand jury and it is hoped this feature of our criminal code procedure will be everywhere abolished and some officer of the law substituted for it who shall openly perform the duty and be held to strict public accountability for his performance of it.

On request by the board of inspectors of the house of correction, the common council of the city designated a special committee of their number to make a thorough investigation. The composition of the investigating committee was of such unexceptionable citizens that the defendants submitted their case without employing counsel, and the district attorney, ashamed apparently of his part in procuring the presentment, did not, either personally or by proxy, appear for the prosecution. A very thorough inquiry was instituted by the committee. Open sessions of the committee were held at the city hall and at the house of correction, where both citizen and prisoner witnesses were summoned and testified, with the result of our complete exoneration. The well-nourished appearance of the prisoners was of itself sufficient to refute the starvation charge.

As to the charge of disciplinary severity, it was unsupported by any testimony of prisoners except in the instance of an illiterate negro who, on the direct examination, by his connected, consistent, and apparently candid statements amazed me and made a temporary profound impression upon the committee. It was truly astonishing that a man of his character could construct such a plausible story, could weave from arrant falsehood such a fabric of apparent truth. He seemed obsessed of some cunning evil spirit from the nether depths. He appeared as rather a reluctant witness, simple minded, artless, and so the more convincing. His testimony occupied the whole of one afternoon and stood well the usual cursory cross-examination. The committee then adjourned and decided to hold an evening session. In the interval I gave informally the history of the negro witness and, in detail, the truth about his prison treatment, and requested that he be recalled and in the light of what I had stated be re-examined by the attorney member of the committee. To my request the committee readily acceded and the whole of the evening session was devoted to his cross-examination. Never was there a more intensely interesting exhibition of skilful cross-examining and subtle fencing of a witness. Gradually, as by painful labor, the truth appeared, utterly refuting his testimony of the preceding afternoon. These experienced men — the attorney and other committeemen — were now, in turn, amazed. They declared the whole performance of the afternoon and evening a new and startling

138

revelation of the danger of such a witness before arbiters who are prejudiced or without previous knowledge of the real truth. With the final testimony of this negro witness, the work of investigation was concluded, and a full acquittal speedily resulted.

My indignation at these charges was soothed by the clear acquittal and the dissemination of better information about the institution and its operations, as well as by the sympathy and strength of general public approval. The experience of this investigation taught the need for the keeping of complete and minute records of occurrences and procedure in all public institutions. In order to be equipped for defense if charges of insufficient feeding should ever again be made, we began at once to weigh each prisoner on his admission and again on his discharge, recording weights and annually summing up the loss and gain, and publishing it in the annual statements and reports. After five years of this practice the following interesting fact appeared: The increase over loss of weight of 3325 prisoners received and discharged was 13,579½ pounds. This aggregated increase of bulk of prisoners called forth from our manager, Mr. Mason, a facetious objection to such feeding. He argued that since the average weight of criminals is near 135 pounds we had unwittingly, by this process of good diet, actually produced the equivalent of one hundred additional criminals!

But a more important improvement in prison records grew out of this investigation, a record of the disciplinary treatment of each prisoner so accurately and minutely kept as to cover every item, even things so trivial as mere reproofs orally administered. This disciplinary record plan was brought to its perfection afterwards at Elmira, and in the early nineties when an attack was made there and investigation lasting full two years followed, such records proved serviceable.

So completely discomfited were the mischief makers in this their first open attack on the house of correction that they were quiescent thereafter, and never again at Detroit was the prison management attacked for alleged fault of prison dietary or severity in disciplinary matters.

However, a revengeful attempt to visit punishment upon me for befriending Mahoney on his trial for homicide was made at the instigation of his relatives, by means of a vindictive prosecution of my brother Hugh, the deputy superintendent of the house of correction, for the alleged killing of a Negro prisoner. This inmate suddenly died after removal to his cell from his place of employment in the prison factory, where he had become so disorderly and violent that his forcible removal was necessary. That the prisoner died of meningitis was clearly shown on the trial and a verdict of acquittal was promptly entered. The accusation and trial attracted scarcely any local public attention, so firmly established in confidence had the management of the house of correction now become. I myself suffered but small anxiety, so that again the purpose to inflict irritation and gratify animosity quite failed of its accomplishment.

The incident seems worthy of mention only for the reason that it suggests the liability of prison officers to vilification and even criminal charges for occurrences which are always incident to prisons and prison management, even in absence of any fault of the officers themselves. This fact, especially menacing in these later days of newspaper sensationalism, might with good reason operate to withhold men who are most suitable and desirable for the prison service from engaging in this important department of public administrative affairs. This opinion was emphasized by a later attack at Detroit from a more influential source but with equally unsatisfactory results to the prosecuting agents.

During the ten years of history of the house of correction the management had been placed so completely in the hands of the superintendent that it partook of the nature of a private institution under personal control. The capital for carrying on the considerable industrial interests was borrowed on my own credit and that of Mr. Mason. The operations were aloof from local municipal political influence and for that reason out of the public glare. That is to say, its detailed operations were not brought up and discussed at the meetings of the common council of the city and gazetted in the newspapers as was the case with other departments of municipal affairs. Moreover, the institution being conducted on methods so much out of the ordinary — on a higher plane of means and purpose than the jails and prisons of that time — was a fact that kept alive a certain slumbering antagonism ever ready to manifest itself on favorable opportunity. The opportunity came at a political campaign when a certain member of the common council was running for Congress. He was chairman of the finance committee to which was referred our monthly house of correction account of receipts and expenditures. Eager for popularity, when he found in our monthly budget a trifling interest payment which he affected not to understand, without further inquiry or notice he publicly proclaimed it as a suspicious circumstance. Stung by the innuendo of his public remark I protested against the injustice couched in such language. The council then ordered that the finance committee should hold a conference with the superintendent of the house of correction and make their report at the next session of the common council. Such a conference was had at the committee room at the city hall on an evening long to be remembered. The alderman himself presided and presented a shrewdly arranged series of interrogatories carefully written out, to which he demanded oral and, in the main, categorical replies. He was much exasperated when I insisted upon my privilege to reply in writing only to his written questions and to make my replies not categorically but in extenso and with full explanations.

It was a stormy conference, extending late into the night, and at the final breaking up I was told by the accusing alderman that I might expect an adverse report in the most scorching language which he was capable of using. He fulfilled his threat at the council meeting which occurred on the evening of the very next day, but in the interval I had prepared a communication which followed immediately the presentation of his report. An acrimonious debate followed concerning the two documents and finally resulted in the appointment of a special committee to examine the accounting at the house of correction and report at their convenience. This special committee was fortunately composed of excellent men who together with expert accountants appointed by the mayor and board of inspectors made such a thorough examination of the business transactions and accounting of the house

of correction as had not probably been equaled in the
history of any other similar institution. The outcome
of this remarkably thorough inquiry is embodied in
two reports which covered examinations of two different periods of operations, these periods covering the
whole history, and are deemed of sufficient importance
to warrant their insertion here.

To the Honorable
    the Common Council
        June, 1872.
Gentlemen:

Your committee, to whom was referred the report of William Wiley and B. Franklin Baker, expert accountants,
employed by the committee appointed by the mayor and
board of inspectors, in January, 1872, to examine the books
and accounts of the Detroit House of Correction, would
respectfully report that they have examined the same, and
would herewith report that the examination is for the first
four years of the business of the House of Correction, covering the years 1862, 1863, 1864, and 1865. These gentlemen
say, "We have found errors in these accounts as detailed in
schedule A, sent herewith. We also notice in the books some
informalities, which have prolonged the examination, although *not affecting the accuracy of the accounts*. But all these
informalities disappear in subsequent books. The whole
number of errors, as set forth in schedule A is twenty-three
(23), varying from two cents to twelve dollars and fifteen
cents ($12.15). The errors occur on both sides of the ledger,
and are stated to be errors from voucher to day book, and
from day book to journal, there being a difference of loss and
gain, if there be any, of four dollars and twenty-four cents
in favor of the House of Correction."

Your committee submit it as their opinion that the report
of these gentlemen is all that could be expected; that it could
not be expected that the superintendent, with the various
duties he must necessarily perform, in the first four years
of his superintendency of the House of Correction, could

detect these small and unimportant informalities and errors, as in their opinion, very few, if any, business houses pass that period of time without more errors occurring in their books.

Your committee feel it obligatory upon them to say that it is to be looked upon as a remarkable occurrence in public institutions to have a thorough examination of the books and accounts made, and found as accurate as have been found the books of the House of Correction, for the first four years of its existence.

(Signed) SMITH R. WOOLLEY
P. PARSONS
CHARLES STRANGE

Soon after the beginning of work by the expert accountants employed they were said to have remarked to their acquaintances in the city that the books they were examining bore, on their face, unmistakable evidence of their integrity. Their remarks and the publication of the first report dissipated in the public mind all effect of the innuendo which had been made by the member of the council. The final report of the committee appeared under date of November 8, 1872, and is as follows:

"To the Honorable the Common Council:

Gentlemen: — Your committee, who was instructed to employ two expert accountants to examine the books and accounts of the House of Correction, from the first of January, 1866, to the first of January, 1872, would respectfully report that they have complied with said instructions, and herewith submit to your honorable body the report of said gentlemen, which is the result of five months' labor. Their report is accompanied by the book in which many of their computations are made, and in which they took the trial balances of the business ledger, and seventy-nine pages of manuscript, containing almost a complete history of the business of the institution.

The report is so complete and explicit, your committee do not deem it necessary to make any extended comments upon it, and beg leave to submit the same with saying that it furnishes the following facts, namely:

(1) That the books have been systematically and properly kept.

(2) It is a complete vindication of the integrity and business management of the institution, and with the exception of the small errors mentioned, verifies the accuracy of the published reports of the superintendent. The errors that were found by the examination were committed by *one* of several accountants employed during the six years covered by the report, and being in favor of and against the House of Correction, resulted in a gain of a little over $100.

Your committee have ascertained the fact that the various vouchers said to be missing have been used for the purpose as stated by the experts, and that the payments were actually made, as charged in the books of the House of Correction.

Respectfully submitted,

(Signed)   SMITH R. WOOLLEY
P. PARSONS
CHARLES STRANGE
Committee

On the publication of this conclusion of the whole matter the local newspapers denounced the groundless attempt to discredit the house of correction and its superintendent, and the large expense to the tax-payers for the unnecessary investigation.

This year, 1871, the last year of the first decennial period of the institution, is noteworthy and epochal in my experience for this remarkable investigation and complete exoneration; for the destruction of the institutional industries as a result of fire, and the quick recovery therefrom; also for the production of an annual and decennial report, which gave also a historical sketch of the progress of laws and prison practice, together with my own mental attitude at that time towards the whole question of prison reform.

So much aroused were all the managers of the house of correction by the attempt to discredit the management, and so determined were they that there should remain no loophole for further attack, that the mayor was asked to invite such citizens as in his judgment were well qualified to join in the examination for the decennial record. The mayor accordingly invited nine representative men to perform this special service. Four were assigned the duty of ascertaining the correctness of the inventory of the machinery, tools, chairs, chairstuff, and lumber, appraising the same, thus covering the materials of the manufacturing interests. Three were assigned the like service in respect of household furniture, general fixtures, horses, wagons, etc. To Mr. King, a crockery merchant, acquainted with house furnishing goods generally, was assigned the duty of appraising the crockery and domestic utensils of the establishment. Four, some doing double duty, were entrusted with the supervision of the examination of books and accounts. The whole body — the nine — together inspected the buildings and grounds. The outcome of the entire examination by these citizens is tersely expressed in the following paragraph taken from the inspector's report of that year:

"It will be seen from the statements herewith that near the close of 1861 the building commissioners turned over to the city the buildings of the institution, which had cost $77,746.60. But it was then in no condition for use. It was wholly without motor power, machinery, or stock. Large additions and improvements have since been made at a cost of $102,150.64. . . .

This whole amount has been furnished from the earnings of the institution, leaving every dollar that has been furnished by the city since its opening, now on hand and represented in personal property as shown by the inventories. In other words, the city has now represented in property of the institution not only the original outlay, but also over $100,000 in acquired value."

This good economic showing was achieved under the discouragement of deranged general business conditions incident to the years of our civil war before referred to, and under the embarrassment of loss by fire at the beginning of the decennial year. On the night of December 31, 1870, and morning of January 1, 1871, an accidental conflagration destroyed the west line of workshops including the steam engine and much valuable machinery, completely demoralizing, for the time, the principal productive manufacturing industry of the institution — the manufacture of chairs. It required $34,153.91 to restore the burned building and equipment, of which only $12,000 was supplied by insurance. Yet, though the industry was so crippled for the first half of the year, the profit or income over expenses and losses for the entire year, based on the inventory and appraisal of the citizens' committee, reached the large sum of $34,855.39.

The investigations so satisfactorily concluded effectually closed every avenue to captious criticism, and we were supplied with better manufacturing facilities by the new, enlarged factory building and improved machinery. The sense of restful relief that supervened can easily be imagined. All account books, records, and documents of every kind, together with reports of expert examiners and committees covering the business transactions from the beginning in 1862 to the commencement of the year 1872, were enclosed and sealed in a strong chest constructed for the purpose and permanently consigned to the vaults of the institution. Surveying this sealed chest with good knowledge of its imprisoned contents, my friend, Inspector Mason, remarked, in all seriousness now, "It is rare in the history of a public official of any grade in the service, that ten successive years of his administration should receive such an exhaustive examination as the past ten years of your superintendency here has received. You may well felicitate yourself on having received the completest possible bill of health for your official acts and your personal standing now — at your age of forty-three years. Such an endorsement of public approval constitutes the best of capital for either a business or an official career." Then with a merry twinkle in his eye he said, "I trust you will not yield to the temptation of the present situation or mistake your certificate for a license."

The tenth annual report, which is also the first decennial published report of the house of correction, printed in 1872, the only accessible copy of which is perhaps the copy in my own possession, and whose contents until recently reviewed were lost to sight if not to memory, is, I am impelled to say of the entire document, the most comprehensive and satisfactory prison report that has ever come to my notice except, possibly, some later reports of the reformatory at Elmira. The statistical and financial tables are unusual examples of accurate accounting and interesting information admirably condensed.

During my period of service at Detroit I was appointed by the Canadian government as a member of the arbitration commission provided to adjust a difference that had arisen between that government and the prison contractors of the Central Prison at Toronto. The commission held a number of sessions in the parliament house at Toronto and made the award which proved satisfactory to the contending parties. In the year 1873 the War Department of the United States designated a commission to prepare plans for a military prison intended to be established at Rock Island, Illinois. The commission was composed of three army officers and two civilians; namely, Col. Nelson A. Miles, Lieut.-Col. William A. French, Mayor Thomas F. Barr, and Rev. E. C. Wines, Secretary of the American Prison Association and Secretary of the Prison Association of New York, together with myself of the Detroit House of Correction. The commission met at Boston and prepared the plans; but the prison was never established because Congress failed to provide the necessary appropriation. The governor of Michigan made me a member of the permanent "Board of State Commissioners for the general supervision of charitable, penal, pauper, and reformatory institutions," to which commission, as already stated, the duty of investigating and reporting on a revision of the criminal laws was committed.

There occurred, here at Detroit, a hiatus of three years in my prison service, the only break in nearly a half century of continuance. Conditions at the Detroit House of Correction seemed unfavorable for such a demonstration of an improved prison system as it was my ambition to show. There was no apparent probability that, within the period of my prospective active life, the indeterminate sentence principle would be applied to the treatment of misdemeanant prisoners; and I felt unwilling to devote my best years to the vain effort to confer a public benefit by managing such prisoners under the disadvantage of the short sentence. The extreme conservatism and narrow views of the city mayor were discouraging factors in the situation. Besides, serious illness in my family and my own prostration by an attack of acute rheumatism made me feel that further residence at the Detroit institution was really undesirable on account of our health.

While in such a frame of mind the opportunity came to me to engage in the land department of one of the Pacific railroads at greatly increased income and with prospect of philanthropic activity in peopling their lands with actual settlers. Meditating this proposition when confined to my room with illness, I had fully determined to accept it. But my friends, James McMillan and John S. Newberry, owners of the Michigan Car Company, desired that I should remain in Detroit and offered me the vice-presidency of their company, naming a salary far beyond my estimation of my own value. I accepted their offer and resigned the superintendency of the Detroit House of Correction at the close of the year 1872.

CHAPTER X

THREE YEARS OF PRIVATE LIFE

1872–1875

ON ASSUMING duty with the Michigan Car Company, December, 1872, the family — wife, two daughters, and myself — removed from the residence at the house of correction to a three-storied house in the Wight Block, 405 Jefferson Avenue, in the city. One adjoining house was occupied by Dr. Hogarth and family, the pastor of the church of our attendance; the other adjoining residence was the home of the Wights, whose mistress, Miss Wight, was actively engaged with us in the mission school. Nearby lived, each in a handsome residence, my friends and associates in business, McMillan and Newberry. The neighbors and neighborhood were all that could be desired. For the first time in our family life we now had a residence apart from an institution. It was a new and grateful change of family circumstances, accompanied with increase of social privileges and of incidental obligations. The changed way of living, release from the cares of a prison, satisfactory outcome of the recent contentions, and the hopeful outlook for achieving a competency, imparted happiness of a calm and peaceful kind as of a tempest-tossed voyager on reaching the harbor.

This more agreeable family life continued throughout the three years, broken only by one incident. Our daughter, Emma, nineteen years old, had just graduated from Sill's Seminary and had suffered a siege of typhoid fever. In order to insure her complete recovery, accompanied by her cousin, Miss Grace Comstock, of about the same age, she went abroad for the benefit of the ocean voyage and six months of travel under the escort of Colonel J. A. Bates, U. S. A., who, with his wife — my niece — was already in London. No familiar escort for the ocean voyage could be found and it was with hesitation and solicitude that they embarked unattended and with the possibility of missing connection with Colonel Bates and finding themselves alone in London. But we were comforted by the assurance of Captain Brooks of the steamer, City of Antwerp, that the young ladies should be treated as his own daughters and that he personally would see that they should find their friends in London or be properly cared for. It is a pleasure to say that this was fulfilled. However, it could not be avoided that, after witnessing the departure of the steamer down the bay at New York, putting out to sea and carrying away our children, we were sobered and still quite anxious. This frame of mind was favorable for the deep impression that was made by Henry Ward Beecher's Sunday morning prayer, at Plymouth Church, Brooklyn, the next day when we all were present. Whether himself moved by his own anxieties I know not, but he paused in the course of the prayer as if overcome with deep feeling, until the great audience was hushed and expectant. Then to our astonished ears he cried: "Oh Lord! our children! Some have separated from the parent stock and are now *sweeping out to sea!"* Then in the tones of his marvelous voice he entreated divine care, preservation, and rescue. It will readily be imagined that that passage in Mr. Beecher's prayer made an ineffaceable impression on our minds and feelings. Crossing the ocean in those days was not a simple holiday affair.

It was with high hope that I entered upon my new occupation. The company's business, already large and profitable, was planned for expansion. Messrs. McMillan and Newberry, the proprietors and managers, combined rare business qualifications; my own previous success in managing prison industries warranted self-confidence; my stipulated compensation was abundant; and a pathway to accumulating a fortune seemed wide open. But the expectation was never fully realized, nor have my purely personal business ventures beyond the salaried employments ever been successful. My father once said that a wise New England forecaster of character said of me in my teens, "That lad will never become forehanded, for he has not the money-getting instinct." And I must acknowledge that all my life long I have been conscious of an instinctive repugnance to mere money-getting.

My first investment of money saved in bank stock resulted in a loss; the second in Western Union Telegraph stock was equally unprofitable; the third, a private partnership in a haberdasher house, was not unprofitable, but involved the risk of endorsement never properly compensated by any profit gained. Another private partnership with the Tallman Furniture House was more disastrous, but a certain service I rendered induced the other partners to assume the monetary loss without such loss to me. Five years a special partner in the Detroit Safe Company, the period of its development, gave me no profit nor did it involve a loss. Again, investment in a glass-works at Wyandotte, a short-lived venture, was unfortunate for all except myself, saved from loss by the generosity of the others. Later, after I left the car company, I formed an active partnership with the old established furniture house of Marcus Stevens and Company, which house proved to be hollow and unsound. With McMillan's assistance I forced a settlement that saved my capital; and after my withdrawal, the house soon failed.

My connection with the Michigan Car Company and the Car Wheel Company continued from December, 1872, to August, 1874, not quite twenty months. The first and chief reason for such short duration of the connection was the general financial depression and panic of that time and the particular difficulty of getting currency for the $30,000 a month pay roll. The great works were temporarily closed, leaving little or nothing for me to do in return for the large salary I was receiving. Such service for the company as was open to me was out of my experience and often distasteful. The most important service I rendered during the twenty months of service was of a negative sort, preventing a heavy loss sustained by an Ohio company that took a large contract for cars which I rejected. The before mentioned brief connection with the Marcus Stevens Company furniture house fills out the remainder of this three years' hiatus.

Thus at the age of fifty years I found myself out of employment; without the requisite capital for any suitable business venture; and with insufficient income for the support of my family. Perhaps the prediction of the New England wiseacre had in my middle life proved true at all events. Avenues of business advancement seemed hedged up from the date of my withdrawal from the prison service. In April, 1876, the Jefferson Avenue residence was given up, our furniture was sent to storage, and the wife and daughters went to our childhood home in Connecticut to spend the summer while I myself, on urgent invitation of my friend McMillan, became temporarily his guest in his home. Such was the rather painful situation which with the early ensuing deliverance is so markedly coincident with what at that time seemed the fulfillment of a veritable prophecy. A few days after beginning service with the car company, I met one morning a familiar business acquaintance who said he had dreamed of me as follows: In his dream we were conversing about my change of employment from the House of Correction to the car company, and I had remarked that I had probably made a mistake in changing; that the commercialism of the new service was distasteful to me and that I intended to re-enter the prison service at the first opportunity. The prophecy of this casual acquaintance flashed into mind when early in May I received by telegraph the offer of the superintendency of the then incomplete and unopened Elmira Reformatory. The dispatch came from Louis D. Pilsbury, son of Amos Pilsbury with whom I had been associated in the early fifties, who was one of the newly appointed board of managers of the reformatory, and who at the same time was the superintendent of the state prisons of New York. I wired my willingness, left for Elmira the same day, and on the following day, May 12, 1876, was duly appointed.

The meeting of the board of managers at which the appointment was made was in the evening, and newspaper reporters were not admitted. But local interest in the proceedings was so great that on his special request a reporter was admitted after the appointment was made to get an account of it. When he had finished his inquiries and his notes he hesitatingly shut his note book and pocketing it surprised us all with the remark, "Gentlemen, will you permit me to say that you have made a fortunate selection of a superintendent. Mr. Brockway does not recognize me but I well remember him. Many years ago I served a term as a prisoner in his House of Correction at Detroit and received good care in the hospital when I was suffering from delirium tremens. I bid you good-night." This seemed another unusual coincidence — the presence of a former inmate, on the occasion of my appointment, in service as reporter on a local newspaper.

The next day, Saturday, I went over to Albany and presented myself at the office of John Bigelow, the secretary of state, to take the oath of office. On signing my name in the book of records Mr. Bigelow remarked that I could be congratulated at signing next under the name of Josephine Shaw Lowell, the first woman ever appointed by the governor of New York as member of a commission.

I had never expressed a desire for the charge of the Elmira Reformatory but had hopefully looked forward to such an opportunity. I had known of the progress of its establishment from the earliest inception, and

in 1870 had inspected the plans at the instance of
General Pilsbury, the building commissioner. The appointment seemed to compensate in some way for the
disappointment at Detroit when I was deprived of
caring for youthful felonious prisoners, the prospect
of whose custody and reformatory treatment was the
chief motive that induced my removal from Rochester
to that city; it seemed to atone for the infelicities of
my experience in the Detroit House of Correction and
the hedging of avenues for other business. It was
opportune in view of my personal and family circumstances. The fortunate deliverance could but be
confirmative of belief in the existent moral order governing the eventualities of every life.

PART II

The New York State Reformatory, Elmira

CHAPTER XI

ELMIRA

1876–1881

THE foundation, development, and administration of the New York State Reformatory at Elmira, in colloquial phrase the "Elmira Reformatory," engrossed my life for nearly twenty-five years, from May, 1876, to August, 1900, so that the story of the reformatory recites my own history for that period.

The reformatory at Elmira is in the interior of the state in a southern tier county, thus diminishing liability to outside disturbance and the numerous annoyances incident to such an institution if very near a large city. Yet the city of Elmira was large enough to supply an influential local supporting public sentiment. It being an important railroad center, transportation facilities were sufficient. And the Woman's College and the school system of the city could and actually did furnish, at allowable expense, excellent non-resident lecturers and other instructors for the reformatory's evening school. Rev. Thomas K. Beecher, a noted preacher and pastor, lived in Elmira. His powerful influence had created in the community a large-minded liberalism and humanitarianism, and a public sentiment that did not by carping criticism hinder the adoption of rational reformatory procedure. Mr. Beecher gave us, at once, his complete confidence and his hearty sympathy with our aims and generally with our methods. His occasional presence and admirable discourses assisted in establishing the desirable institutional tone. In 1893, likewise, when a certain newspaper published serious charges against us, he publicly defended from his pulpit both the reformatory and myself. Lucius Robinson, the state comptroller, who was an Elmiran and quite in sympathy with the reformatory plans, was influential at Albany in procuring from the legislature the necessary appropriations. In November, 1876, Mr. Robinson was elected governor of New York, which was an additional favorable circumstance. Judge George R. Bradley of Corning, twenty miles away, was that year our senator at Albany. He fathered our bill for organizing the reformatory, which included the indeterminate sentence principle. Senator Bradley's high personal standing, his acknowledged ability, and his supreme court juridical career largely contributed to the enactment by the legislature of the law as it is.

The site of the reformatory was happily selected two miles from the city hall, on a plateau on the hillside seventy feet above the road, overlooking for twenty-two miles the charming Chemung Valley with distant headlands in view. In the rear, to the westward, there rises a hill one hundred feet above the level of the plateau, covered with a dense growth of hardwood trees. This hillside background adds picturesqueness to the turreted, gray-lined, massive buildings below, at the same time affording comfortable storm protection. Attractiveness of site and of architecture while not primarily designed for the delight or cultivation of the taste of convicts, may to some extent be useful in that particular. The myriads of impressions of sight and sound and surroundings contribute immensely to the formation of tastes; and it is axiomatic that good taste is essentially of a moral quality. Certainly such attractions of situation, as relates to the prisoners, are harmless, and are undoubtedly useful for forming a proper public sense as to the treatment of prisoners. The very outward appearance of the reformatory — so little like the ordinary prison and so much like a college or a hospital — helps to change the common sentiment about offenders from the vindictiveness of punishment to the amenities of rational educational correction.

By the act of 1869 the governor of the state appointed commissioners to locate and purchase a site. The present site of 280 acres of land, worthless for agricultural use, was purchased at a cost of $38,052. Some 30 acres of the tract were assigned for buildings and surrounding grounds, 13 acres of which were to be enclosed to form the prison yard. By the act of 1870 building commissioners were appointed who adopted the plans of architect W. L. Woolett of Albany, New York. The plans made provision for only 500 prisoners, and the blocks of cells were so arranged in separate divisions as to facilitate some kind of classification of prisoners, but without complete separation of the different groups. The commissioners in their first report (January, 1872) asked the legislature for a building appropriation of $500,000.

The building commission was soon (act of 1874) superseded by a superintending builder, J. R. Thomas, who continued in charge of the construction until by the act of 1876 the board of managers was created to complete the structure and to organize and administer the reformatory for its intended purpose. Mr. Thomas had carried on the building operations according to the Woolett general plan, but had changed the materials for the outer walls from stone to brick, greatly reducing the cost. Mr. Thomas' choice of materials was approved by the board of managers. He continued as advisory architect for a few months, but from the date of my appointment as general superintendent, May, 1876, the labor of prisoners transferred from the state prisons was utilized in the rough and simple mechanical work of construction. This necessitated my own immediate agency both in building and organizing, so that ere long the services of an architect were no longer required, and consequently Mr. Thomas retired. All the constructive work afterwards done until my own retirement in 1900, with the exception of the building by contract of the south wing extension, was done by the prisoners aided by a few citizen mechanics, as ordered by the board of managers and directed by the general superintendent. By utilizing the labor of prisoners in developing the material properties, a measure which later was greatly facilitated by the instruction in trade schools, a hundredfold more was accomplished with an equal expenditure of money than by intervention of contractors and their workmen.

The reformatory was established with a total expenditure of a million and a half, or a little more. (Since 1900 another half million or so has been expended in a similar manner for additional accommodation.) Built as it was without the intervention of building contractors and largely by the labor of prisoners, and with special regard to the intended uses under the reformatory system, it may safely be said that the facilities possessed at this institution for rational reformatory processes probably exceed those of any other known prison. So unusual and admirable are these facilities, and so interesting was the work of introducing, adjusting, and combining them for the main purpose in view, that it is now difficult to refrain from a detailed description of it all. But that must await a later place in this narrative.

When, in 1876, the board of managers was created, and I, as general superintendent, took active charge of everything that related to the reformatory, the buildings and grounds were inadequate and quite unfit for the reception of prisoners. But after a few simple preparations, prisoners from the state prisons were brought to the reformatory to engage in the building operations. The first instalment of such prisoners arrived on July 27, 1876, when the institution went into commission. The laws governing it were tentative and quite inadequate. No suitable organizing legislation had been had; none had yet been framed nor indeed conceived of by the general public, the state government, or the board of managers elect.

Early in the nineteenth century a reaction against sanguinary punishments produced the penitentiary system, but so crude was it that during the first half of the century it was a conceded failure. Official reports declared that "if human ingenuity were tasked to devise means by which the most profligate of men might be rendered abandoned to the last degree of moral infamy, nothing more effectual could be invented than the system then in vogue."

At about the commencement of my prison service, in 1848, there were in existence two plans of penitentiary treatment both of which were intended to obviate the grosser defects of the first penitentiaries, but without satisfactory results. I refer to the solitary or separate system typified by the Eastern Penitentiary of Pennsylvania; and the Auburn or silent system which in the United States has been more generally adopted. Discussion as to the comparative desirability of the two systems was rife and still somewhat engages the attention of penologists, particularly those of Europe. The separate system is more favored in Europe and has advantages for temporary disciplinary purposes and for continued confinement of certain incorrigible prisoners. But it is not adapted to the training of prisoners to become orderly free inhabitants. Mr. Cassidy, for many years the warden of the Pennsylvania Eastern Penitentiary, estimated genuine reformation under that system to be about 4 per cent. The Auburn system, especially under Superintendent Louis D. Pilsbury's administration of the New York state prisons, achieved admirable financial results, — the greatest productive results from employment of the prisoners' labor; but in public protection from crimes by deterrence, or the reclamation of prisoners, the Auburn was no better than the Pennsylvania system. One of the most experienced and capable wardens of an Auburn system prison (who will not permit me to use his name) told me that in his opinion 60 per cent of his prisoners were as sure to resume crimes as they were sure to be discharged from prison; that another 30 per cent would in all probability do the same; and as to the remainder he could not form a confident opinion.

The public and the prison authorities looked to the religious precepts of chaplains and to the penitential effect of prison labor for the desired reformatory result. Indeed, prison labor was at first introduced into the prisons mainly as an aid to religious ministrations; but "hard labor" produced no penitence and proved not a punishment but a boon to the prisoners. Ere long the prevailing motive of the prison labor systems with the state government, the prison managers, and the prison contractors, became excessively mercenary. The mercenary sentiment was fostered by the movement of the time establishing county or district penitentiaries for short-term prisoners. The Albany Penitentiary established in the forties by Amos Pilsbury, where under his management short-term prisoners' labor was made so pecuniarily productive, stimulated the foundation of similar prisons elsewhere, as I have already explained. The pecuniary results obtained in these county prisons served to spread and confirm mere profit-making with, of course, the traditional notion of punishment as the end and aim of imprisonment. Prevalence of this notion hindered for a time ready acceptance of the reformatory system — the detention of prisoners until they were adjudged fit for safe inhabitancy. Release of prisoners was constantly urged by outsiders on the ground that one or another had already been "punished enough," but there were of course different ideas of just what is "enough." Prisoners came imbued with the idea that they were imprisoned for punishment, and this idea, until it could be removed, proved a hindrance to their interest and progress in the means adopted for reformation.

Yet another, more favorable, phase of public sentiment must have been abroad throughout the state, or the laws and appropriations to establish the reformatory could not have been made. A certain diffused, indefinite, religio-philanthropic sentiment had been created by the work and publications of the Prison Association of New York through its very efficient secretary, Rev. E. C. Wines. This was remarked by Senator Schoonmaker, who declared that the influence of the Prison Association had prepared the public mind for even such a radical reform measure. Dr. Harris, who succeeded Dr. Wines as secretary of the Prison Association, said, when the bill for establishing the reformatory had been enacted into a law, that the fact constituted a modern miracle. Every senator present voted for the bill, and in the assembly the vote stood 73 in favor and only 15 against it. But what seemed miraculous to Dr. Harris has a rational explanation. Confidence in the good judgment and advocacy of Judge Bradley, our senator, of Mr. Pilsbury, state superintendent of the three state prisons, and of the petitioners wonderfully helped it along. There were 347 influential petitioners for the Indeterminate Sentence Act. Of this number, 113 were well-known lawyers or trial court justices, 97 practicing physicians, 50 city or county officials, clergymen, merchants, or very prominent private citizens, 20 supreme court judges or ex-state officers, 67 active state officers or military commanders and other officials of highest rank. It was phenomenal that so many distinguished men should so readily petition for the enactment of such a radical change in the criminal law.

There never was a time when, probably, a direct vote of the people to establish a reformatory at an original outlay of $1,500,000 and an entailed annual expenditure of $200,000 for current support could have been obtained. Yet such an expenditure and more has actually been made and entailed by action of the people's representatives without one word of public protest. It was sagely said, at the time, that however sound might be the philosophical basis of our system, it was such an innovation, so far in advance of the common conception, that the work of establishing the reformatory and administering it would no doubt be attended with much perplexity.

The board of managers had five members. Louis D. Pilsbury of Albany, president of the board, was a state officer under the new constitution — superintendent of the state prisons, and of life-long familiarity with prison management. He was the best living exponent of the Auburn Prison System, and pre-eminently successful in managing the labor of prisoners for the state and in their disciplinary control. But he was not specially interested in the reformatory idea, and was so engrossed with his duties as a state officer that he could not, even if he had desired, devote himself to the details of our reformatory organization and management. Ex-Judge Ariel S. Thurston, the secretary, Rufus King, a leading local attorney, Dr. W. C. Wey, very prominent in the medical profession, and Sinclair Toucey, president of the American News Company of New York City, were all, save Mr. Toucey, residents of Elmira. None of the managers, except Mr. Pilsbury, had previously given attention to prison matters, yet all were by temperament and general capability well qualified for their supervisory duties.

At an early meeting of the managers, at the instance

of Mr. Pilsbury, the principle was adopted of free executive managing direction by the general superintendent, upon which so much depends and without which the reformatory could not have achieved its subsequent success. This supplemented the principle of institutional autonomy of the act of 1877. The institution itself was individual, unique in its purposes, and independent of the governing authorities who controlled the other state prisons, and was not subject to the supervision of the state board of charities. Afterwards the managers voluntarily acquiesced in the inspections and published reports of the state board. The following resolutions, adopted at the second meeting of the managers, are here inserted to show how completely the superintendent was vested with executive freedom. Instead of dividing into committees and dictating details the managers direct the superintendent:

1. To prepare a code of rules and regulations.
2. To employ such assistance as he deems necessary to open the reformatory for the reception of prisoners, at such compensation as is requisite and within the limits of the laws.
3. To make purchases in his discretion.
4. To proceed, within the law and appropriations, with the completion of the reformatory structure.
5. That the general superintendent organize the prison productive industries.

Such freedom of initiative, throughout my incumbency, was always awarded me. Thus in the internal management of the reformatory I was privileged to submit my theories when the application of them was tangible. In this connection it seems worthy of note that, by this means, so long ago as 1877, the test of penological truth was made substantially that of the more recent phase of pragmatic philosophy; namely, the practical results.

The freedom and leadership conferred by the board of managers gave me a sense of duty and responsibility which completely dominated my mind and activities. Then and throughout my entire term of service I was untrammeled by any private business interests; any consideration of social or political advantage; and held myself aloof from diverting church and charitable endeavors in which at Detroit and Rochester I had taken such active interest.

The indeterminate sentence act of 1877, precisely as I drafted it with the exception of a maximum limitations clause, which had been inserted not as sound of principle but necessary as policy, put upon the managers the function of determining the duration of imprisonments on the basis of public safety, and left open to the managers the selection and use of measures to fit the prisoners for safe discharge. And this high function of the managers had by their action become also mine; that is to say, in the detail of execution. Thousands of men in the years ahead — youthful men — were to be placed in our custody directly for the public protection but also for the purpose of forming and reforming of their characters, so determining their earthly career. Deprived as they were of the formative influences of a normal social condition, the responsibility for their reformation was profoundly impressive. I absolved myself from any feeling of responsibility for the original interference with their individual liberty and normal social situation — the acts of the police and the courts. Nor did I allow my mind to dwell upon the averred responsibility of society for their crimes. With the faultiness of society we had nothing to do in our relation to the prisoners; but such complete control as was devolved upon the managers and myself over the entire outer and inner life of the prisoners greatly oppressed me. Reverend T. K. Beecher, who clearly perceived the extent of this relation, quaintly remarked: "Why, you, here at the reformatory, are a little tin god on wheels!"

The indeterminate sentence law also gratifyingly changed the usual relation of prison governor and prisoners from antagonism of desire to accordance of interest. If disagreement should occur as to the conditions of release, it was or would be only a surface disagreement, for at the foundation both the prisoner and the governor desired his progress. The responsibility and changed relation ennobled the office of the governor and made necessary the closest scrutiny of reformative principles and of prison management. Could we possibly discover and adopt some guiding basic principle? Twenty-five years of experience with felon and misdemeanant prisoners; with dependents and defectives in charitable institutions; and much knowledge of such persons in their haunts and living places, had operated to somewhat impair my confidence in certain of the popular specifics. My attitude in this respect was somewhat as follows:

Although the reformatory belongs to that department of a state government named "the department of justice," yet the administration of justice could not be made the central guiding principle. It would conflict with the spirit and intention of the indeterminate sentence law; and there exists not within our human ken any reliable standard of retributive requital. Equally, the deterrent principle was inconsistent, and its inadequacy had long been observed. Evangelism would not do. The American policy of separation of church and state should be respected in organizing and conducting a state institution, and the religious instrumentality in prisons had not so generally effected a change of moral character and behavior with prisoners as to commend evangelism for the central guiding principle. Nor had the combined influence of punishment, moral maxims, precepts, and personal persuasion, with the intended introspection, been so effective as to warrant reliance upon such means wielded directly upon the minds of prisoners. Such agencies and considerations would of necessity remain to some extent incidentally operative, but none, nor all, could satisfactorily accomplish the purpose of the state in founding the institution. Beyond any influence of these, something more concrete and effective must be found. Already hopefully loomed the formative value of good habits duly confirmed and the ennobling influence of established individual industrial efficiency. These last principles became dominant and were pursued with increasing confidence and accuracy of application until the final firm belief was reached as formulated in a paper prepared for the International Prison Congress of 1910.*

It is of course not impossible that the foregoing synopsis of my remembered mental attitude may, unconsciously, be colored by the later confirmed

---

* An abstract of this paper, The American Reformatory Prison System, will be found in Appendix IV, p. 419.

impressions; but this at least is true, that at the time of assuming management of the Elmira Reformatory I had emerged from the traditional theological or fictional stage of mental attitude into the evolutionary second stage — the metaphysical, or stage of inquiry; and I was then open to impressions in outreach for the practical and more scientific system later evolved.

During the initial twenty-six months, from July 24, 1876, to October, 1878, it was not practicable to enter upon the projected reformatory plans. The prison structure was not completed; the required facilities were not at hand; the presence of so many prisoners from the state prisons who were under definite sentence, was an embarrassment; the building operations interfered; and a supposed need to produce income for current maintenance by utilizing the labor of prisoners also hindered. It is to be confessed that at that time excessive reliance was placed on mere common schooling as in itself a reformatory agency. Only very slow progress was made until the commencement of the last year of the series, October, 1880; then and afterwards more improvement took place. Up to this date the reformatory differed only in name from a common, rough, state prison with an unusual percentage of exceptionally bad prisoners; yet during this incipient stage much public attention was directed to the institution and its theories. But our earnest investigations continued and the study of means and methods which were subsequently put to use. Before taking up this subject, however, the reader is invited to an inside view of prisoners, bad and good, with an account of occurrences such as are not usually portrayed by address or publication.

CHAPTER XII

DIFFICULT PRISONERS

URING the first half-year of the reformatory, 194 definite sentenced prisoners* were received, all but ten of them transfers from the state prisons at Auburn and Sing Sing. Those selected for transfer from Auburn by Warden Durston, were fairly suitable for the common laborers' work intended; but the prisoners from Sing Sing were not only unaccustomed to such labor, but they were city criminals ill-adapted for laboring work, besides being specially vicious and untamed men. The removal of these prisoners certainly relieved the officials there of disciplinary trouble; and whether deliberately intended or not, foisted upon us at the reformatory prematurely a class of men calculated to discredit the new institution at the very beginning. Prison officers at the state prisons were antagonistic toward the reformatory, and their transferred prisoners came with only contempt for that which in their view the term reformatory signifies — the usual Sunday school notion. Fifty prisoners in railroad transit from Sing Sing, observing in the distance the reformatory on the hillside with its

---

* It should be explained that prisoners under definite sentence were committed to the reformatory by the state courts until, in 1877, the Indeterminate Sentence Act became a law. The federal courts, however, committed definite sentenced prisoners there after that time.

wooden stockade inclosure, shouted in derision both at the frailty of the enclosure and at the avowed purpose of the place. These prisoners — 471 in all — who were definitely sentenced men, were a seriously disturbing element. The insecurity of the place and the confusion occasioned by building operations, incited vicious activity and gave opportunity for insurgent combinations. Safe custody and the avoidance of evil influence necessitated strict discipline, itself additionally irksome and not easily maintained with the assistance of only the inexperienced prison officers of that time; all the more difficult because we deferred too much, as the sequel showed, to our own and the common dislike of resort to physical coercive measures.

A hundred or more of these prisoners were permanently possessed of the insurrectionary mood which, limitedly, was communicated to the others. The existence of the mood was known to the management notwithstanding the efforts to conceal it. It never reached a destructive ascendency because the incipient manifestations were quickly discovered and repressed. Note the following instances:

Once when one hundred prisoners were engaged as laborers and masons in building a division wall under armed guards stationed upon the walls, their muttering attracted attention and a brewing plan was discovered to attack the guards with bricks and then escape. I replaced one of the guards with a veteran army sharpshooter who reluctantly took temporary service with us, when, as by magic, the seething restlessness immediately subsided. The prisoners could not possibly have known the qualifications of the new guard, except by the instinctive perception of animals and men by which they measure danger and safety, yet the effect of his appearance on guard post was instantaneously quieting. Mr. Cook, the guard, soon resigned, disgusted, as he said, that he had wasted a full month of his time without a single shot.

Later, a dozen of the prisoners attempted to scale the stockade within one hundred feet of a guard armed with repeating rifle, who held a certificate of excellence at the Creedmore range. He fired at them, but his shot went wild of its intended mark and two of the prisoners scaled the enclosure unharmed. They ran skirting the nearby woods, pursued by Mr. McKelvey, the principal keeper, who brought down one by a shot that inflicted only a flesh wound. The other got away, but a few weeks afterward was arrested in New York City and returned to us. Here we have again the prisoner's instinctive perception, this time of the inefficiency of the Creedmore guard.

All the prisoners were assembled every Sunday for a religious service, on the guardroom floor. I myself was always present upon the platform with the preacher. At one of these Sunday afternoon religious services, during the long prayer when all heads were bowed in apparent reverence and devotion, I observed furtive glances among a group of the Sing Sing transferred prisoners, who, disturbed by my observing them, discontinued their communications. At the close of the service these prisoners were detained and searched, when knotted cords and implements were found and their plan to seize and bind all the officers and accomplish a general jail delivery was revealed. The attempt that was to be made that day during this devotional part of the religious service was only prevented by the quick detection of their furtive glances before they had completed their arrangements.

The warden of the Massachusetts state prison told me of a similar scheme in his prison which reached the stage of open assault in the prison chapel during the closing prayer. The leading insurgent interrupted the prayer, when the chaplain was tenderly pleading for divine protection and guidance for the loved ones at home, loudly called upon the six hundred prisoners assembled to revolt, and he himself with many others rushed to the platform where, with the chaplain, the warden and deputy warden were seated. The prisoners were armed with improvised stilettos of various kinds and seriously wounded the deputy warden, but the warden, an experienced army Indian fighter, by his bold manner and his revolver checked and quelled the revolt. Some years previous to the above named occurrence Mr. Walker, the deputy warden, was stabbed to death on the chaplain's platform in the chapel of that prison at the close of a religious service, and Warden Turner soon after was assassinated while passing through one of the workshops.

At the reformatory occurred another instance of grouped opposition by these transferred prisoners, which, however, was early overcome. At the noon turn-out after dinner, while the other prisoners were moving to their respective employments, I was told that twenty of these state prison convicts, who were locked up and dined in adjoining cells in a remote part of the prison, had combined and refused to leave their cells to resume their work. Quickly impressed with the serious insurrectionary significance of this incipient revolt, I took from the hand of the officer the cell-keys and went unattended, as with winged feet and increasing conscious impelling force, to the scene of disturbance. On reaching the gallery of the cells and abruptly opening them one by one the rebellious convicts without parley or hesitation, but with a surprised expression of countenance, obeyed my command, came out, and formed in line in the corridor below. Then they marched to their place of employment and resumed work. The insurrectors, full-grown men, had agreed among themselves to resist the authorities, but thus confronted, their united purpose was relinquished and the reformatory was saved from a probable general disturbance which at that stage of the institution would have been very disastrous.

In this connection, in order to correct certain erroneous impressions about the administering of truly effective reformatory treatment to adult male criminals, it appears incumbent on me to describe the bad behavior and troublesomeness of some of the convict class, who, when firmly held to the observance of the salutary régime established for all, which was so opposed to their habits and inclinations, were recalcitrant and not infrequently obstreperous. The recital will offer no novelty to experienced prison managers; but, unattractive as it undoubtedly is, may prove informing to the inexperienced and be serviceable in correcting misconceptions produced by moving stories, exaggerated or truthful, of altogether exceptional individual reclamations; and may correct mistaken opinions derived from fallacious theological theories and excessive sentimentalism.*

---

*Names of prisoners mentioned are in most cases fictitious.

Two men, Rafferty, transferred from Sing Sing, and Reddington, from the Blackwell's Island penitentiary, were typical ingrained recalcitrants. They were each about twenty-five years of age, of slender but muscular physique, black-bearded men of Celtic, sanguine temperament. Rafferty, because of his frequent conflict with the prison guards, spent much of the term of his imprisonment in the seclusion cells, and occasionally an outburst of insubordination was overcome for the moment by confronting him with the muzzle of a revolver. On his release at the expiration of his definite sentence Rafferty returned to New York City, and soon afterwards at an early morning hour he was discovered suspiciously trespassing on the premises of a lumber yard at the upper west side of the city. When ordered off the grounds, he viciously assaulted the proprietor, but in the fray received a blow from the brass-bound board rule in the proprietor's hands which fractured his skull and caused his death. The occurrence was followed by an extended and expensive trial of the proprietor with the result of his acquittal. Rafferty was not recognizably insane, but pugnacious and untamed. He was doubtless unable, as he was indisposed, to restrain himself without the aid of extraneous agency. Therefore he may not have been quite responsible for his conduct.

Reddington, whose inborn or inbred defective disposition was like that of Rafferty, had additional exasperation by reason of his definite ten years' sentence. His four years' career at the reformatory was turbulent. At no time did he get interested in work, recreative opportunities, or in the improving agencies. This sour temper kept him in constant trouble.

Finally, in 1881, for inciting a very dangerous affray in the foundry, where about one hundred and thirty prisoners were engaged, during the exciting hour when the melted iron from the cupola was being distributed to the molds, he was permanently placed in a light and roomy cell in the division for separate confinement, where during the daytime, while other prisoners were at work, he was manacled as a precautionary measure. On a bright August Sunday afternoon the thought of his discomfort took me through the long corridors to the remoter division of the cells where Reddington was confined. I hoped to find him in a mood that would warrant the removal of the restraints. He was found not in a promising frame of mind but, in the hope that he would appreciate the consideration and prompted more by sentiment than judgment, I directed that he should be released to the freedom of his room. As usual, I was spending Sunday afternoon in cell-door visitations. On reaching my office half an hour later I learned that Reddington had hanged himself and efforts for his resuscitation were unsuccessful.

Another phase of discordance is represented by three young men, Carr, Abbott, and Simmons, who are representative too of criminals at large in the community who ruthlessly kill when committing their crimes, or, if imprisoned and opposed, are homicidally dangerous.

George W. Carr, of fair complexion, light weight, symmetrical proportions, and attractive appearance, admitted to the reformatory in June, 1878, was at once intractable and was reduced to the third or convict grade in December. Incited no doubt by the hope that misconduct would result in his temporary transfer to the Auburn State Prison where, as was known, the prisoners were indulged with freer communication among themselves; where tobacco was allowed and distributed, and where correspondence and visits with outside confederates and influential comrades could be had; Carr having secretly provided himself with an improvised razor-like knife, picked a trifling quarrel with a fellow prisoner working near him, and then suddenly assaulted him, slashing his throat and inflicting a dangerous, though fortunately not a fatal wound. For this felonious assault Carr was tried and convicted in the county court and committed to the state prison,— not temporarily, as he desired, but for a definite term of years. There he murdered a prison keeper and was duly sentenced to death by electrocution. The commissioners of lunacy declared him not insane in the legal sense of insanity, so that after some delay the sentence to electrocution was carried out.

Carr possessed unusual but misdirected native capabilities. His egotism, a quality commonly offensive and obtrusive with criminals, was so excessive that it suggested, simultaneously, heroism and illusion. Within the more limited range of capabilities, restricted opportunities, and consequent different manifestations, he showed similar traits of character to the intriguing, violent Alcibiades of classic literature. It is not improbable that, had Carr been an inmate of the reformatory ten years later, under the perfected and more effective disciplinary régime, he might have been saved to himself and to society, and have achieved a useful, possibly a brilliant career.

Joseph Abbott was a vagabond, certified as seventeen

years of age but in reality in his twentieth year; tall, well developed, muscular, swarthy as an Indian, brutal, deliberately malicious, the inheritor of criminal tendency — his father was then serving a life sentence in the Connecticut State Prison. Abbott was committed to the reformatory in 1879 for burglary in the first degree, which, under the indeterminate sentence system, involved a maximum imprisonment of twenty years and a minimum of one year, dependent on achieved fitness for release. One day, shortly before the evening closing hour, Abbott as leader, the before mentioned Carr, and John Dunn, a prisoner transferred from the Blackwell's Island penitentiary, all troublesome, dangerous prisoners and all employed in the hollow-ware finishing factory, boldly left the work room and attempted to scale the outside enclosing wall, twenty feet high, and guarded with armed guards. Carr and Dunn were quickly apprehended, but Abbott, though proceeding under aim of the guns, nearly reached the crest of the enclosure, where he would have been shot had not a guard upon the ground pulled away his scaling ladder and secured him. An impeding clog was attached to Abbott's ankle and he was then returned to work. Afterwards he killed a fellow prisoner, the circumstances of which crime are detailed in the proceedings of the supreme court on his trial for the murder. I quote from the charge of the judge:

"The prisoner and the deceased George Reed both worked in the same prison shop, the hollow-ware department, each having a lathe, or machine on which he worked, situated on opposite sides of the room about 19 feet apart. On the day of the homicide Reed took a kettle not suitable for his own machine, but fit for

Abbott's, and left it there. Abbott angrily pushed it away and broke it, but at the time no words were passed between the two prisoners. An hour or so afterwards Abbott took his turning bar, four feet long and an inch thick, and went where Reed was working. Approaching stealthily from behind with the bar he struck a powerful blow on the back of the head, following with two other blows as Reed fell to the floor, crushing his skull. Abbott then walked coolly back to his own place of work, put on his coat, folded his arms, and awaited his arrest and removal to his cell."

For this "unprovoked, cowardly, wicked murder," the judge said, "there could be no defense for there were no mitigating circumstances." Abbott was found guilty of murder in the first degree, was removed to the county jail, and in October, 1880, he was executed.

The third example of this evil class of young criminals of homicidal tendency is Edward Simmons, committed from New York City in 1879, for burglary. He was more evidently degenerate, but otherwise, physically and mentally, very similar to the prisoner Carr already described. He was soon reduced to the lowest grade of prisoners for persistent bad behavior. After fifteen months of malingering and miserable misbehavior, the only immediate consequence of which to himself was closer cellular confinement, on May 6, 1880, he stabbed to death the principal keeper, Mr. McKelvey. Simmons had served a short term in the New York City prison for an assault with a hammer upon one Henry Holtzer, and he had spent some weeks there awaiting trial and committal to the reformatory. Through his own experience and associations, he had become familiar with the lazy life and free communication in ordinary prisons, which added to his disappointment and the

184

distastefulness of the intense activities, the systematic daily work, the schools and disciplinary restrictions of the reformatory. In order to avoid these things and get the indulgences of the state prison he sought to force his transfer by bad behavior. He feigned illness, spoiled his work and injured his tools, simulated stupidity, and disregarded the regulations, all without effecting his object. Then, unobserved, he improvised and secreted a stiletto, refused to work, and intentionally got himself removed to the cell where during the working hours every day he was made to stand handcuffed to the cell door, on restricted diet, until he should comply with the requirements. On the fatal morning at eight o'clock Mr. McKelvey, the principal keeper, entered Simmons' cell to put him in the prescribed position, when with the weapon he had prepared and secreted, he stabbed McKelvey over the heart, causing his death almost immediately.

Simmons was quickly indicted for murder in the first degree, was removed to the county jail, and at the term of the supreme court, January, 1881, the trial came on. He was defended by a notorious criminal law firm of New York City, assisted by a local attorney. The chief member of the firm himself appeared and conducted the case. The trial aroused much local public interest and was attended by crowds. The temper of the trial was extremely hostile on the part of the defense, and the irritability was communicated to the crowds, so that the following incident of the trial was unusually dramatic.

Mr. Griscom, the overseer of the shop where Abbott and Simmons worked, had testified truly as to the character and bad behavior of Simmons, but the surprise came on his cross examination by the defense. Griscom was a large, fine looking man, favorably and generally known. He was selected for the difficult duty of overseeing the rough work and ruffian prisoners of the hollow-ware shop on the recommendation of the warden of a wellknown state prison, who however had not mentioned the fact which was brought out on the cross examination, in the following colloquy:

Mr. Griscom was asked: Did you ever live in the city of Auburn, New York?

Ans. Yes, Sir.

Q. In the prison there? A. Yes, Sir.

Q. For how many years? A. Eight years.

Q. Were you a voluntary inmate of the prison?

A. No, Sir, I was there for an offense.

Q. As a convict? A. Yes, Sir.

Q. Sentenced to seven years' imprisonment there?

A. Instead of seven the sentence was ten years.

The witness was then dismissed. He passed immediately out of a rear door of the court house and was never afterwards heard of!

The verdict of the jury was, guilty of murder in the second degree. Simmons was sentenced to imprisonment in the state prison during his natural life. Not long after he was committed to the prison at Auburn, through outside influence he was transferred to the asylum for insane criminals, at that time on the grounds of the Auburn Prison. He was allowed exceptional privileges there. His relatives were allowed to visit him for several days at a time, and entertained as guests of the medical superintendent of the asylum. On the occasion of one of these extended visits Simmons and his visiting relatives drove away in a carriage in the night and he escaped from custody. After a year or two a rumor was put afloat that Simmons had died in one of the southern states. Neither the fact of his escape from the asylum nor the manner of it has ever been satisfactorily explained.

Since the main purpose in telling these incidents is to impart accurate information from inside experiences which shall be corrective of current fallacious notions about prisoners and prisons, let me here interject a comment on the case of Griscom, the overseer and witness, and also a brief reflection as to discharged prisoners generally.

No doubt the state prison warden sincerely believed that Griscom would prove an excellent officer for our reformatory, and it was out of consideration for the man that he withheld the fact of his previous imprisonment at Auburn and afterwards in the Michigan State Prison. But it was not quite fair as between two friendly governors of prisons to conceal the fact; and, towards Griscom himself, it was mistaken kindness. Had I known of Griscom's career he would not have been employed with us, or if employed as he was, the early discovered lack of metallic quality in his governance would have been better accounted for and guarded against. In a sense the prison warden's humanity and Griscom's concealment are responsible for the tragedies of the hollowware shop. To allow a prisoner fresh from prison to conceal the fact is unjust to the employer, hazardous to the community, jeopards permanency and certainty of employment and social rehabilitation, impairs the prisoner's conscious integrity, and keeps him, always, on the margin of calamity. At least the first employer should know. A certain actual mutual friendliness springs naturally from the mutual confidence. When after a sufficient lapse of time the discharged prisoner gets industrially and socially well adjusted, then the fact of his previous unfortunate history may become encysted — lost to observation and, if possible, to memory itself.

Prompted by the central purpose already mentioned, and for historic truthfulness, I must briefly mention other experiences as illustrations. It is a familiar truth that throughout our northern temperate zone from February to June all nature feels and makes response to an awakening mysterious stir. In normal beings normally circumstanced it is the source of their best ambitions and enterprising endeavor. But in defective human beings and animated things and the unfavorably situated, the same impulse develops into evil, or at least troublesome, behavior. The months from February to June are months of special liability to this in military camps, on shipboard, in institutions where defectives are housed — including prisons, and wherever there exists much density of population. At this season a single act of violence is specially contagious. It may be that the throat-slash by the prisoner Carr started the other reckless acts and individual instances of insubordination in the early months of that year. During the spring of 1880 personal acts of convict bravado were particularly rife. More dangerous knives and improvised stilettos were in some way obtained, secreted, and offensively used by prisoners than had been known in all my prison experience.

Another manifestation of such bravado, imported into the reformatory with the prisoners from Blackwell's Island and from Sing Sing, had its run that year. It is carried out somewhat as follows:

A prisoner in his cell on the gallery of the open corridor, within hearing of hundreds of other prisoners, boisterously disturbs the quiet and openly defies removal. Having barricaded entrance to his cell, armed with knife and bludgeon, he announces his dare to all prison authorities. Parley but excites his sense of self-importance, strengthens his opposition, and stimulates admiration and imitation among certain others of his kind. It becomes necessary therefore to use what force is required immediately to remove him.

The serious trouble such an entrenched prisoner may occasion is shown by an occurrence of the kind at the Missouri State Prison when it was at Alton. The prisoner there was a beardless youth of fair complexion and good appearance. He had drawn into the cell with himself one of the prison guards of about his own stature, barricaded the cell entrance, and had completely intimidated the guard by inflicting now and then flesh wounds with the knife he held. Whenever the cell was approached he threatened and even cut the captured guard, thus warding off outside attack. The prisoner demanded that himself and his captive should be enveloped exactly alike in cloak and hood and conveyed at midnight, unaccompanied but by a selected driver, to a designated uninhabited waste of the prairie and there released. It is said that the stripling prisoner, holding the life of the guard as hostage, kept the prison officers at bay three nights and days. Finally at a favoring moment the risk was taken, the entrance forced, and the guard though severely wounded was rescued alive. Not long afterwards, when casually visiting the prison at Alton, I saw and conversed with the prisoner referred to. It seemed scarcely possible that such a lad could create so great a disturbance.

This stereotyped malicious convict prison trick is known in every established penitentiary where the proper control of prisoners is exercised. It was frequent — almost epidemic — at our reformatory in that spring of 1880. In some Italian prisons chloroform is used to fill the room with fumes to anesthetize the prisoner. R. W. McClaughry, long a warden at Joliet, Illinois, at the Huntingdon, Pennsylvania, Reformatory, and for many years warden of the United States Penitentiary at Fort Leavenworth, Kansas, used the fumes of burning turpentine—a ball of candle-wick saturated and ignited that produced a sense of suffocation. Such measures I never used for fear of fatal consequences; but formerly, before the killing of McKelvey and the presence of so many knives with the prisoners, threats and offensive preparations were disregarded, and single-handed entrance was forced and the prisoner overcome. But latterly this risky summary method was prohibited. Once, when the prisoners Reddington and Carr in their separate adjoining cells both tried this form of defiance, we flooded the cells with water from a hydrant until it reached the armpit, when they gave up their weapons; but the splash and confusion of the water-measure precluded its general use. Then the use of a hook-implement was permitted, the same as was used at the Connecticut State Prison after General Pilsbury was cut when he was removing a turbulent prisoner from his cell. The implement was gaspipe, long enough to reach the rear of the eight-foot cell, bent at one end for a handle and at the other so as to encircle the body. The method was to bring the prisoner up to the door, disarm and remove him. Whenever the prisoner resisted by securing the long lever end and putting it aside, the hook was heated so hot that he could not handle it. This simple, harmless device was later exploited by an unfriendly newspaper, and alleged to be a cruelty!

Three suicides of reformatory men at this early period attracted additional attention outside and increased captious criticism. Such suicides elsewhere got only passing notice, but for us the fullest exploitation. One, a prisoner on parole in New York City, who violated his obligations, was taken for kindly investigation to the secretary of the Prison Association, at the rooms then situated in the third story of the Bible House. While awaiting the secretary's convenience the young man suddenly dashed through an open window to his death on the pavement below. The newspapers made a sensational account of it and inquired why, if the reformatory was as it should be, a paroled man should voluntarily go to his death rather than be returned to treatment there. Another, a resident prisoner under a definite sentence, hanged himself in his cell. The coroner's jury absolved the reformatory management from any blame, but the hungry newspapers magnified the incident. Hughes, a prisoner from Albany, of feeble intellect, hanged himself by his suspenders in his cell. The remains were forwarded to his parents, working people at Albany. The condition of the remains on arrival, by reason of the manner of the death and futile extraordinary efforts by our physician, Dr. Wey, for his resuscitation, led to the mistaken opinion that he had suffered ill treatment at the reformatory — an opinion which, though contrary to the coroner's verdict, was entertained by his parents and was mentioned sensationally in the newspapers of Albany.

Besides these three actual suicides, so many attempts, real or feigned, were made that suicide seemed for the time epidemic. I traced the abnormal activity to, (a) instinctive imitation, (b) craving curiosity, (c) mischievous desire to excite alarm, (d) intent to create sympathy and obtain favors, (e) a certain subjective abnormality induced by secret pernicious practices. These suicidal attempts were completely stopped by notice in the institution newspaper that thereafter they would be followed in each case with physical chastisement.

The foregoing unattractive pages,— the detailed accounts of vexatious prisoners at this period,— shall now close with a brief discussion of one more similar condition, but with a precautionary word. During the five years preceding 1880 eight out of a total of 1238 prisoners went insane and were transferred to the asylum for insane criminals. Two of them were serving under definite and six under indefinite sentences. Though this ratio of insanity among the prisoners was small,— smaller than is usual in prisons,— and was greatly increased afterwards at our reformatory, as naturally it would be, the insanity was disquieting. The same subjective defectiveness that induced the suicides and numerous feigned attempts, led to the few cases of real mental disturbance and to very considerable feigned insanity. This was difficult to deal with because of the intricacy of the problem — the difficulty of just discrimination between the true and the false. Feigning might unwittingly produce the real disease. Voluntary surrender of the habitual if supposititious conscious self-determination might unleash mental regularity, increasing derangement. The study of alienism then became a necessity. Thus the few cases of insanity, together with the feignings, served to widen for our investigations the field of "new psychology," particularly the department of it known as physiological-psychology. The study was never afterwards relinquished, and while there could not be traced to the few instances of suicide and insanity any important public disfavor, the events doubtless contributed to the sensitiveness of public opinion towards the reformatory, where both in fundamental principles and in prison procedure such a new departure was instituted.

In order to guard against a possible wrong impression from the preceding recitals it should be said that in our northern American prisons not more than 10 per cent of the prisoners are so defective and intractable as to require extraordinary disciplinary methods, and not more than 1 per cent are so extremely recalcitrant as those just mentioned. Such prisoners are constitutionally abnormal and habitually anti-social. The governing authority of a prison, who unnecessarily either directly or by subterfuge and indirection discharges such dangerous prisoners into a free community, is himself heinously reprehensible. Whenever at the commencement of a curative régime such prisoners are subjected to the necessary repression or stimulation, they are irritated, their evil nature is shown, but not created, as is too often alleged. The effect is as of reagents in chemistry; it reveals the nature and extent of defectiveness. It is unfortunate when the general régime is reduced to avoid friction with these exceptionally troublesome men. The story when written and read is apt to be exaggeratedly impressive. Prison managers being familiar with such men and evils treat and meet them calmly one by one as they arise. The vexing occurrences already mentioned may fairly be attributable to the excessive proportion of bad prisoners brought from the state prisons, to incompleteness of the prison structure, to a disciplinary régime which was not strict enough, for it was before our system was perfected, and further, to our hesitation to use the simple, harmless, physical method of coercion, which in the later years of my administration was freely introduced and effectively employed. There is small doubt that but for that hesitation, Reddington, Carr, Abbott, and Simmons would *not* have committed their tragic crimes, at least five human lives now lost would have been preserved, and the reformatory would years sooner have reached the adult stage of its greatest usefulness.

CHAPTER XIII

THE BETTER AND THE AVERAGE TYPES

CONTINUING my description of prisoners as they were and are, it is pleasant to turn now from considering the inimical specimens to the gratifying recollection of other prisoners of a much more promising type.

Those committed under a definite sentence, both transferred prisoners and those directly from the courts, were discharged, of course, at the expiration of their respective terms, and others took their place who were committed under the Indeterminate Sentence Act of 1877. As the former diminished and the latter increased, the effect of the new law was very apparent. The atmosphere, the surrounding element of influence, changed for the better and favorably affected all the prisoners. But those now to be particularly designated were, evidently, of a different native quality from the troublesome men I have described. Three "definites" and three "indefinites," to be mentioned, shall comprise the present allusion to this better exceptional class.

J. E., one of the prisoners of the first gang transferred from Auburn in 1876, had nearly completed his long sentence there for horse stealing. He was a native American, about thirty years of age, with coarse, strong, shapely physique, an untiring worker, familiar with every kind of farm work; a natural boss of rough men at rough work he was well fitted for a public works contractor's foreman, and had he been so employed earlier in life would probably not have become a criminal. Without the advantage of much schooling he yet possessed good reasoning powers and in every day practical affairs he had superior judgment. Every task assigned him while with us as a prisoner, or afterwards in our employ, was well and faithfully and thoroughly done. He was good-natured, obliging, watchful, and careful of his employer's interest, a man of honest intentions and practically so, temperate, and without a known bad habit except what is commonly considered profanity, a peculiarity that requires particular mention. His remarkable volubility and use of expletives found little opportunity of exercise while he was a prisoner, because of restricted intercourse among the inmates, but afterwards as an employe it gained freer use. The profuse interjection into his speech of objectionable qualifying adjectives was so innocent, so rhythmical and artistic, so similar to the arranged punctuations of rhetorical expletives in eloquent oratory, that it was devoid of offensiveness and was even entertaining to world-wise ears polite. For instance, the highly cultured instructor of the famed ethics class at the reformatory, a non-resident, for whose convenience a carriage was sent on Sundays, often asked that J. E. be sent as driver because he so enjoyed his "conversation."

On the expiration of his period of imprisonment with us in 1877, I gave J. E. employment in charge of the reformatory farm property which includes some 280 acres of farmland and hillside forest, together with the gardens and lawns of that portion occupied by the reformatory proper. The farm portion was a worn out pasturage unkempt and unpropitious for cultivation, but under his intelligent and efficient direction the barren farm land became more and more productive, the forest was pruned, protected, and beautified, the farm buildings repaired and new ones constructed, and the farm was well stocked with animals and agricultural apparatus. He soon became known to farmers and others living in the vicinity of Elmira and he was rated as one of the best farm managers in the county.

He remained in our service in charge of the farm more than twelve years, until 1889, when his commendable career suddenly collapsed. He had married a worthy young woman who, in the sequel, proved of too sensitive a nature for such companionship. Three children were born to them. The family occupied a moderately comfortable cottage near the reformatory, and it is not known that there was any domestic disagreement, but evidently he could not appreciate the more refined tastes and social hunger of his wife and, not understanding, did not minister to them. So it came about that when the youngest child was still an infant, the wife, no longer able to endure the monotony and, possibly, other incongruities of her lot, took her own life, leaving the three young children to the sole care of their father. He was not equal to this crisis in his affairs. Not that he was overwhelmed with grief at his bereavement; he was deeply disturbed, but not profoundly broken in his sorrow. His deportment was not singular but normal to his nature. During the preparations for the funeral of his wife he came to consult about some of the details accompanied by his three or four-year-old little daughter towards whom as we talked he manifested restrained genuine fatherly affection. Soon after the burial he took a fat steer from our herd (it should not be characterized as stealing) and sold it for an amount about equal to the balance due him for his services, and absconded, utterly abandoning the motherless children. It is gratifying that I am able to add that a friend of J. E. cared for all the children and educated them at his own expense.

J. E. was a rough, bluff, good-hearted, up-state hard worker, remarkably free from common corrupting vices. Instinctively he was sufficiently honest, but early in his life for a technical fault he was handicapped by a criminal conviction and state prison service. He himself had never intended an injury to any one and was not normally conscious of the injury his conduct occasioned. He typified a small class of exceptional prisoners who are criminals while remaining subjectively non-criminous. At his first conviction could he have been subjected to the training of the developed reformatory system instead of to state prison régime he would, undoubtedly, have been saved from other crime. The recollection of him, as he was known to us for twelve years, is chiefly of his manly qualities. It is pitiful to recall the calamities to himself and his family and the sorrowful disappointment of the unhappy outcome of his career.

Among the transfers from the state prisons at this early period of the reformatory was the prisoner L., who is representative of a still rarer class of prisoners. This all too brief mention is prompted by my respect for his memory, my regret that I did not at the time better know and reward him, and for the sake of recording, again, what is believed to have been one of the occasional errors of criminal court procedure.

L. was originally imprisoned for a homicide the particular circumstances of which are immaterial since he himself had not disclosed a single trait of viciousness. He was an old man, towards seventy years, a Frenchman, a professional and very competent horticulturist; a gentle reticent character of much native refinement. While yet a prisoner he laid out the grounds about the reformatory and ornamented them with shrubs, flowers, and a rosary. On the expiration of his sentence I employed him on a salary, and it is a regrettable reflection that I did not provide for him and his wife, who occupied a cottage near, more liberal and so more suitable compensation for his valuable services. Soon after he left our service he returned to the place of his former residence on the lower Hudson River. Erelong his good wife sickened and died, which was a grief he could not endure. A few weeks after the death of his wife L. went to her grave and there committed suicide. Had the court, at the trial of this choice old man, had a scientific, psychical examination made of his mental condition, he would no doubt have been sheltered in an asylum instead of being sentenced to a prison. It will be observed that the aftermath of the imprisonments in the cases of J. E. and L., as has so frequently occurred with discharged prisoners who do not resume their former associations and life, was the tragedy of suicide.

Another prisoner, of the definite sentence class, was received at the reformatory in October, 1876, convicted of larceny from the post office where he was employed. He had been sentenced by a United States court to one year's imprisonment, but privileged to the statutory two months of abatement should he prove worthy. He was certified as sixteen years old, and was a delicate, well bred lad of good heredity. His record during the few months at the reformatory even in that rough and formative stage of it was absolutely perfect, so that he earned the abatement time and was discharged in August, 1877. He was immediately lost to our sight and knowledge. After more than twenty years had passed I learned of his history since his release from the reformatory. Accosted one day on the public street by a stranger who proved to be a relative of the discharged prisoner here referred to, impelled as he said by the desire to give me the gratifying information, I learned that my young prisoner of 1876–1877 was at the time the honored pastor of an influential Congregational church in a western state, and the happy father of a family of promising children. He gave me the address. Ten years later, thirty years from the date of his discharge, information about him derived in another way confirmed the original statement and showed a continuance of the pastoral relation. I am also credibly informed that once within the period, this young man of my erst reformatory acquaintance, but grown to full maturity, had, on a Sunday when visiting relatives here, filled as supply preacher the pulpit of a church in Elmira.

It need scarcely be said that such an outcome of imprisonment for crime, especially under the unfavorable circumstances at that time, must be classed as an unparalleled event. It is the only instance of persistent, consistent, religious devotion that ever came under my observation out of the tens of thousands of prisoners I have known. While this particular instance calls for commendation, the impulse occasionally shown by prisoners to engage in religious, moral, and charitable activities should be discountenanced as incompatible with their history if known; hazardous to any community where they may dwell; and, by the concealment and strain of the situation, dangerous to the good continuance of the discharged prisoner himself. Inconspicuousness is more appropriate and promising. This very exceptional instance, however, once stood me in good stead when before a legislative committee at Albany the prison labor question was under hot discussion. The demagogic agitator against trades instruction for prisoners turned to me and roared the question, "Why do you always teach occupations that serve to bring the prisoners, on their discharge, into competition with tradesmen? Why not, for instance, make preachers of them?" I was able to surprise my interlocutor with the reply, "That is precisely what we at the reformatory have already done," citing in proof the case above related.

Of prisoners serving under the new indeterminate sentence who were quickly responsive to the law and treatment and after their discharge were worthy inhabitants, so many rise to memory that any selection savors of partiality. Over against the excessive proportion of recalcitrants there were, at that time, more prisoners of exceptional good quality and promise than any subsequent resident ratio. With the passage of years the proportion of such good men gradually diminished, as is equally true at each of the three prisons I have opened, organized, and for a time conducted. Such a trend is perhaps to be accounted for by the increased density of population in cities, the habitat of offenders,— a well recognized controlling influence of the criminal ratio,— by the increased influx of aliens unassimilated to our Americanism, and to leniency of laws and court practice. This tendency of things warrants the prediction that the populations of prisons will in the future be composed of still deeper dregs of society, only such as cannot be reclaimed in the open; and that penology must be more practical, more scientific, better knowing the real constituents of criminousness to effectually restrain it.

The outcome of imprisonment on the three following specimens of the very superior class cannot fail to be of interest. They probably belong, in Professor Tarde's classification, with the accidental criminals, or "criminals of occasion," whose imprisonment under the usual penitentiary conditions is quite sure to result in their becoming habitual criminals; but under the rational reformatory system we were developing, they are, as these were, readily reclaimable.

Two of the three, denizens of a populous interior city, were habitual companions, with worthy but not wealthy family connections, and their associations were within the good middle class of inhabitants. One was fair and the other dark complexioned; both were of good form and appearance and each possessed educational attainment equal to the usual full high school course. They were office men in good employment, popular and free

participants of the reputable social life of their community, but additionally were inclined to high-seasoned
entertainments — frequenters of theaters, and acquainted behind the scenes, where simultaneously the
two became enamored with a susceptible actress. One
of them having obtained $2500 by forging his employer's
name, the two, with the actress, fled to Canada. On their
arrest at Montreal they voluntarily returned to face
their crime and on arraignment both pleaded guilty
and were among the first hundred committed to Elmira under indefinite sentence. Here their behavior
and record were so satisfactory in every respect that in
about one year — the minimum under the regulations
— they were adjudged quite fit for the usual conditional release. But since the law required and prudence dictated that on the release of prisoners by the
managers some regard should be had to the effect upon
the community, correspondence on this point was had
with unprejudiced leading citizens of the city to which
they would return. It was ascertained to be the unan-
imous opinion that in view of their former social standing and the attention which their crime had aroused,
their return so soon would be injurious. When made
acquainted with the decision that they must remain at
the reformatory somewhat longer and with the reason
for it they made no complaint, though they were greatly
disappointed. After twenty hours for deliberation one
for both made at my request free expression of their
feeling about it. Here it is:

"Our offense, so generally known as it was, wrought
undoubtedly a certain moral injury, to atone for which
we ought to be willing to make the personal sacrifice
the impartial inhabitants and the correspondents deem

requisite. We are therefore willing to bide the time." They entered again upon the institutional routine, smothered their disappointment, and made no allusion to their coveted release for a full year, nor until the authorities took up the matter. Then both were paroled to go home to employment which we had arranged for them; and after six months on parole they received their absolute release, after which, of course, they were completely absolved from our control and from any further legal consequences of their offense.

Ten years after their discharge, though they were widely separated and differently occupied, it was my pleasant experience to meet and converse with each of them. One called at the reformatory, but so matured and changed that at first he was not recognized. His apparel, bearing, and conversation bespoke the prosperous business gentleman. Interestingly he described his inward conflicting agitation as his train neared Elmira and the triumph of his determination to stop over and afford me the pleasure of renewing our acquaintance under the changed circumstances. On my invitation, he with some hesitation accompanied me inside the reformatory where ten years previously he had been in custody. The visit inside was a trying one to him, but gratifying to me for the manliness of his mood. In the corridor, in sight of the cell he had occupied, we paused and he sorrowfully remarked, "Is it possible that I was ever an occupant of that cell?" Then straightening himself he answered his own question, saying, "No! The occupant of that cell then was quite another personality." The remark though probably not a product of philosophic contemplation was nevertheless an honest expression of his veritable

Zebulon R. Brockway, 1878

consciousness; and considered in connection with the doctrine of possible alienation, alternation, and substitution of personality, stimulated within myself hopeful inquiry and further experiment as to scientific reformatory methods even to the extent of absolute renovation of personalities. Again, five years later, in 1892, reliable information was had of the continued, complete, permanent rehabilitation of this prisoner.

The other of the two confederates, the stronger, probably the instigator, and certainly the leader in the crime, returned when he was released, to the city of his former residence, and resumed clerical work for the employer he had betrayed. His necessary appearance on the public streets produced at first a painful sense of personal abasement. When persons whom he had known now failed inadvertently to recognize and greet him as of old, he thought them alienated, and himself despised, and he felt the hurt of it. When old acquaintances cordially accosted him he attributed it to their pity and charity and his humiliation was intensified. Soon, however, he correctly concluded that he was taking himself too seriously; that he overestimated and probably misinterpreted the interest others really felt and the lack of recognition he observed. Gradually, though modestly, his good sense and manhood gained the ascendency; the sense of humiliation wore off, but enough remained to restrain and steady his ambition and behavior.

Here let me say that the too common belief that such unpleasant consciousness usually attends discharged prisoners seems to call for a corrective statement out of my own unusually extended observation of prisoners. Such sensitiveness and sound good sense are as rare except with the very unusually good men as the prisoners themselves are exceptional. The sensitiveness which this man felt is so inconsistent with the egotism of common criminals that it proves, as his whole career also shows, his healthy normality of character.

The manliness of the man is further shown by the letter that he independently wrote to the legislative committee which, years after his absolute release from all obligation, was conducting an investigation of affairs at the reformatory. The letter came out through the hands of a committeeman of the same city, an old acquaintance of the discharged prisoner, and contained a plain statement of the facts as the prisoner himself had observed them, contradicting the allegations made during the mendacious attack on the reformatory. The intervention of the voluntary letter led to renewed inquiry about the man himself and his situation. It was learned that his good character and abilities had taken him into the larger field of insurance management. In the service of one of the largest English insurance companies doing business in Canada and the United States he was the general agent in charge of a wide division of their territory. At his Canadian headquarters I saw and conversed with him in 1887. He was living with his mother, very comfortably, in their own hired house situated in a good residential part of the city, and most assiduously devoted to his occupation. Years after, he was promoted to a still more responsible insurance supervision. Full fifteen years' knowledge of the careers of these two men and occasional incidental hearsay still later, warrants my confidence that they, felonious offenders in their earlier years, now grown to middle life and established in business, are, if living, so

merged in the current life of the times that the faultiness which we endeavored to correct is completely
covered out of sight.

The third and last of the typical prisoners of the
exceptional class to whom I shall refer, was admitted in 1878 among the second hundred prisoners
received. The story of this man is so interesting and
suggestive that the account may not inappropriately be
somewhat extended.

Twenty-nine years of age when received at the
reformatory, this prisoner was small of stature, — only
5 feet, 5 inches tall,— weight 125 pounds, but of fine
form and innate good quality. His speech and his
bearing were instinctively those of a gentleman. Mentally he appeared considerably cultured and without
the common self-conceit of convicts. His mind was
astute rather than profound, but without chicanery.
In short, he appeared to have healthy-minded and well-
developed intelligence. As to morality he was neither
obtuse nor sensitive, but intelligently voiced the commonly accepted notion of the right and wrong of things
and this with the usual superficiality of appreciation.
Theological theories of a Deity offended by reason of
his sinfulness gave him no uneasiness, but he keenly
felt the misfortune of his mistake, the unworthiness,
and the folly of his offense; yet he philosophically submitted himself to the inevitable consequences. At the
age of fourteen, obedient to the *wanderlust*, he ran away
from home on the Ohio River to a large interior western
city where, for a time, he joined the gamins, subsisted
by peddling newspapers, and otherwise as gamins subsist, until he got the job of bell-boy in a large hotel.
Soon, fortunately, the interest of a benevolent perma-

nent guest at the hotel, a faculty member of the university, was enlisted, and under his influence and friendly guidance the bell-boy earnestly entered on a prescribed course of study. His native and acquired expertness as accountant enabled him to increase his meager income by extra work evenings and Sundays. With the increased earnings and some friendly aid he entered the university as a student, was creditably graduated, and became a full-fledged member of the university faculty. His recurring vacation times were spent at a fashionable mountain summer resort where, because of his excellent social qualifications, facility in games and amusements, and his ability at accounting, he was given compensation. Attracted by the pleasures and elegance of life at this resort, with the warm personal friendship and promise of ample pecuniary investment by a guest of the hotel, a multi-millionaire of about his own age,— a little wearied too with the monotony and the small salary of his professorship,— he resigned from the university, purposing with his wealthy friend to open, as they had already leased, one of the largest and best modern hostelries in the west. Suddenly, before the arrangements were completed, his wealthy friend died. The project was necessarily given up and he was turned adrift with less than a thousand dollars of savings, which were soon gone. He made his way to New York City where he readily obtained employment as bookkeeper in a large wholesale hardware house.

The taste and propensity for gentlemen's gambling acquired at the summer resort he indulged in in New York at the haunts of professional gamblers. On one occasion he lost, gaming, $40 of his employer's money, properly in his possession, but improperly put up and lost. No entry had been made of the $40 paid in at the store after the closing of the safe. From day to day he deferred the entry in hopes to win back the money and restore it. For this he borrowed from the till and lost again, until his cash shortage reached the sum of $600. Finally, alarmed at the fearful position in which by his indiscretion he had placed himself, he went on a Sunday evening to the uptown residence of his employer, made a clean confession of his undiscovered fault and besought the opportunity to earn and refund the amount. To this the employer, on Sunday evening, assented, the arrangement to be perfected at the office on Monday. But on Monday things were different. In his business mood the employer was offended, and the clerk, afraid, failed to appear as he had agreed, but by messenger asked for the interview elsewhere. Instead he was arrested and in due time arraigned for trial in the court of general sessions. Here he pleaded guilty, explained truthfully all the circumstances, and, considerately, was committed to the reformatory instead of to the state prison where ordinarily a prisoner so near the maximum statutory age limit, convicted of such a crime — grand larceny — would have been sent.

Now if the kind reader will recall the poker game incident at Guilford, Connecticut, recorded in this narrative, where more than thirty years before I had risked and lost precisely the same amount of my employer's money, but with a very different and much more fortunate denouement, it will not, I am sure, be thought singular that I should have had a lively appreciative sympathy with the situation of this man. The closest scrutiny showed him completely non-criminous, and this together with his remarkable competency as an accountant were considerations that elicited and, as the sequel proved, justified full confidence, and led to his assignment to the quasi-confidential expert work of assisting to organize and perfect in detail the very complete system of recording and accounting then under advisement at the reformatory. His trustworthiness was soon subjected to the severest test. On a moonlit summer night, in the outside unguarded office, with open windows overlooking the sparsely populated valley, we were planning and arranging the accounting, when unexpectedly I was summoned to the city. Being unwilling to lose the evening's work I left the prisoner alone until I should return, which I expected to do at once; but I was detained until near midnight. It was not without anxiety that I came back. There, still at work at the solving of our problem, but in an agitated state of mind, I found my man. Nothing, absolutely nothing, but his honorable choice and his forecasting wisdom prevented his escape. He told me of his fearful battle with himself the evening long and tearfully besought me never again to subject him to such a trial.

Thirteen months from the date of his admission to the reformatory, having in every respect acquitted himself with credit, the first impression that he was not and never was subjectively criminous was quite confirmed. Based on this opinion, and possibly somewhat influenced by my desire to requite the suffering I had unwittingly caused him by that summer night's temptation; maybe, too, remembering the similarity of his situation at the time of his crime with my own more

210

fortunate poker game experience, nearly forty years before, I asked the board of managers to take exceptional action by granting his absolute release without the usual parole period. This was done promptly, thus terminating our control, and he left New York for his native place in another state.

Altogether voluntarily, for many months afterwards, he kept me advised of his progress and prospects by occasional letters. Naturally as time passed and he became more and more engrossed in business his letters were less frequent, and our correspondence practically closed with one announcing his betrothal to the daughter of a leading banker, one of the best men of his community. I learned from him and also from the father of the family into which he married, that before his marriage, at a family gathering which he had arranged for that purpose, he had acquainted them all with the fact of his crime and committal to the reformatory. And, singular to relate, he told me, when we met many years after, that from the date of that open explanation no reference to this portion of his history had ever to his knowledge been made, either within or without the family.

The last knowledge I had of this man was on November 14, 1903, after the lapse of twenty-five years, when he called on me at my private home in Elmira. Fifty-four years of age, rotund, matured, and prosperous, I did not recognize him until his voice recalled his identity. With warm hand grasp and smiling face he said, "Reaching Buffalo last night on my way from New York to California, I yielded to the impulse to interrupt my journey to make this call on the twenty-fifth anniversary of our introduction to each other at the 'college on the hill.'" He was much pleased that on hearing his voice I should so quickly pronounce his name. Our interview extended through the day and was most gratifying to me. He told me of his business, his difficulties and disappointments, his triumphs and his success, some of which I had already known of. He was or had been treasurer of a realty promoting company, chairman of the ways and means committee of the common council, and as I already knew from others, had been delegated to negotiate in New York City a considerable block of county bonds of his locality. He spoke of his happy family life and showed photographs of his two grown daughters soon to be married. Then mentioning his happily changed relations I hesitatingly referred to the reformatory experience of the earlier years. We freely talked about it all. He said that at the time the contrast between his customary cuisine and the reformatory food and cooking was distasteful and irritating, and then he felt that the stringent regulations required to be observed as a condition of release were unnecessarily minute and exacting. In retrospect, however, he was grateful for the plain nutritious diet and general régime which restored his good health, and he felt that the disciplinary experience had since been of the greatest service in his prosperity. As the talk went on it seemed that he dimly discerned that some mysterious intelligence had determined every item of his entire career, and doubtless beneficially determined it.

The hours of conversation, all too short, over, and the time for his departure near, I gladly walked with him to the depot, where we parted, in all probability never to meet again.

THE AVERAGE TYPE OF PRISONER

The bulk of the prisoners were and are of a character between that represented by the vicious and the very susceptible specimens just mentioned. The general public and also prison boards and managers are apt to be too much occupied with these extremes — the troublesome and the attractive criminals and prisoners — to the neglect of desirable attention to the main body of them. The former compel and the latter attract too absorbing consideration. Numerically the two exceptional classes of prisoners, taken together, are but a small minority which, faultily, has been and is yet the chief determinant of criminal laws and prison systems. No lack of suitable thorough attention to the needs of the men of the dual minority was or ever could justly be chargeable to the management of the reformatory during the twenty-five years of my official incumbency. But, developing and developed, the Elmira reformatory scheme has always mainly directed its effort with regard to the major middle class of the prisoners, the great bulk of the prison population.

This mass of prisoners at the reformatory neither was nor is composed of boys. That term applied to them is a misnomer. They were and are adult males committed for felony. To quote from the 1893 year book:

"The reformatory prisoners are *felons*. They are, all of them, committed for state prison offenses. They are not, as is erroneously supposed to be the case, sent here for small misdemeanors, but for high crimes. Neither is it true that they are simply accidental criminals; nor are they all first offenders. Fully 45 per cent of them have been imprisoned, asylumed, station-housed, arrested, or in some manner have been previously in conflict with the law and in contact with its restraining agencies."

It is true that the statutory limitations of age are sixteen and thirty years; also that the average age of the resident population ranges between twenty and twenty-two years. Some are thirty years old, married and fathers, and many are of voting age. The reformatory prisoners as to age and crimes are like the majority of prisoners in the state penitentiaries. By the sentence and committal of these prisoners to the reformatory they are practically withdrawn from the state prison populations, yet after thus taking away the twelve to sixteen hundred here confined, the proportion of the remaining state prisoners between the same ages, sixteen to thirty years, is about 60 per cent. Most common crimes are committed by persons of the age of our reformatory prisoners. Lombroso's investigations show that the crime age is between fifteen and thirty years.

Considered in crowds prisoners are inferior. More closely scanned, the inferiority appears as physical, mental, and moral imperfection, derived, some of it, by inheritance or from early formative circumstances concededly beyond the prisoner's control. To quote again from the year book of 1893:

"They are not, generally, reasonable beings, in such sense that rational considerations habitually control their conduct, either before or during their imprisonment. Sixty-eight per cent were on admission practically illiterate; 75 per cent were without regular and remunerative occupation; 92 per cent were reared

214

without the restraints and benefits of good home surroundings; 75 per cent were below the average of their class as to susceptibility to ordinary moral motives and the same ratio not sensitive. In short, the prisoners sent to this reformatory were individuals out of adjustment with their environment; were considered by the courts as belonging to the unsafe-citizen class and as requiring, every one, a course of training in observance of law and the recognized proprieties of the community.

"These thousands of young felons fallen into or following crimes, recruiting the habitual criminal class, unwilling or unable to subsist by their own legitimate industry but, instead, stealing the possessions of others — these, who are regardless of their statutory and moral obligations, and pitiless for the grief and damage their crimes produce, are committed to the reformatory, not for punishment, but for restraint and training, to be continued until there is evidence of such changes in their dispositions and capabilities as give promise of self-support and orderly behavior if released. It should go without saying that such a training for such men involves use of the strongest motives and, in many instances, of positive compulsory measures.

This conviction of the inferiority of the prisoners, previously acquired and long maintained, was repeatedly emphasized, and greatly shaped and regulated the reformative activities. World-wide inquiry into the causes of crimes arising from defectiveness of the criminals, particularly the investigations of Lombroso, quickened my own inquiring attitude and stimulated rationality of reformative procedure. I offer now not tabulated details, but only a summarized or general statement of the deficiencies of prisoners whom I have observed. Without argument or citations the inferiority might be assumed from the one fact of their criminal behavior. While situated when at large substantially the same as are the vast number of their class who remain at liberty, under restraints and motives sufficient for the others these were irresponsive and have fallen. Like wind-falls of the fruit orchard, some defectiveness at the core or elsewhere has weakened the hold, so that under stress one kind will stand, the others give way.

Compared with college students of about the same average age the prisoner's average height, weight, lung capacity, strength of chest and back, are considerably less. In measurements and strength the reformatory prisoners closely resemble the measurements of the women of the New England women's colleges where such measurements are taken and recorded. Many of the prisoners show a sort of feminine face, with little beard. Some have features, gait, pose, movements of the hands and head, manner of dressing the hair on the forehead, voice and speech that are not masculine. They have certain organic peculiarities, and perverted inclinations are so prevalent that the inquiry forces itself whether many of them are not the product of a faulty generative process which has left the sex determination uncompleted. The femininity of male and the masculinity of female prisoners is quite commonly observed. So, too, the manifest excess of asymmetries, distinctive of a collection of prisoners, more than the similar asymmetries of any common miscellaneous crowd of free inhabitants, additionally indicates congenital deficiency. Evidences of interrupted organic development are plentiful: the cranium, long, broad, conical, sparrow shapen, knotted, variously irregular, crowned with coarse hair grown far down at the nape of the neck, low upon the forehead, coming to a point there. The face shrunken, right and left sides of different size, shape, and expression; eyes small, narrow, rodent-like, or parti-colored — I have observed one eye gray and the other hazel — the ear with adhering lobes, rimless, projecting out of due proportion, too large or too small; the nose awry, turned to one side, convex, with the extremity elevated or depressed, a humpy and undulating ridge; chin receding and weak; irregular and defective teeth and ill-formed palate; the skin, particularly the hands, moist and clammy, or dry and scaly; the whole corpus suggestive of degeneracy and susceptibility to disease.

An examination of photographs in the reformatory year book for 1892, of 100 of the prisoners who gained their release on parole, the good average of this middle-bulk-class we are now considering; and again, in the year books of 1893 and 1895, photographs of representative specimens of selected degenerates, will doubtless sufficiently confirm the allegation of inferiority. But for the sake of further assurance and affirmation also of mental inferiority the following summary of facts, the result of a scientific examination of 8000 reformatory prisoners concluded in 1908, is now given. Of these 8000, 25 per cent gave evidence of previous physical injuries and disabilities; 22.7 per cent were either ill or bore symptoms of disqualifying illnesses; 12.8 per cent had defective eyesight, 5.4 per cent defective hearing, and 57.8 per cent had defective teeth; 19.9 per cent were tuberculous and 43.7 per cent were affected with some form of venereal disease.

Certain discrepancies of physical characterization of the prisoners between statements taken from the year books of the reformatory and the last above quoted summary of facts from the 1908 examination may be attributed to different standards of comparison and to difference of the respective examiners. The tables are made on the basis of comparison with the exposed deficient class of free inhabitants from which the prisoners chiefly come, the result of outward observations and of measurements made by non-professional examiners; while the examiner of the 8000 men, more recently, was a competent medical officer, and the later examination is possibly the more accurate. Moreover, during the intervening sixteen years between the two gatherings of facts a considerable change had occurred in the character of the inmates admitted. The large modern influx to the metropolis from which so many are sent to the reformatory of immigrants from southern Europe and from Asia, has perhaps effected the change. Yet even in the decade of 1890 it was discerned that about one-third of all the prisoners could not without very special and quite exceptional tutoring, keep pace with the moderate requirements of the educational, mechanical, and disciplinary established régime.

The examiner of the 8000 prisoners, who reported the results in 1908, gave 37.4 per cent as the ratio of prisoners received whom he adjudged to be mentally defective. It is interesting to note the substantial agreement of ratios as between that above stated derived from scientific inquiries, and the one-third proportion ascertained from application of the practical test of the demand of the institutional régime. But quite beyond any statement of ratios, it was my own opinion in 1880, afterwards abundantly verified, that, as might reasonably be inferred from physiological unfitness, the mental gauge of the whole mass rates below and is less promising than the average of their class in the general population. The mental incompleteness of the mass may be concisely stated in three phases.

First, those who during or soon after their adolescence appear to have reached their own low maximum of feeble mental capacity. They seem to have suffered an arrest of natural intellectual growth, either by reason of congenital limitation or more probably, as I have observed, from the degrading effect of pernicious personal habits that affect the tone of the nervous action. Sometimes the effect of these habits reaches to complete dementia; they are dullards, wooden-like; their life is vegetative, or at best but animal.

The second, the most interesting and dangerous class, are the men who only specifically and sporadically are deranged. Deficient in a single important mental quality they readily gain confidence which is sure to be betrayed. Like the effect of a lost cog in the wheel of some complicated revolving mechanism, which is only felt when the movement falters, their loss of faculty is only disclosed by some trying exigency. The common run of such defectives, the men of moderate ability, are frequently unable to make progress in mathematics; they do not reason correctly; their judgment is at fault. Or if the specific fault is loss of regulative faculty, or of prudence, the subject, though not intrinsically vicious, may habitually disregard important proprieties and obligations and be an uncomfortable free inhabitant or disorderly prisoner. The strenuous training at the reformatory was especially serviceable to such men.

An interesting specimen of still another but very

scarce variety of this second class was Alfred Goslin. He was a young man in the twenties, a Frenchman, of pleasing appearance and engaging manners, born and bred in Paris of excellent parentage of an upper social grade. He was well educated, both in the schools and by the attrition of habitual association with patrician Parisians. His career was so notorious that it cannot be injurious or indelicate to give his true name and briefly trace his course.

In Paris, dealing for his employer on the Bourse, he is said to have robbed him of above 70,000 francs. He fled to England, thence to Australia, and afterwards in company with his brother reached New York, where soon he was engaged in the family of a well-known magazine publisher as French tutor for his children. In this employment he obtained fraudulently, by forged checks which his brother negotiated and otherwise, some thousands of dollars of his employer's money, for which crime both Alfred and his brother were committed to the reformatory. His conduct in all the requirements was such as his superior mind would warrant it to be. His record was absolutely perfect. He was a ready but unobtrusive debater of the more abstruse topics that came up in the ethics class of nearly five hundred, and there revealed remarkable intellectual ability, keen, logical, resourceful, and well balanced. His analytical power, exactness, facility of expression and good taste of arranging, was shown in the publications he was assigned to edit, in the translations from French to English which he made, and in the ideas and composition of certain articles that he wrote.

When in due time Goslin had fulfilled the obligations

required by the regulations he became an eligible candidate for parole and conditional release, and his case and character were for that purpose carefully reviewed and considered. It was clear enough that he desired and purposed to live a law-abiding life, but he evidently lacked intensiveness, and his liability to vacillation led to the issue of a limited parole. He was given employment at the reformatory, salaried, and allowed all the privileges and liberties of other citizen officers and employes, except that he should not absent himself from the premises. After six months of such limited liberation he was permitted, but with some misgiving, to return to New York City to employment provided. On the eve of his departure, late at night, alone together, and after an hour of interesting intercourse, when complete mutuality of mind and feeling was attained, I said as impressively as I could, "Tell me, now, Goslin — as man to man and confidentially, do you yourself really feel that you can withstand the temptations of the great city?" To this he replied after some hesitation and with much repressed agitation, "Yes, I *think* I can, unless in some way I get into close relations with banks and banking."

The next day he departed for New York, and after a few months, as was inevitable, he did get in touch with financial fakers just outside of legitimate Wall Street business. He was several times arrested, but with the exception of one short term in the county penitentiary, managed by use of much money to avoid the more serious consequences, until at last he was indicted for an offense he could not cover, when he fled to Paris with what was estimated to be a full million of his fraudulent accumulations. He had been living in New York several years then, luxuriously combining in himself the characteristics, self-indulgences, and sharp practices of the two historic scoundrels, Lovelace and Cagliostro. Or, more charitably and possibly more accurately, it might be said that he simply lived and illustrated the concentrated form of the extreme of that which is stigmatized now-a-days as rank commercialism or "high finance."

A third manifestation of alleged inferiority of the middle bulk of prisoners — deficiency of the commonly recognized moral sense — might be assumed, without over-presumptuousness, from the fact of their physiological and intellectual defectiveness beyond the average defectiveness of the social grade of free men to which they belong. It is shown by their habitual unscrupulousness and want of pity. Also, if morality may be considered to be conformity to the statutory demands and to the standard of current behavior of the community, these prisoners must be classed as excessively immoral because they disregard such obligations. But, if morality be viewed subjectively — an inner dominating sense of moral accountability to the Supreme Moral Governor — I cannot speak so confidently, for I do not know to what extent, if at all, the average free inhabitant governs his conduct by such a consideration. Rather, in this respect, I should rate the prisoners as *non-moral* than immoral, not having ever discovered in any of the thousands of prisoners I have known the supposedly abiding sense of moral obligation, unless the notion of *luck* may be so construed. And this notion was never observed based on a rational concept of the right or wrong of things; it was purely whimsical.

The middle mass of the prisoners at the reformatory in the year 1880 — the close of the first five years' epoch — were, notwithstanding the imperfections already named and others which more discriminatingly might be named, more simple minded and interesting than the prisoners I had known at Wethersfield, at Albany, and at Rochester. Their physical degeneracy, intellectual weakness, moral insensateness, together with their industrial inadequacy, disclosed the complexity of and at the same time intensified the interest in the problem of the reformation of criminals. With renewed clarity it was seen that both for safety and contentment a well-closed and secure corral must be maintained, and that in order to arrest the customary harmful habits and to initiate salutary corrective activities, a fine-meshed disciplinary régime must be planned and executed; in fine, to the end that genuine rational enduring reformations should be wrought, devotion and skill of administering were indispensable.

CHAPTER XIV

IMPROVEMENTS AND HINDRANCES

FROM July, 1876, to the close of the year 1877, approximately a year and a half, there were distributed to the prisoners books, magazines, and selected expurgated newspapers, and the nucleus of an excellent library was provided. Later all newspapers, except the institutional weekly newspaper, edited and published by the prisoners, were excluded on the ground of their hindrance to the necessary attention, concentration, and complete control of the mental processes. Religious Sunday services were regularly held, conducted by Elmira preachers of the several denominations. These usual means — the library and Sunday services—were supplemented with the general superintendent's unusual personal attention to each individual prisoner. From May 14, 1877, when the indeterminate sentence law took effect, its leavening influence gradually increased, inciting many to good and some to bad activities as has already been stated. The mark system was formulated, with its division of the prisoners into three classes or grades, according to merit and demerit in their records for labor, school, and demeanor. The mark system necessitated closer scrutiny and so made possible a better judgment as to the present and potential capabilities of each prisoner, his proper place in a free community, and the wisest training therefor. The school, two evenings a week, was organized and given in charge of Professor Danforth, the superintendent of the schools of Elmira. Brush making, a productive prison industry, on the state account system, without intervention of contractors, was introduced and carried on, but without any appropriation of public funds for an operating capital.

In the year 1878 the developing prison industry emphasized the need of capital; it revealed the industrial inefficiency of prisoners, and consequently the need of appropriate means for their bodily and mental preparation. It was one of the surprises of the year that so many of the prisoners, who it was thought would be actuated by the powerful inducement to advance themselves for release, not only failed to comply with the moderate conditions of advancement, but retarded their progress by conduct which made necessary their reduction to the lowest of the three grades. This was another most convincing indication of their supposed general inferiority. During this year the system of instruction by lecturers was instituted, which further on became a distinguishing representative feature. Dr. Ford of the Elmira College was regularly employed as non-resident lecturer in physical geography and in natural science.

Faint mutterings from unsatisfied religious denominationalists were heard that year, from both a Protestant and a Roman Catholic visiting preacher. They had quickly scented the rational flavor of the developing reformative system and were sensitive at the change in the procedure, so different from their dogmatic formulas.

Healthful institutional development characterized the next year, 1879. The building operations advanced; the hollow-ware industry, heavier and better for the older and stronger prisoners, was introduced; the brush making was profitable and there was a good prospect that income from labor of the prisoners would soon be sufficient to support the reformatory without any appropriations from the legislature.

The number of prisoners had reached 485. Professor Ford of the nearby college took entire direction of the prison school, which so enlisted the interest of the prisoners that their educational progress was concededly remarkable. The effectiveness of the indeterminate sentence, and of the mark system with its stimulating and discriminating effects, was more and more evident. By the mark system the unfit were gravitated to the lower grades similar to their free social grade; and many others moved up to the grade corresponding to a better free social grade. Movement instead of inertia characterized the mass; and a very desirable personal relation of prisoners and the management was manifest. In regard to this the board of managers in the year book for that year say:

"It is astonishing how willing, nay, how anxious he (the improving prisoner) becomes to unbosom himself to and consult with the superintendent and managers, whom he now begins to count as friends interested in his welfare, about what he had best do when he is set at liberty."

The solicitousness referred to should not be mistaken for mere provident economic forecast. It was a product of the tension of the régime, of a desire to earn for discharge and have the required employment definitely pre-arranged. Up to this time no very marked general interest in the reformatory had been manifested, though from wide distances leaders in penological and charitable undertakings, sociological instructors and students, and influential educators made inquiries and paid visits for examination. Occurrences of the next two years, however, focused upon the reformatory greatly increased general attention and somewhat particular close scrutiny. The manufactured output in 1880 was $226,153.60, yielding for the earnings of prisoners $62,610.49, a volume of manufacturing business that could no longer be sustained without an operating capital. A crisis was thus reached and earnest demand made upon the legislature for $100,000 of funds for this purpose, a request that led to the appointment of a legislative committee composed of two senators and three assemblymen to "investigate the affairs of the reformatory."

The member who moved for the committee was elected from Cohoes, the principal brush making community in the state. If the ultimate design was to relieve his constituents, the Cohoes brush makers, from the competition of our brush business by discontinuing it altogether, he accomplished it. The procedure of the committee, together with the allusions to the reformatory in the report to the legislature, are so interesting and informing as to such methods and as to the estimation of the reformatory at that time, that they warrant some additional consideration.

The report and testimony cover 58 printed pages in the volume of assembly documents for that year. The investigation was thorough and with the exception of the discontinuance of our brush business was altogether fair. The report is partitioned into what is named the "Moral Question" and the "Business Question." The committee unanimously commend the reformatory as to the former, and offer but one simple recommendation in relation to it; namely, a "good time" allowance to prisoners who are transferred to the state prisons from the reformatory. The committee says:

"We take pleasure in commending the management for the excellent condition in which the buildings and grounds are being maintained and for the skill, thoroughness and efficiency with which the work of the Reformatory in reclaiming the inmates is being carried on. . . . We are convinced that its object is being attained to a greater degree than its best friends anticipated."

Then after a statement about the buildings, facilities, food, the régime — particularly the indeterminate sentence feature, the report concludes as follows:

"In general we have none but words of commendation for the *reformatory* work of the Reformatory. The experiment is being proved a success. Young men who have fallen into bad ways are being saved to homes, friends, and society, instead of being crushed in spirit and prepared for deeper shame and greater crimes. The principle on which the Reformatory is being conducted should, in our judgment, be extended into the other penal institutions of the State."

The words "in general" in the above paragraph were used in order to prepare for the recommendation to extend the good time law to the transferred prisoners. The italicising of the word "reformatory," together with the fervent commendation of this feature, was evidently intended to magnify the idealistic aim, thus to minify the pecuniary side for the intended sacrifice in the interest of the Cohoes brush makers. In order to accomplish this object a majority of the committee recommended the change from the "state account" to the contract prison labor system. No brush manufacturer would contract for prison labor because free labor, of women and children, could be procured so cheaply. The recommended change was ordered by the legislature of that year (Act 585) over the protest of the committee's minority report, signed by W. S. Andrews, the only committeeman who seemed to have proper appreciation of the intimacy of relation of the labor system and the reformatory régime, and also against the views of the reformatory management communicated to the legislature in the cogent memorial of February 21, 1881.

This legislative interference hindered the general development and was a disappointment. The calamity was, at the time, somewhat compensated by increase of favorable attention to the reformatory, incident to the fact of the investigation and the commendatory report; and in retrospect it is seen to have been really beneficial, a preliminary to the legislation of 1888 — the practical abolishment of productive prison work in all the prisons, releasing to us the entire time of the prisoners of our reformatory, numbering then 828, for direct reformatory training and a completer development of the rational reformatory system. At the close of this five years' period, 1880, the best developed and most striking feature of the system was the school training as it was directed by Professor Ford of Elmira College, and by Professor D. P. Mayhew of Michigan, the latter employed as resident moral instructor.

Professor Mayhew was remarkable for his emanant goodness, and he was an impressive instructor. As the principal of the State Normal School of Michigan he graduated there not only capable teachers, but teachers with a rare quality of enthusiasm and undying attachment to himself. He succeeded in bringing in orderly mental processes among pupils who were frivolous and scatter-brained; he readily interested and instructed even primary class pupils in mental and moral discriminations — work similar to that so admirably done with the prisoners at the Detroit House of Correction. All this gave high hopes for benefits from his services at Elmira. Professor Mayhew devoted the few months with us to the experimental effort to quicken and increase the moral and spiritual susceptibilities which prisoners in common with all humanity were believed to possess, — at least as a rudimental vital element of character. He says his object was, "Not to give extended metaphysical instruction but to clearly discriminate (to the comprehension of the prisoner pupils) the mental powers we use, and so define them that each shall be clearly seen and the mode of growth and way of development plainly given." His lectures were on psychology, ethics, and Biblical-spiritual interpretation. The experiment proved valuable, but not so successful as his similar work at Detroit had been. The difference should be attributed to Professor Mayhew's advanced age, increased deafness, and clearly to the fact that the Elmira prisoners were more absorbed in earning merit marks in the other departments as well.

The regular prison school of letters was held evenings only, which made it possible to employ the very best teaching ability in the adjacent city. Besides Professors Ford and Mayhew the corps of teachers embraced three principals of Union Schools and five college graduates, lawyers apt and willing to teach, who on school nights were conveyed to and fro in a special conveyance provided by the reformatory. Dr. Ford, who at first was somewhat doubtful as to our unusual educational plan for the prisoners, gradually gained complete confidence as is shown in his report on the schools in 1880. He says:

"The main work of the school, reading, writing, and arithmetic, has been supplemented by elementary instruction on the laws of thought, morals, and health, using the lecture method, with gratifying success. There has been a steady eye given to the practical use of these in the affairs of civic life. . . . The best of order and a growing desire for a plain common school education is now the marked feature of the reformatory school. *It is wonderful, in most cases, how it revives and brightens latent manhood.*"

CHAPTER XV

AGITATION, PUBLICATION, AND VINDICATION

1881-1882

THE two years immediately after the first five years' period — 1876 to 1881 — marked a transitional epoch in the history of the reformatory and in my own life. They were characterized by incidents then thought impeding and annoying, but which proved to be in reality auspicious and helpful. Newspapers published sensational notices of occurrences which drew an amount of critical attention to the reformatory greatly in excess of the attention such occurrences in the usual state prisons would have attracted. This resulted from misapprehension of the felonious character of our inmates, derived from the title "reformatory" — so commonly applied to schools for the confinement of juveniles committed for venial offenses, and considerably, no doubt, because the current fanciful notion of reformation was not yet distinguished from the more realistic and correct conception of our procedure. A better public appreciation dawned later, but even now — 1912 — it is not fully effulgent. This better public understanding was promoted by troublous events at the reformatory some of which have been already referred to in the mention of bad specimens of prisoners. Critical public attention was further stimulated by newspaper notices of investigations — the one already described and another which took place in 1882.

This second investigation by the joint legislative committee on state prisons — nine senators and assemblymen — representative men, brought out in their report to the legislature the complexion of the intelligent public sentiment of the time about prison management and towards our reformatory. After citing the law and emphasizing their opinion of its intention in founding the reformatory,— that it was not for punishment but for reformation, they add: "Therefore a milder and different disciplinary régime should be expected to exist." The belief is expressed that "cruel and inhuman treatment might consist in a moral régime of undue severity, and in an unusual and undiscriminating administration of the system of grading on the record of merits and demerits, as well as in the infliction of excessive punishment."

The report goes on to say that, "since the contract system of prison labor has an important bearing upon the subject of prison discipline" it falls within the proper scope of their authority to investigate it, which they proceed to do with the result that, later in the report, the committee are unitedly in opposition to it, — unitedly opposed to the labor system which on recommendation of the investigating committee of 1881 the legislature ordered to be introduced in place of the state-account plan which the board of managers had adopted and preferred. The inquiry was pursued with great thoroughness to the very conclusion. The report contains all the testimony that relates to complaints made about the prisoners Hughes, Reddington, Tibbetts, Hill, and Minch, and gives the finding that, "The allegations of cruelty are not proven," and adds, "While we fully acquit the officers of the Reformatory of the charge of cruelty in the treatment of prisoners, we deem it our duty to make some suggestions in reference to the management of the institution with the view to its increased efficiency in its special work." Three suggestions or recommendations are then made:

"(1) Opposition to the contract system of prison labor. (2) That while under the then present management the system of marking and grading is in the main judiciously and successfully administered, etc., the general superintendent should be supplied with competent assistants, such as a resident chaplain, schoolmaster, and inspector of labor. (3) The Committee find that the prisoners are not overworked, but suggest giving consideration to the lack of inspiration and of energy induced by a rewardless occupation.

"As to the alleged improper committals by the courts, non-transfer of such to the state prisons, and the proposition that it be made by law compulsory to immediately transfer them, the committee find that the managers are best qualified to judge whether a prisoner should be transferred or not transferred."

The report concludes with a consideration of "corporal punishment." The committee say, in regard to this, that though cognizant of the instinctive general sentiment of revolt in the community at recitals of details of punishment, the committee incline to defer to the weight of opinion of men of large experience who favor it. The finding as to this at the reformatory is that no instance of excessive severity has been discovered and that only ten instances of "paddling" had occurred during the five years of the institution. The report is signed by all the members of the committee as follows: John McDonough, Daniel M. Kelly, John Raines, R. D. Clapp, John O'Brien, E. R. Keyes, J. Higgins, E. O. Farrar, J. E. Sheldon.

It will not have escaped the observation of the reader that the committeemen were quick to discern the particularity of the scheme of training and the thoroughness of the administering. They saw how completely the life of the prisoners was controlled by the management through the central directing mind of the general superintendent. While the very searching examination disclosed no fault and elicited no censure, the committeemen were evidently impressed with the delicacy and the skill required for proper management, and also convinced of the desirability of providing very competent assistants. They saw the incongruity of a contract labor system, and they appreciated the necessity of leaving untouched the wide discretionary authority vested in the management by the organic act of the legislature. The committee's interpretation of the intention of the law and the founders of the reformatory as so different from the design of the penitentiaries, reveals that punishment and leniency were uppermost in the minds of the committeemen as they were in the general public appreciation. This traditional mental attitude was felt to be the chief menace to the new institution and system in the reformatory scheme. The agreeable or disagreeable experiences of the prisoners were always rated as casual, never primal, considerations. It was not quite clear to these gentlemen that the aim — reclamation —

should be and always was in supremacy, and that the transitory comfort or discomfort of the prisoners must remain incident to the reclaiming process.

This second investigation and report, the study and conclusions of nine such intelligent, impartial, representative men, emphasized again to the management that our theory and methods were so much in advance of the common appreciation that more attention must be given to disseminating accurate information about them. So it came to pass that this transitional period was notable for the policy of publicity then inaugurated.

Previously, not secrecy but comparative silence had been the policy. During the early experimental stage it was obviously wise to proceed quietly, thus avoiding judgments likely to be formed from observing incomplete progress. Mere silence might be construed as secrecy, always a ground of suspicion. It had become evident that, as a city set upon a hill cannot be hid, our reformatory on the hillside at Elmira must henceforth be opened to American curiosity and public observation. Pursuing the policy of publicity, the annual reports to the legislature were made more explanatory. And later, when issued from the reformatory press, the reports were elaborated, illustrated, and 3000 or more copies of each annual issue were distributed to members of the legislature and public officials; to the judiciary and professional men; to public institutions, newspapers, and libraries throughout the state; and to correspondents at home and abroad. Already the reformatory was famed, visited, and favorably commented upon by inquiring delegations. The year book for 1881 contained a full explanation of the law and reprinted the act of that year that changed the labor system, together with the managers' protesting memorial to the legislature, and excerpts from commendatory publications by the following: The Prison Association of New York, the California legislative committee, the special committee of the Connecticut legislature on contract convict labor, and the commissioners of prisons from Massachusetts, New Jersey, and Pennsylvania; also Governor Hoyt's message to the Pennsylvania legislature recommending the establishment of a similar reformatory institution in that state. Also excerpts from the report of the visiting state board of correction and charity of Michigan; the report of Mr. Longmuir, inspector of prisons and asylums for Canada; and approving comments of the Howard Association of London, England, whose leaflets were widely distributed in this country as they were in England.

Visitors who came from curiosity were freely admitted and conducted over the entire establishment, and given painstaking explanations; and many thousands of such visitors availed themselves of the privilege. Interviews between prisoners and their relatives were permitted without the presence of an official listener. Moreover, and this is important to be noted, the practice established at the very beginning was continued throughout the twenty-five years of my superintendency of keeping a record open to the prisoner clerks, the officers and employes of the establishment, the members of the board of managers, to visitors, and to the relatives and friends of the prisoners, — a record of each prisoner's disciplinary treatment, entered in his account in plain detail, however serious or trifling it might be, showing even reproofs and admonitions as well as the use of coercive measures. The record includes also, of course, every item of merit and demerit marking. This wide-open policy proved to be serviceable for defense against mendacious attacks; and it stimulated carefulness, fidelity, and thoroughness of administering.

The following extracts from the year book for 1882 best show this, and the preparation for further expansion. The board of managers' contribution is a concise statement of the business affairs; an explanation of the need of and a formal request for appropriations; and gives their opinion that the reformatory is useful and shows the basis of its usefulness. The managers say:

"The appendant reports of the general superintendent and certain heads of departments show conclusively that the Reformatory, as organized and conducted, is a real advance from the usual treatment of the class of criminals here confined, is already of actual service in the repression of crime, and is destined to be still more useful in the same direction. The Reformatory system meets a demand of enlightened public sentiment which favors the idea that young offenders, though felons, shall be wisely and humanely treated, be supplied with incentives and opportunities to reform, and, as far as possible, the unworthy and determined criminals shall be subjected to lengthened detention in prison, and all, when released, be properly supervised until they are established in industry, respectable associations, and good behavior.

"There are many agencies which contribute to the gratifying success achieved here, but the supreme influence, the real foundation of hope and fruition, is found in the Act of 1877 with its indefinite sentence and subsequent supervision features," etc.

The general superintendent describes the reformatory plant, its extent, attractiveness of situation, architecture, and apartmental arrangement; the date when first used for confinement of prisoners; and the amount of recent additional outlay for construction ($288,644.33). Some benefits betokened by the Act of 1877 are mentioned; namely, it is a first step in New York towards classifying for treatment states prison convicts; it makes prominent in the criminal laws the better purpose of public protection in place of punishment of offenders; it protects prisoners from the inequalities of the definite sentence system; it establishes the principle of conditional release; it changes the mental attitude of prisoners towards the prison government and the state from antagonism to accord; and it supplies the strongest known motive and the best probable encouragement for self-help to reformation. Attention is again called to the popular misapprehension of the really criminal characteristics of the prisoners; to the great danger or damage to the community occasioned by the stream of unimproved prisoners discharged annually from the prisons of the state. The salutariness of the mark system and the abundant precautions taken against errors or injustice are fully explained. Passing mention is made of the excellent school organization, the lecture work, and the admirable corps of educated and experienced teachers. But it is declared, "No reformatory system is complete that does not train each subject of it for a specific industry, actually induct him into it, and maintain supervisory control over him long enough to insure a good degree of permanence and success." The most earnest recommendation is made, "*that there be erected and fitted with facilities an establishment, within the enclosure, for instructing inmates in industries that promise reasonable income and respectable associations."*

The general superintendent concludes his report with the confident remark that a unified administration of juvenile and adult reformatories, together with adoption in all the prisons of the principles of the indeterminate sentence law of 1877, would, within a few years, effect an important reduction in the volume (ratio to population) of crime. The report contains a condensed statement of the financial results of the year's operation (the maintenance cost, $95,099.63; income from labor of prisoners, $64,445.96). It also gives interesting statistics relating to the prisoners; their heredity, environment, and condition on admission, their average rate of progress qualifying for release (16 months) and the average detention of the prisoners in hand (only 17 months). Pertinent facts concerning them are included; as for instance, that 94.5 per cent of the crimes were against property; that 40 per cent were on admission more than twenty years old; that of those released on parole 81.2 per cent were probably living properly, and that including those still in custody the state has good protection from 91.2 per cent of the whole number treated up to that date.

Dr. Ford, the school director, wrote encouragingly of the schools, their history, course of study, and grading, adding specimens of examination papers of pupils in ethics, geometry, elements of psychology, and health, single entry bookkeeping, United States history, elements of physics, psychology, elements of political economy, and geography.

Mr. White, secretary of the summer school, wrote

similarly about the newly adopted educational department. The librarian, an educated prisoner, reported
on the library, its needs, the plan of distributing books,
the awakened and awakening new taste and wish for
reading, and he gives duplicates of three library cards
from the three school divisions which show the effective
use of the library.

The Protestant and the Catholic non-resident chaplains wrote briefly, each giving his impressions of
religious ministrations; and the physician gave an
account of his work for the year and made his recommendations. In the appendix is included a synopsis
of rules and regulations; the new overwork rule; summary of the daily institutional routine; specimens of
the forms in use for regulating and communicating the
performance and progress of the prisoners, and of the
parole certificate for conditional release; and a reprint,
for information and convenient reference, of the indeterminate sentence law of 1877.

Following this two years' epoch with its attendant
accusations, inquiry, and vindication, besides inspections by home and foreign visitors with resultant
commendation; and after the above mentioned full
descriptive report had been widely distributed, things
became more normal.

Undoubtedly the annoyances and all the experiences
of the two years were, in the ordained orderly movement of human affairs, a necessity, and as the story of
the reformatory, which is also the story of my own life,
proceeds, it will be seen that the total experience was
also salutary.

CHAPTER XVI

RECOGNITION

1883–1888

THE dominant characteristic of the reformatory during the years between 1883 and 1888 was that of adolescent institutional development. The period was rife with experiments, interesting incidents, and with annoying embarrassments. But the reformatory forced its way to a permanent place in the prison system of the state and was recognized, if somewhat reluctantly, as a new departure in the treatment of adult male felonious prisoners.

The number of inmates reached 829, an increase of 65 per cent. The gross annual maintenance cost grew to $135,217.58, and although in 1883 the structure was completed according to its original design, there was additionally expended for the new south wing and other items of construction, $267,912.77. The unique characteristic of this period of adolescent development was the *educational idea* of it all. It was at that time, as has been shown, something new to use such a system for adult prisoners, men convicted of high crimes. For this reason a full account of it seems justified.

At the start, in 1883, the managers in their report to the legislature said:

242

"The educational work carried on in the Reformatory, with a few changes in the use of terms, describes that of many high schools and academies scattered over the state which are patronized by pupils who expect to be fitted in them for engaging in the many occupations which give character to the citizenship of our republican form of government. This distinguishing feature of the Reformatory exists in intimate association with specific branches of industry and the most exact requirements of discipline and deportment. The Reformatory is a training school with varying appliances to meet the necessities of illiterates as well as those who have already enjoyed the advantages of education to a certain extent."

This encomium does not mean smug satisfaction but an examination incident to progress.

In this year (1883) under the direction of Professor N. A. Wells, art instructor from Syracuse University, a most interesting experiment was made to test the educational value of industrial art for illiterate prisoners. Two small classes were formed, a primary and an advanced class. The primary class numbered fifty men who were chosen for their dullness of perception and backwardness in common school branches. The advanced class was composed of ten selected from the most intelligent and best educated; men possessed of some mechanical and artistic skill. These were quickly interested and were serviceable as monitors and aids in instructing small groups of the primary division. Drawing tables and instruments and clay for modeling were supplied. Instruction was given orally and without printed patterns, except that the advanced pupils made portraits in hammered copper from photographs. The experiment continued eleven weeks.

The primary pupils received eighty hours of practice lessons, and the advanced class forty hours. Professor Wells gives the results as follows:

"Out of the whole number there were but three men in whom it was impossible to develop that state of receptivity which is the result of permanently aroused interest, one of these being so refractory as to necessitate his expulsion from the class. . . . About 80 per cent of the whole number showed marked intellectual growth, and more than a dozen of these voluntarily expressed a desire for the higher educational privileges. . . . Eighty per cent of the whole number also made marked improvement in manual skill, showing that manual skill and mental development keep even pace with each other. And about 20 per cent of the whole number developed a high grade of artistic feeling and skill. Improved tendencies were quite apparent as shown by the daily record of deportment, as well as by the greatly changed bearing and expression of countenance exhibited by a majority of the men."

The vivifying influence of the experiment so generally evident was also shown by particular effects. Its force had necessitated the expulsion of one pupil, but produced the uprise of others. One instance may be related. On entering the class room one summer evening with Professor Wells, who had picked from the shrubbery outside a bit of leafy trailing vine and was playfully twirling it, we observed a pupil apparently stalled. On the paper before him he had drawn a six-inch square with bisectional lines, but now stood puzzled and discouraged. He was a massive, swarthy, morose man of nearly thirty years of age; strong of limb, slow of motion and speech, and apparently of sluggish mind. The instructor approached and deftly held the vine within the square, offering a brief suggestion as to how its form could be incorporated within the drawing of the square, then passed on to other pupils. Half an hour afterwards on returning to the stalled pupil the instructor was surprised and pleased at the delicate skill the drawing now displayed, and he so expressed himself. Some silent evidence of responsive feeling was manifest but the trifling occurrence was soon eclipsed in the teacher's memory. But whether by cause or coincidence, from this point the prisoner progressed well in drawing, in the school of letters, and in his daily work of iron molding. On his parole, which was duly issued, I employed him at regular mechanic's wages to instruct novices in the molders' trade. He lived in the neighborhood, married respectably (but not with happy final results), found steady employment in the city later at his trade, and ever since, now twenty-four years and more, he has maintained his liberty and supported himself by means of legitimate industry.

This industrial art school experiment, covering only eleven weeks of time, encouraged the scheme of oral, manual, technical, and disciplinary education which in its later development distinguished the Elmira Reformatory, and when carefully studied by leading educators and economists had their approval and was declared to be a model much in advance of any educational organization then to be found in our free society.

School books were discarded, being replaced with printed outlines prepared for each lesson by the teachers. These outlines were printed on the reformatory press and distributed to the pupils, not as texts for study but as programs only. The prisoners took notes of the oral teaching and submitted written examinations monthly, the marking of which had effect as to their progress towards release. A number of subsidiary classes, composed of specially selected pupils, were formed for particular additional tutelage; and the principle of small classes and intensive teaching was generally adopted throughout the school of letters, in the industrial training, and even in the endeavors to effect directly a moral and religious impression. These subsidiary classes were, of course, subordinate to, or better, supplemental of the larger classes and assemblages, such as the Sunday afternoon popular assembly for religious address and service, and the Sunday morning assembly of all pupils of the higher school classes — the brightest — numbering from three hundred to five hundred for consideration and discussion of practical morality. This class, which was called the "ethics class," was so remarkable in method, in the extraordinary interest it awakened, in the surpassing fitness of the instructor, in its revealing of the true inward character of some insidious minded prisoners, and in the powerful effect that it had on the intellectual and to some extent the moral tone of the establishment, that a rather full account of it seems justified.

THE ETHICS CLASS

The practical purpose of the class was not, as might at first thought be supposed, directly to inculcate moral maxims in expectation that the prisoners would consciously adopt the maxims and afterwards shape their conduct in accordance therewith, but rather to create in their minds a habit of qualitative moral discrimination. The attention of this class, that year, was directed to the lawful and unlawful, or what a man may do as determined by rules and principles drawn from the Scriptures, from the laws of society, and from equity and natural reason. These topics, under the remarkable guidance of the instructor, in free discussion, became of absorbing interest to the men.

Mr. Charles A. Collin, then a practicing attorney in Elmira, afterwards resident law professor at Cornell University, and through the terms of two state governors their legal adviser, took charge of this class and of another in political economy just for the love of the work. Able, original, and vivacious, Mr. Collin took the attitude of a sincerely interested investigator rather than a teacher,— a fellow inquirer with his pupils. He had the tact to seize upon, unfold, and sometimes gleefully and gracefully to surrender to an incisive thought or argument by any pupil, however crudely it might be suggested. Knowing the instinctive contradiction of such awakened minds, with high trust in the self-propagating power of truth, he at times advocated undesirable views with all his trained controversial skill until I myself became uneasy and the class solicitous for the real truth.

The secretary of the schools, himself a prisoner (of whom more anon) says in his report that year:

"The lectures on practical morality given to the Sunday class have served to show how efficient and stimulating and incisive scholarly treatment of that subject might be made, even for men unencumbered with any metaphysical baggage. The discussions opened with an inquiry into a man's place in nature and society, and were pursued through the themes of social collisions, revenge and forgiveness, the equilibrium of social forces, retribution, and truthfulness. . . . The main questions were uttered as from a strictly intellectual, non-religious point of view, but the religious bearings which were naturally suggested as the discussion progressed, were not wholly ignored though never intruded; and the endeavor was then made to reach the truth through disputations, in which the audience took part."

Members of the class were encouraged to send to the lecturer written criticisms or suggestions which were read aloud at the opening of the following lecture.

In after years, as the inmate population increased, this class numbered some five hundred men, and the attractiveness of the discussions became an incentive for inmates in the lower school divisions to qualify for admission to it. It was also for the class members a most powerful intellectual stimulant. While the assemblage was always sufficiently orderly it was at the same time, by the extraordinary tact and inspiration of Mr. Collin, the teacher, in originality of thought and utterance the freest possible assemblage. A striking feature was the complete absence in the debaters of any show of bashfulness or discomposure. Naturally a large majority of these pupils were members of the higher social institutional grade — as was apparent by their distinctive better apparel, which fact, together with their advanced educational standing, imparted a certain social tone above that of the common herd. Yet a recreant paroled man arrested and returned in disgrace, with hair cropped and clad in the glaring red clothing of the lowest grade, would and did on his first attendance in the ethics class participate in the debate

THE ETHICS CLASS, ELMIRA REFORMATORY
Professor Monks lecturing to five hundred prisoners

with an air of the utmost sang-froid. This general characteristic revealed again the lowered sensibility of the average prisoner and partly accounts for the want of pity and probity that characterizes their crimes.

The ethics class exercises were of additional service in disclosing the real character of these prisoners who, from the fact of their advanced standing, must soon be considered for conditional release. The class work was so useful in this particular that I was rarely absent from the sessions. Moreover, the entertainment and instruction of the ethics class hour incited my attendance. The late well known prolific author, editor, and lecturer, Charles Dudley Warner, was occasionally present and declared himself surprised and delighted at the freedom, facility, and incisiveness of the prison debaters. Professor Jeremiah W. Jenks of Cornell University said of the principal prisoner debaters that in this respect they equalled the senior pupils in his classes at the university. Mr. Collin himself, on his retirement, said that he had gained from their lively, unharnessed, original minds, more of value than he felt he had imparted to them.

On his acceptance of a call to a chair in the faculty of Cornell University Mr. Collin wrote a review of his impressions of the ethics class. Since only occasional allusion to this remarkable feature of the reformatory's educational work will again be made in this narrative, his clear and interesting description is here inserted:

"Ethical study calls for a keen, critical, dissecting spirit, and it is thereby precisely adapted to receive the immediate attention of a prison audience. Not merely learning moral maxims nor listening to good advice is meant, but the culture of that temper of mind and soul designated by the great modern teacher, Arnold of Rugby, as 'moral thoughtfulness.' Answering back their arguments firmly and sharply the audience will be curious to see what one of their own number will say. Their interest will be transferred to the replies of the teacher. Men who say nothing will begin to think what they might say. . . . To have attracted interested attention is more than half the battle. . . . Expressly discarding oratory, stories and similar nonsense, I set to work dryly but cheerily and heartily to discuss, on a low plane, the most comfortable methods of living. At the outset I ignored all authority, the Bible included, and took up the problem of life as though for the first time. . . . I proceeded with reckless intellectual honesty. For instance, I gave a fair exposition of the argument for temperance as opposed to total abstinence. My pupils had hitherto listened with dubious interest, but now began to scent rank heresy. . . . I was rebuked for encouraging intemperance and we had some very forcible total abstinence lectures from members of the class. I took my castigations meekly, and conceded that total abstinence was, possibly, the only true rule for any one, and was certainly the only safe rule for very many. By this time my pupils had decided that their teacher was not smart nor particularly good. . . . The practical morality class became decidedly unpopular for the difficulty they foresaw of passing their examinations in this study. It was known throughout the institution as the class in 'Practical Rascality.' . . .

"The discussions naturally passed from physical health to the health of the soul. Here I met with a spirit of skepticism (doubt as to existence of soul). Strange to say, the proposition that man has a soul troubled *me* for several Sundays in spite of the assistance of the orthodox majority of the class. I finally clinched the proposition as follows: 'If I called you a fool, you would say I insulted you. Then there is something of you besides body, and this something can be happy or suffering, healthy or diseased. Let us call this something, whatever it is, *soul*, without regard to whether it continues to exist after the death of the body.' . . . The leader of the skeptics said to me privately as we were passing out of the class, 'Well, I see that in the sense in which you use the word soul, man has a soul, but whether man has a soul in the religious sense or not I do not know, and I am going to wait and see what I can make out of it.' . . . What he finally made out of it is indicated by his contribution to *The Summary*, allegorical of his own hard struggle with himself, as follows:

"GOD AND THE ROBIN

Early in the morning before the lazy cock crows, you may hear the robin singing his welcome to the sun. All is quiet until his music rends the air, and as you listen you are inspired with thoughts of Him who made the robin and you. Perhaps the sweet song is a prayer of thanks to God for sheltering them from the dangers of the night. Do they know of God? Who can tell? Perhaps He is the cause of what we in our ignorance call instinct. Once as I listened to their music I fell asleep and dreamed of a house near the sea. It had a lawn in front, on which was a robin hopping in search of food for her young. But as she hopped about the sky seemed to grow darker. I knew that a storm was approaching, and when it came I saw the robin cling to the tree for shelter. But the wind was fierce and it tore her from the branch and in spite of all her efforts bore her out over the ocean, farther and farther from the land, till at last when its energy was spent, its fury gone, it left her on the ocean with no land in sight to guide her to her home. And as she flew she thought of her little ones at home and of her mate. She thought she was flying to them, but every little effort was taking her farther away though she knew it not. In her frightened cry I seemed to hear her say "O where shall I rest my weary wings?" But in the murmuring of the ocean she heard no reply. So she could but fly on.　The darkness came, when utterly exhausted she fell upon the cruel waves and died.　And He who made her will receive her when the course of life is past.　Cannot that little robin find in that house of many mansions a place to rest her weary wing?　Is heaven made for man alone?　Are not these little creatures who never offend God, but worship Him with the purity and happiness of their little hearts, entitled to the joys of the hereafter?　Who can doubt it?"

The remarkableness of the foregoing production, which evidently is a mixture of quotation or suggestion from the Sunday school library publications and the prisoner's own originality, consists in its parallelism with his own experience; his recognition of and brooding over it.　The writer was eighteen years of age, physically a low type, affected with a chronic skin disease, and with a peculiar head, the back of which dropped vertically into the cervical line.　He was of criminal heredity, environment, and habit; his father was a professional burglar, his mother a professional blackmailer, and both of them were then in state prison. He himself said that his grandmother was also a thief. This youth had been in the House of Refuge before admission to the reformatory, where on his admission he was pronounced thoroughly criminal and devoid of moral susceptibility though intellectually bright.　His career both in the House of Refuge and at our reformatory confirmed the view.　With us he oscillated between the highest and the lowest grade for fifty-one of the sixty months of his possible detention, with fights, gross insubordination, and attempted arson in his track.　He was unbalanced and quarrelsome, and with intervals of noble impulses and manly behavior, he was subject also to violent passionate outbursts.

From the first he was an active participant in the practical morality class debates. A few times he made himself so objectionable that his exclusion was imperative. In December, 1885, he was removed altogether from the reformatory as incorrigible and of evil influence and was transferred to the Auburn State Prison, where he died about two months later.

This man possessed, most markedly, a double personality, very bad and very good, of which he was thoroughly conscious. In each he was equally sincere. Notwithstanding his youth he was the most dangerous of all supposedly sane prisoners I have known. His native intellectual capability was equal to any, and he was an exceedingly interesting specimen of the criminous character. I recall a conversation with him, when he was in a good mood. Referring to his recent attempt to incite a mutiny among his fellow prisoners in the foundry, I warned him that a second attempt would cost him his life, for the guard had been instructed to unhesitatingly shoot him. He replied with a pleasant smile upon his face, "Superintendent, if it were not for the smart of the spanking which my procedure would bring upon me, I could and would in a short time disorganize and destroy your entire reformatory scheme here."

The membership of the class soon reached five hundred, and intense interest was manifested in the discussions. That its popularity was increasing, may be inferred from the following note given verbatim:

"General Superintendent: Please allow me to attend the lectures on Practical Morality Sunday forenoon. I ges I can pass examination. I would much like it, as I think Morality is my weakest point. Yours truly ——"

Continuing now Mr. Collin's account:

. . . "We continued the readings from Socrates on punishment as a remedy for diseases of the soul. That a man should run to a judge to be punished, as he would to a surgeon when wounded, and should do the same for his friends and relatives, was a strange and new doctrine, and the professionally orthodox could not tell which side to take. The only trouble with the discussion now was to control it. Half a dozen hands would be up at once waiting for the teacher's nod and even the superintendent could not always keep his seat. . . . I soon went floundering into the terra incognita of business morality, with unaffected ignorance hunting for some standard of right and wrong whereby to test the morality of business transactions. I took positions confidently and abandoned them freely. Some called me socialist and communist, but they soon found that names did not trouble me in my search after substance, and that I was desirous to follow only my intellect wherever it might lead, wholly regardless of my landing place. . . . We all plunged together into the unstable waters of doubt and inquiry, but slowly came out again into the solid ground of New Testament doctrine. . . . A discussion of the fundamental propositions of religion naturally followed, indeed could not be avoided. . . . I confined the discussion as closely as possible to the points in which the principal religions agree."

This religious discussion precipitated, as the discussion of morality had not, denominational partisan asperity among the pupils, which for a time threatened to wreck the class, but none openly denied the existence of God and the life hereafter. One pupil suggested that a man can only reverence, not love God — a remark that brought out in the next issue of *The Summary*, the institutional newspaper, a sonnet copied and sent in by a third grade man who, after remaining many months in the lowest grade, was forced out of it and developed unusual literary taste and capability. He became the chief editor of *The Summary*, was made the librarian, and given charge of the class in English literature, which embraced all the prisoners who could use the library with fair intelligence. Here is the sonnet:

"Back from the door that bound the sepulchre,
Wherein my soul was gyved with chains of sin,
This morn of Life the rock of Death has been
By hands seraphic, rolled away fore'er.
From out the dark cold sleep I cried aloud
Unto the Lord, within whose hand doth rest
A myriad worlds; who doeth for the best
All things! He cast aside my bond and shroud;
And Death's armed sentries, who through all the night
Had watched beside my prisoned spirit's cave,
Fled, blinded by the rays of Heavenly light
That circled him who stood beside the grave
With angel cohorts, come my soul to save
And wake from out the sleep of Wrong to Right."

It is interesting to note that, following the religious trend of the day's discussion, this low grade man should find and sufficiently interest himself in the lofty theme of the sonnet to copy and contribute it to our weekly publication. The subsequent successful career of this man shall be given later, but let us first attend to the concluding portion of Mr. Collin's description. He says:

"The Socratic philosophy took sharp hold of the class and was used freely as the basis of discussion — selected passages from the Apology, Crito, and Phaedo — and without special intentional guidance the class sessions more and more took the form of the Socratic colloquy. A very practical friend inquires: 'Well, after you have got through with your moral and intellectual gymnastics, what is there in these men to show for it? What is the final outcome of sharpening the wits of such men with your high-toned discussions?' My answer is somewhat to this effect: However it may be with religion there is no such thing as a sudden conversion to morality. Morality means firmly set habits acquired by long practice and severe discipline. Men cannot be kept steadily thinking with a genuine interest on higher and better themes, with reference to better ends, without acquiring better habits of thought."

He might have added that the mass of mind of the men then belonging to the ethics class was held in a favorable attitude of receptivity for the permanent good impression desired to be made.

No more striking example can be given, confirmative of the truth of Mr. Collin's definition of morality as a habit of mind which may be induced by pressure and practice, than the recovery to sound moral rectitude of the prisoner above referred to — he of the sonnet. He was twenty years old, undersized, with hands and feet strangely deformed, but with an excellent cranium. For years he had been an inmate of the Protectory at Westchester, less for any unlawful conduct than for abandonment by his faulty parents. Discharged from the Protectory into the streets of New York City he gravitated immediately to vicious and criminal associations, and soon, technically convicted of burglary, was committed to our reformatory under the indeterminate sentence law, with the maximum statutory limitation of five years. Unfitted by reason of his deformed hands for any mechanical work he was assigned to messenger service which gave free opportunity to communicate with the other prisoners. His good fellowship for his own kind led to violations of the regulations, disregard of his individual progress and welfare, and effected soon his reduction to the third or lowest grade where, because of continual irregularities of behavior, he remained for two years or more irresponsive to the motive-obligation and to the moral persuasions with which he was plied. Could it properly be said of him and such as he that he disregarded his own welfare for the sake of maintaining equality and fraternity with his chosen class of fellow prisoners? He did, whether deliberately or instinctively, prefer the liberty to do as he pleased, the supremacy of his personal will, to the freedom achievable by self-subordination. Have we not, up to this point in his history, a man in conflict with government, yet actuated by the noble love of essential liberty, equality, and fraternity? If such motives must be classed as good and the conduct intolerable, the usual appeal to the moral consciousness might be ineffective.

Approaching the meridian of his detention period, on passing which the motive of the indeterminate sentence must wane, I summoned him for a private interview at which I endeavored to impress a sense of obligation in the larger relations and to urge the motive of his own true interests and welfare, but not with any appearance of satisfactory success. To clinch the matter, since I was fully purposed that he *must* now amend his conduct and gain some improvement, he was advised that resort would be had should he make it necessary, to physical coercive measures. And to focus the matter he was notified that a given number of just demerit marks would precipitate the treatment of which he was then forewarned. It thus remained, it was explained, quite with himself to avoid or qualify for this physical treatment. The interview occurred late at night and before noon the next day he qualified and immediately received the treatment. Not a punishment, but a compelling physical experience within the comprehension of animals and of men so animal and inconsiderate as to require it. This simple, altogether harmless, physical shock served to convince him that a radical change in his personal behavior was indispensable and it perhaps made possible such a change by the incident molecular commotion in changing the channels for the flow of nervous energy.

It wrought no immediate changes of a subjective conscious moral quality, but a change of outward behavior. He held fast to his choice of criminal associations, but now, for the sake, as he afterwards said, of qualifying himself for a notable criminal career, took earnest advantage of the educational opportunities of the reformatory which until then he had only perfunctorily used. Satisfactory conduct and natural adaptation induced his assignment to the editorial rooms of *The Summary* and to some minor additional work. Macauley, the prisoner editor, an Oxford man, took him under his tutelage. He was studious and after a time succeeded Macauley as the principal editor and in charge of the literature class, as has already been said. A close reader of the best books, a ready writer, his native literary taste and ability were soon plainly manifest, together with glintings of unusual imaginative and philosophic insight. His editorial criticism of current events and sociological incongruities was keen and convincing. The governor of the state on receiving *The Summary's* criticism of his own veto message said, "Did a prisoner write that? If so, he ought to be pardoned." On his discharge from the reformatory, he entered upon journalistic employment, moderately at first, but soon rose to a permanent remunerative place on the staff of a great metropolitan newspaper, where he remained continuously for full twenty years until his death.*

Let us briefly review this case for the suggestive lessons of it. Douglas, for that was the name by which he was known to us, was handicapped by his bad heredity — his parents were dissolute; by his deformities; by early parental abandonment; by the ineffective tutelage of the Protectory; by poverty and homelessness in the great city; by his unavoidable criminal association and by his own crime and its consequences. He never was what is ordinarily understood as intrinsically bad, only extraneously so, for he was subjectively nonmoral. But when he felt the pressure of impelling lawful requirements brought to bear in our reformatory the superficial faultiness became also the inward impulsion. His case illustrates the Pauline principle (Rom. 7:9): "For without law sin was dead. . . . When the commandment came sin revived and I died." Now when the institutional impulsion became in his case compulsion his vagrant inwardness took definite evil direction, but his outward behavior

---

*During the period when the Elmira Reformatory and the superintendent were under investigation as the outcome of newspaper criticism, the journal in question made an attractive financial offer to Douglas to testify against Mr. Brockway. He repelled the offer with indignation, saying a man should be judged by the best he had accomplished and not by his mistakes.— I. C. B.

necessarily changed for the better. The first effect was general orderliness of mind and demeanor, but there remained real if unrecognized disharmony of outward probity and inward perfidy. Such incongruity could not indefinitely continue, for it is contrary to nature.

Gradually, without conscious intention of moral exercise, but by means of the properly regulated demeanor, the influence of improved mental occupations, saturation with good literature, his somewhat improved daily associations, with prospective and after a time actual better remuneration, the inward evil purpose became abraded, worn away, while the better state developed into a dominating habitude. Many months were required for the process, and not until they had passed did he awaken to the change that had been wrought within him. His appreciation of it and solicitude for his future were disclosed by his inquiry made at one of our late-at-night interviews. While we were conversing of his own future and that of others, suddenly he put forth his deformed hands and excitedly asked whether probably his deformities but typified his mental and moral abnormality. It was a pleasure to assure him that such important changes had taken place in his personality that in reality he was then a new creature; that whatever should betide never again could he become his former self.

His own estimate of the mental tension maintained throughout the reformatory, and particularly the molding influence of the compulsory literature class, were presented in his report as instructor in English literature, included in the publication of that year, which is the epitome of his own now recognized experience.   He illustrates his conception of the theory and results of his deportment by citing a particular instance that accurately represents himself:

"Consecutive No. ooo was admitted in 1883. The initiatory examination of the prisoner revealed the low moral condition with intellectual activity only in the literary direction. From the cradle he had lived a life that was marked by the absence of those controlling influences, mental, moral, domestic, and social, which are present to some degree in all but the lowest lives. It could readily be seen that the problem of reformation here was the adjustment of the disordered mind and soul of the individual to healthful conditions of law and order of society. He was placed in the English literature course. . . ."

After describing the plan of this department he proceeds:

"The inexorable demand for continuity and uniformity of mental action cannot be evaded. . . . The only course left to pursue is that of earnest work though the motives are very often unworthy, sometimes as in this case actually criminal, and only in isolated instances is the motive of a character at all commendable. It is not long before the effect of this sort of mental athleticism is seen in the formation of new intellectual habits and perception and corresponding moral appreciation. This man had never been trained to think and act on system, and there is some natural rebellion of his uncultivated mind to work in harness. But after alternate and varied intellectual elevation and depression he is finally got down to a steady gait — and now what? Would it be reasonable to suppose that there has been no change? Is it not palpable that a radical alteration of mental perception and method must be accomplished, some development of moral understanding and feeling? Is it not true that in nine cases out of ten moral obliquity proceeds from mental incompetency? This man has been forced upward and upward, and he does not himself know how far he has climbed till he stops to rest and looks down. When he sees from his pinnacle of mental and moral culture the ignorance and weakness and degradation of the past, do you think that he will have any desire to descend? . . . In my work with the class in English literature I proceed on the basis that the earnest obligatory *study* (let me emphasize the word "study") of mental and moral beauty develops or creates the mental and moral faculty of appreciation, and furthermore, the mental and moral habits may be formed just as certainly as physical habits and without any more conscious co-operation of the individual than is required in physical practice."

The lecture method grew more and more into favor. Professor J. R. Monks succeeded Mr. Collin and for twelve years, until his death, was our stated lecturer, often coming four times a week. His course covered topics literary, historical, biographical, ethical, civic, and scientific. Judge Seymour Dexter and other professional men in Elmira favored us with short courses or specific lectures to the advanced pupils. The prisoners of less ability in the lower classes also received ample attention. The educational status at this epoch is best described by a prisoner school secretary, whose personal usefulness and moral unworthiness were notable characteristics. He says:

"Special effort is made in the lower division of the school to compass thorough and comprehensive teaching. . . . Pedagogical traditions are disregarded and much mere rubbish of the schools and text books finds no place in our method of teaching the rudiments of knowledge."

Of the pupils and instructors he further remarks:

"The manner of thought of most of our men is hardening into concrete shape or is already hardened on their admission here, while the mind of the ordinary pupil in a free school is yet plastic and retentive. The hardening process must be arrested; the mind of our subject must be arduously and patiently worked before it will assume the proportion and balance that lead to proper modes of thought. The results of our school training may be described from its observed effects upon the two classes, the ignorant and superficial. The first is stirred by it from a sluggish, sometimes almost from an animal, torpidity and grossness of mind into increasing activity of thought leaving the mind pliable and receptive. The second class may be said to be recast as a type whose sharp edge has been worn away; the united effect is a cleansing out of the intellectual avenues which open upon the aesthetic and higher yet moral faculties of the soul. . . . On the whole the character of our scholastic régime is less that of a common school than an academy or college, the maturer age of the pupils and the enforced decorum operating to this end."

This school secretary who was so capable, useful, and appreciative of the effect upon the pupils of "opening avenues upon aesthetic and higher moral faculties of the soul" was himself an interesting but not very promising character. He came to the reformatory in May, 1880, under the name of Macauley, an Englishman whose ancestry and previous personal history could not be easily traced. His crime was burglary, second degree, which involved a possible maximum term of imprisonment of ten years. Tall, bearded, athletic, and symmetrical, with a reserved, dignified mien, neither confidence nor suspicion was suggested on a casual acquaintance. In his possession was a certificate in his name of a degree from Oxford University, and as afterwards appeared he was in fact a fairly educated man. He earned and received his parole in a minimum of time by the rules, that is to say, in June, 1881. But for violating the conditions of parole he was arrested and returned to the reformatory in November of that year. After sixteen months, in May, 1883, he was the second time paroled on condition that he take employment at the reformatory on agreed wages, to remain thus more immediately under our supervision. He was made secretary of the schools, librarian, and editor of *The Summary*, which Macauley originated and organized. He instructed a class in drawing, lectured to five hundred upper class inmates on the history of art, edited the annual report of the managers and officers to the legislature, and edited pamphlets on penology prepared for distributing information about this new institution to the citizens of the state and abroad. While thus employed on parole he married and lived in nearby apartments outside the reformatory.

In February, 1884, on complaint of his wife, Macauley's parole was again canceled and he was placed in custody within the enclosure and put in the initial grade of prisoners, still exercising his school, secretarial, and other functions. In August, 1885, he was the third time paroled and employed on wages and remained in such relation for fifteen months, until November, 1886. After six years with us, the influence of the "indeterminate sentence" gradually weakening by its fault of having a maximum limit, the parole condition was changed, and he took employment in New York City.

He endured for a while, but failing to make his monthly certified report of himself, he was on our order arrested in New York in April, 1887. His blandishments induced the magistrate to discharge him before our officer arrived to take charge of him, and we lost sight of him, and he was beyond our further authority at the expiration of the ten years' maximum, May, 1890.

Macauley typifies an exceptionally small class of incorrigible criminals. Such offenders, could they be committed under the absolute indeterminate sentence plan, would be continuously held under enough of custodial restraint to protect the public, and it would also be promotive of their own individual welfare. If thus conditioned their capabilities may be made available for the benefit of others also in custody, as was the case during Macauley's parole and employment at the reformatory.

CHAPTER XVII

ADVANCE AND SOME DISQUIETING EVENTS

1883–1888

RECURRING to the beginning of this period (1883–1888) no momentous change of importance had taken place with the managers as to the commonly conceived reformative agencies. It was held necessary to maintain strict discipline, and a school of letters was considered indispensable. It was thought that "the general religious service should not be dispensed with, but might be changed to a popular praise service so conducted as to enliven and exalt the mental state instead of depressing, as sermons and stereotyped religious services often do. . . . The general religious service and the exercises of the practical morality class were made to act and react on each other to the benefit of both. The management was much impressed with the importance of the unified, balanced wield for the central, practicable objects, of all agencies — the disciplinary régime, the religious, ethical, and educational means, and, indeed, the industrial activities."

The original intention of the management to more effectively utilize prison industries as a means of reformation, strengthened as that purpose was by the successful industrial and educational experiment conducted by Professor Wells, an aim signally accomplished later on, was felt to be annoyingly interfered with at the beginning and throughout this period; but, in the sequel, the interference proved promotive of the original intention. It should here parenthetically be stated that by the act of 1876 the managers were left free to adopt such a prison labor system as in their judgment was most conducive to reformation. In the exercise of this discretionary authority, as has been previously explained, the public account system had been adopted, looking to a plan of co-operative employment for all the prisoners. But in 1881 the legislature ordered the contract system. This discouraging action, however, brought out the idea of the "piece-price" plan, originally suggested by Mr. Hawkins, who was an expert brush maker then connected with the reformatory as instructor of industry, contractor, and managing agent. In my report of 1883 I recommended the "piece-price" plan to replace the per diem contract system. Mr. Hawkins' suggestion, somewhat modified and elaborated, was afterwards very successfully applied in the perfected wage-earning marking system.

Another act of the legislature, in 1884, abolished the contract system but declared no other prison labor policy. The then existing contracts continued until their term of expiration, September, 1886. Now in reorganizing the industries on the originally adopted public account system, care was exercised to diversify them both for the advantage of trade training and avoidance of irritating competition. Six several branches of industry were introduced for the employment of the 711 prisoners in custody, but we were without sufficient operating capital,— only $90,138.30 for the conduct of the whole six.

Disregarding for the moment the chronological order, I will add that the so-called "Yates Law" of 1888 prohibited all productive labor in all prisons of the state. The following year the legislature enacted the "state supply system" which will be explained in a later chapter.

Besides the troublesome derangement of the industrial organization occasioned by fluctuating legislation, embarrassment was felt by lack of facilities for trades training, the importance of which for reformation was more and more apparent to all the managers and to the superintendent, as will appear from the following brief quotations from their utterances that year.

"The managers most earnestly ask the attention of the legislature to the matter of a permanent suitable labor system for the reformatory on account of economical and disciplinary considerations; but more especially for promotion of the legitimate reformative work of the institution."

The general superintendent said:

"There is not any proper education and test of character that does not include training in industry."

Then, citing the considerable but only partial benefits and the inadequacy of the existing conditions, he concludes:

"We should have facilities and all needed authority to train every inmate to some suitable trade or employment, and prisoners should be held in custody until a

268

demonstration in each case is had of a capacity and sincere purpose to earn by voluntary, honest work sufficient for the living and something saved. And each prisoner should, on his enlargement, be introduced into his calling in the free community."

Troublesome complaints were made by their relatives and others that prisoners were retained in the reformatory solely for want of progress in school. So persistently was the punishment notion of imprisonment held that we had discarded that explanation, and argument did not satisfy. Even two of our managers, excellent men, but of limited education, quite hesitatingly deferred to my own view of the necessity of school progress as an evidence of changing proclivity, and it was only by unremitting insistence that this and other tendencies to superficialism were effectually stayed.

Another disquieting annoyance occurred at about this time, the early eighties, to which, reluctantly but for truthfulness, I must refer.

Stephen T. Arnot, one of the managers, who was originally appointed by the governor and the senate, possessed great wealth and influence. He had taken no special interest in the reformatory but was known to be not in complete accord with the advanced penological ideas of the management. It was charged that, quite unknown to himself, he had been appointed a manager in expectation that his known bias might be made available for furtherance of a private personal interest. But Mr. Arnot was not to be so used. He was a man of positive and strong character, great personal independence, and high sense of honor. When, in his official relation, he was fully informed, he became the open and most earnest advocate of the reformatory system and bluntly opposed the self-seeking scheme which led to his appointment. A bill was then clandestinely before the legislature, intended to make possible the use of patronage of appointments and purchases at the reformatory. Fortunately, when the bill was reported in the senate, a friend of the reformatory was present in the lobby and immediately telegraphed to me the information, which reached me when the full board of managers was in session. Mr. Arnot at once pronouncedly fathered a protesting telegraphic response, which effectively stopped the legislative action. In this connection it is certainly worthy of remark that throughout my entire incumbency there never was to my knowledge, with one trifling exception, a divided vote of the board of managers on any question. Such unanimity is believed to be altogether exceptional and must be credited as an important factor in the successful management. Near the close of the year 1884 Mr. Arnot died suddenly, after about four years of valuable service.

Still another, the most menacing vexation of that time (1884), was occasioned by the excess of prisoners over the number of rooms or cells, a fact that necessitated two in a room, the very worst thing so far as communication is concerned. Of the 667 prisoners, 326 were thus associated. Enlargement was in process but the number of resident prisoners increased faster than cells could be provided, so that the serious evil increasingly continued; and notwithstanding the utmost care in selecting room-mates, the necessary doubling was a great embarrassment to reformation.

Besides the individual corruption the necessary doubling proved to be a perplexing dilemma on account of its disintegrating general effect. It also occasioned an improper discharge of the prisoners, either by premature release or by transfer to the state prisons; the former to the danger of the community, the latter at the risk of thus abandoning to incorrigibility really reclaimable prisoners, a risk emphasized by the following incident.

Twenty odd years ago, at a stressful period of Mr. Collin's ethics class, fifty selected prisoners ready for transfer on Monday to the Auburn State Prison were, on Sunday morning, confined in contiguous cells in the passage to the ethics class room. On our way to the class services Mr. Collin saw through the open-grated cell door one of his pupils, and paused for a pleasant word with him. Standing apart and observing, I seemed to see in the prisoner's face a hopeful indication and I directed his removal from the transfer gang. Thenceforth that prisoner gradually improved, earned his conditional, and finally his absolute discharge. His kind remembrance of us is betokened by the interesting clippings, notes, and letters he has for years past occasionally sent to me. Quite recently, after the lapse of many years, he called on me here with his family, when journeying in his vacation time. He is altogether a worthy man, a very capable journalist, and in every way a good inhabitant.

This is in great contrast with what in all probability would have been his character and social status now, but for the accidental Sunday morning incident twenty odd years ago. The following letter in his own beautiful script is of interest:

Z. R. Brockway, Esq.

Elmira, N. Y.

Dear Sir: — Just a line or two to let you know that I have not forgotten you, although sixteen years have passed since my "graduation."

Looking back I can hardly realize the flight of years, but I more and more realize what my stay with you meant to me. While I was a member of your family I felt that my lot was rather a hard one, a feeling that lasted for some time after I left, but I know now that I could never have held the situations I have filled if it had not been for the education I received while with you.

Since I left the "college" in 1888 I have occupied every possible position in a newspaper office from printer to publisher, have mastered the business in every detail and am at present holding a responsible position on this paper.

Quite a difference from a tough Fourth Ward kid, whose only, or I might more properly say, highest ambition was to be a truck driver.

If some of the boys on the hill could only look forward they would not bemoan their fate, but would make the most of the advantages.

I regret that circumstances have always prevented me from visiting you, even though I passed and repassed Elmira, en route to and from the West.

I enclose you a clipping which I thought might interest you.

Sincerely yours,

(1140)

The excess of prisoners — the overcrowding — is largely the cause of what has these later years grown to be a very serious fault; namely, superficiality and ineffectiveness of the reformatory régime, with premature and improper release of prisoners; too free transfer of prisoners to the state prison or to the Napanoch Reformatory; impairment of the tone of the institution, and the opening to the mind of prisoners of ways of release otherwise than by meritorious effort.

In 1884–85 we were confronted with another alternative, — either to suffer relaxation of requirements and consequent institutional disintegration, or resort to more coercive measures to maintain the established standards. The latter of these alternatives was deliberately chosen regardless of the not unforeseen criticisms that subsequently followed, the product of nescience, of sentimentalism, and of mendaciousness. It is now commonly known and is not actively criticised that, on the advent of a new and more politic management three years after my retirement, the former alternative was chosen and the intrinsic disintegrating process was allowed to proceed.

The reformatory weekly newspaper, *The Summary*, edited and printed by the prisoners under proper censorship, distributed to every prisoner in lieu of all other newspapers, was established in 1884, and proved stimulative to educational endeavor and to good use of the institutional library; but this year an experiment in a more intensive use of literature for reformative effect was also instituted. A brief description of the development and influence of this experiment cannot fail to interest any reader who is patient enough to pursue this narrative.

The class in English literature formed at first of about sixty advanced pupils, had increased in 1885–86 to more than five hundred men. The course of study was made obligatory, subject to examinations that would affect the grade standing and progress towards release. Two lines of study were planned, one of English literary history and the other of texts of great literary masters. The study was pursued in private from leaflets and books, with helps through *The Summary* and in interviews with hesitant and backward pupils. At first the pupils generally received this new assignment of study task as a fresh infliction, making the earning of merit marks more difficult, a veritable nuisance. Some refused to open the book or leaflet. Others opened and threw it aside as a task beyond their powers. But under pressure of the indeterminate sentence with its marking system, assisted and encouraged as much as could be, hopeful interest was soon aroused and a class momentum produced which was accompanied with phenomena quite unique in any prison. Passing along the corridors and galleries when the prisoners were in their cells in the evening, fully 90 per cent of the entire prison population might be seen engaged in study, and these literature pupils, note books in hand, were delving into the best English literary productions. The spectacle, curious as it was, gave also to the whole place a still and tense air that was most impressive. At the library it was not unusual to see a prisoner who entered the prison a tough, now advanced through the school classes, ransacking the shelves for specimens of early English and text book aids for his examination exercises. The awakened literary taste while contributed to by all the cultural agencies, was particularly furthered by discussions in the ethics class, where the argumentative powers were quickened and a sharp relish given for high examples of good expression and incisive thinking.

I may quote and endorse the remarks of the prisoner school secretary:

" It may truly be said that as a resultant of the English literature class in its harmonious working with the class in practical morality, the intellectual life of the reformatory has been visibly changed in the course of the year; that it has developed a new function which affords the highest improvement and pleasure in its exercise. Signs of this elevation in social and intellectual tone crowd upon us, affect our system favorably at unexpected points, assist our work by a many-sided reflex action. . . . When it shall be so that every inmate of the institution must be a member of the English literature course, when it shall be ordained that every man who reads a book must read it in the best manner possible for him, as may be shown by appropriate tests, then we shall be in condition to reap the highest profit from this with us new form of mental activity and our ideal of prison library organization shall have been fairly reached."

The library was enlarged this year by an expenditure of $500 from the prison funds; and by large additions of English classical authors, the gift of Mr. Valentine Lawson. The whole collection of books was scientifically catalogued, classified, and shelved, and a new system of distribution established, insuring to each prisoner the most beneficial short course of reading for him.

Intellectual leverage at this period was enhanced by lectures and suitable stimulating discourses and exercises, held on Sundays under the ablest leaders. Eight of the leading preachers and teachers of the vicinity spoke, and twelve prominent preachers from pulpits outside the city within a radius of about one hundred miles. There were addresses from Bishop Taylor of Africa; from four University men — three from Cornell — and President Webster of the Union

University at Schenectady; and from five editors — Lyman Abbott of the *Christian Union;* J. M. Buckley of the *Christian Advocate,* New York City; H. L. Wayland of the *National Baptist,* Philadelphia, Pennsylvania; S. J. Barrows of the *Christian Register,* Boston, Massachusetts; F. B. Sanborn of the Springfield *Republican;* also from Charles Dudley Warner, author, Hartford, Connecticut: Charlton T. Lewis, editor, lawyer and scholar, and F. H. Wines, secretary of the State Board of Charities of Illinois. Besides these extraordinary addresses, professional readers appeared, and high class musical entertainments, stimulating and refining, were held.

The animating possibilities of skilfully conjoined instructive ethical and religious exercises are suggested by a memorable Sunday at the reformatory. The practical morality class in the forenoon, led by Mr. Collin, was visited by Charlton T. Lewis of New York, who with a prepared discourse had come from New York City for an afternoon address to the prisoners. The morning ethics class exercise — purely intellectual that day, unusually casuistical — reached a very high point of interest by means of Mr. Collin's suggestiveness and the responsive flashes of original bright mentality among the pupils. Mr. Lewis observed this and was much impressed, as he said, with the incongruent fallowness of the mass of mind before him. He put aside his prepared discourse and prepared another during the recess interval, a lawyer's brief of an argumentative address that should match on to the discussions of the morning hour. This address, the product of his remarkably able mind, judicial habit and training, and felicity of language, was of the

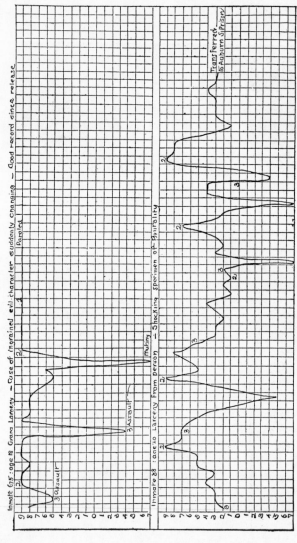

CHARTS SHOWING RATE OF PROGRESS OF TWO PARTICULARLY DIFFICULT PRISONERS

very highest excellence. And when in the afternoon it was eloquently delivered by a man so profoundly aroused as he was, and of such attractive personality, it constituted an ethico-religious discourse of apparently irresistible influence.

The exercises of that day culminating with the remarkable discourse by Mr. Lewis can never be effaced from memory. It was and remains the source of increased confidence in the impressionable possibilities contained in powerful public address upon a mass of common minds.

An interesting if minor incident of the year was the preparation by a prisoner of diagrammatic charts published in the report of that year, showing the fluctuating progress under the marking system of a thousand prisoners, shown in groups and by special individuals. The ingenuity displayed in the charts is interesting and the charts themselves are "a great study in a moral and psychological sense, for, at a glance, they show the whole story of the depressions and aspirations which prompted the course of men through shorter or longer stages, towards a common, but always attainable end."

Sustained "personal touch" between the general superintendent and the prisoners and their free access to the managers, were features of the reformatory not then usual in other prisons. Every prisoner was supplied with pad and pencil, and receptacles for their notes were distributed at convenient intervals throughout the establishment. The notes bearing special requests, or asking for an interview, were daily gathered and responded to. Every written com-

munication from every prisoner was promptly steno-
graphically answered, and every request for a personal interview was duly granted. During the year
1884, with the population less than 600, fully 7000
private interviews were had; and at the termination
of the six years' period (1888) when the number of
prisoners was just above 800, the number of private
interviews reached 12,672 for the year. It is scarcely
needful to remark that these interviews, together with
the minute marking system, always supplied accurate
knowledge of the prevailing institutional tone and,
also, very intimate acquaintance with the real characters of the individual prisoners.

My published report of that year records two
emphasized impressions: that most of the prisoners
were unable of themselves, unassisted by some exterior
compelling force, to effectually resist, even if they were
so disposed,— which in general they were not,— their
inner tendencies; that they were creatures of instincts,
very limitedly amenable to ordinary purely moral
inducements. This conviction gave additional emphasis to the importance of a strict régime to prevent
the play of evil impulse, and so give open opportunity
for improved activities and habits. Most of the
interviewers came over and over again to tease the
superintendent for unmerited indulgence as to their
record. On failing to properly earn merit marks they
became persistent and unscrupulous beggars. So
pronounced and general was this characteristic that
afterwards, to avoid the cultivation of permanent
mental and moral mendicancy, interviews were restricted to purposes in the note of request which
were approved. But throughout all the years of my

official incumbency the prisoners always had very free access to the general superintendent, individual managers, and the associated board of managers at their monthly and quarterly sessions.

Since incidentally with this story of the development of the reformatory I am retracing the evolution of my own inward attitude, I will here remark that at the close of the year 1885 I had a greatly enhanced estimation of the reformative value of rational education. This was an outgrowth, partly at least, of proceedings in our ethics class for the more capable men and the observation of the insufficiency of the ordinary pedagogical humdrum methods for the men of least intelligence. The new impression was also associated with chagrin at the lateness in my prison service of this clear conviction and my long neglect to utilize this efficient means. It is a pleasure to reproduce from my published utterance of that year the concluding paragraph:

"I am glad to be able to close my report with the declaration that never before in my long prison experience has the problem of reclaiming to society a large majority of convicted criminals seemed so probable of solution."

The next year, 1886, strenuousness throughout the several departments of the administration was well maintained; unification of processes progressed, though it was not quite perfected; the innate tendency to superficialism was effectually resisted; a good degree of thoroughness was preserved; some additional trades classes were formed; and the important feature — scientific physical culture — was introduced. The initial experiment, under the direction of the physician, Dr. H. D. Wey, consisted of scientific physical treatment for mental and moral betterment. It was continued that year only five months, and was applied to twelve selected inmates of lowest type, apparently incorrigible prisoners. The experiment was so successful that, aside from the benefits of it to the twelve pupils, it resulted, later in the history of the reformatory, in establishing the comprehensive physical culture feature that so distinguishes the Elmira Reformatory system. This experiment, condensed from Dr. Wey's interesting account of it, was briefly as follows:

The class consisted of ten white and two colored men. The average age was twenty-two and nine-tenths years; nineteen and twenty-nine years, respectively, being the extremes. One was committed for assault in the first degree, five for burglary in the third degree, four for grand larceny, one for rape, and another for attempted rape.

When at liberty they were tramps and street loafers. Upon a scale of three, zero would represent the class collectively as well as individually in moral susceptibility, and .008 in sensitiveness. They all were well nourished, and had no indication of real disease; their functions were normal; but five had cutaneous disorders and one had ichthyosis or fish skin. Some did not know the state or county where they were living; they were without purpose or ambition, content to vegetate. Nine of the twelve were in the third or lowest institutional grade and three in the second grade.

The treatment included a special dietary, weighed

out and fed under supervision; baths, Turkish and Russian, as ordered by the physician; passive exercise, such as kneading the muscles, working the joints, and friction of the skin over the entire body, done by a professional trainer; continued regular school exercises; military setting up drill, and specifically prescribed calisthenics.

The effect was an average loss in weight of 4.87, but two gained slightly. The baths and stimulation of the cutaneous system brought the skin to a high degree of functional activity and all integumentary disorders quite disappeared, muscles were developed and hard, the carriage and bearing were improved, the careless, shuffling gait was gone; stolidity of countenance was replaced with a look of animation; they became interested and made advance in their studies, showing increased mentality. In education the average class marking which at the commencement of the experiment was 42.16, rose to 74.16 at the end of the training.

Every one of the class had greatly improved, but the exceptional mental awakening of an ebony African calls for particular mention. Physically a good specimen of his race, mentally he was marvelously stupid. After a year and a half of schooling in mental arithmetic he could only multiply to the fives. Under the physical treatment he gradually progressed in arithmetic and in language, made progress in the grades, and after the year required by the rules, received his parole and went to the employment provided for him, — lumbering in the forests in northern New York. His monthly report letters were well composed and written by himself and his good record was duly certified by his employer. The last of these letters — the report that immediately preceded the issuance of the absolute release — contained an original remark, a paraphrase of Seneca's philosophic wisdom of which he could know nothing, a proof of mental activity. He said: "I have learned since I first went to the reformatory that to be good to myself I must be good to others."

The disquieting incidents of the year 1886 were: the disturbed and uncertain industrial system; the continuance of the evil of two prisoners in one cell, occasioned by increase in the number of prisoners to 711; and a virulent newspaper attack on the management of the reformatory for political partisan advantage.

Politicians hungrily desired to get control of the considerable patronage which hitherto they had been unable to wrest to their use. When, that year, I peremptorily discharged the principal keeper for malfeasance, and the mechanical supervisor for gross insubordination, which naturally stirred their antagonism, the local politicians quickly availed themselves of the disaffection of the two discharged employes. A Sunday newspaper under their control printed an attack, mainly upon myself, of a column or more of matter in every issue for fully a year. Finally, in the belief that their newspaper fusillade had affected public opinion in their favor, a conference was held in Elmira at which the governor of the state, David B. Hill, himself an Elmiran, and formerly an active leader in local politics, was present. I have it from one who was also present that when Governor Hill was appealed to to remove the non-partisan management and substitute partisan control of the reformatory, he refused the request. Thus that crisis was passed and we were able to continue our progress. I have in my files a letter from the editor of the newspaper in question, dated August, 1893, expressing regret for the attack upon me made in 1886 in his paper.

Already, by means of wide distribution of the published annual reports of the reformatory; the distribution of *The Summary;* and the first of a series of pamphlets entitled "Papers on Penology," edited by Macauley, the school secretary, which contained two articles by Charles Dudley Warner, reprints from the *North American Review* and *Harper's Monthly* (one "A Study of Prison Management," the other "Education as a Factor in Prison Reform"), an original article by Charles A. Collin, "Moral Education in Prisons," and the report of the Committee on Labor in Prisons and Reformatories, read at the thirteenth National Conference of Charities and Correction, 1886, our reformatory had become well known. The knowledge too was greatly extended by this unsuccessful attack. It brought additional visitors for inspection, — officials and commissioners from many states. The governors of several of the states recommended legislative action similar to ours as to the system of sentences; new reformatory prisons were being established in other states, and foreigners began to take notice. Massachusetts had converted her new prison at Concord into a reformatory. Pennsylvania was then building the reformatory at Huntingdon, which was opened in 1887. Ohio on the fourth of November laid the cornerstone of the reformatory at Mansfield;

Kansas had adopted plans and made appropriations for a reformatory which was promptly constructed. The discipline of several state prisons was modified and some others of the states were moving to establish institutions similar to the now famed Elmira Reformatory. The annoying newspaper assault unwittingly promoted prison reform throughout a very wide expanse of territory.

During 1887 still further additions of trades classes were made. The advanced theory and methods of the educational system excited interest and attracted as visitors professional educators from beyond the vicinity; useful if unusual instruction of prisoners increased, and the perplexity of another investigation was experienced and endured.

It had already been demonstrated that under the indeterminate sentence system prisoners could be utilized in the conduct of a reformatory far beyond and differently from any known prison use of what were known as "trusties." Two incidents of this year, 1887, went to confirm that confidence.

When Macauley departed on parole the vacancy in the school secretaryship was filled by another prisoner, Butts by name. Butts had been a country schoolmaster; he belonged to the accidental offender class. He was of an even temper, possessed but moderate mental energy, yet was very capable and faithful. His assigned sphere of duties was more limited than Macauley's, but still important both for record-keeping and instructing. The management of *The Summary*, the library, and the literature class devolved on the prisoner Douglas, the story of whose remarkable personality and career both within and without the reformatory has already been given. Butts, the new school secretary, performed his work well and soon earned his conditional, and duly his absolute release. On his final discharge he went to a middle western state where ere long he was appointed to a subordinate place on the staff of the superintendent of the reformatory there. His previous imprisonment with us remained for a time quite unknown to his new acquaintances. By merit he was advanced to the office of assistant superintendent of that reformatory. Curiously enough, in the course of my friendly casual correspondence with that superintendent, the chief officer, he chided me for my supposed neglect to train suitable citizens and prepare them for reformatory officers. Feeling quite sure that no injury would result to Butts, I enjoyed defending myself from the charge of neglect by informing the western superintendent that since I had trained an inmate of our reformatory fit to be his excellent assistant superintendent he might feel inclined to absolve me from that blame.

Another more remarkable instance of the somewhat similar service of an inmate occurred the same year.

The legislature of another of the middle western states had enacted a phase of our reformatory organic law which required the adoption of a marking system for that prison. On request of the warden for an expert to aid him in the matter, I loaned him for two months a paroled prisoner whom we had in our own clerical employment. He fulfilled the commission faithfully, and in an entirely satisfactory way.

CHAPTER XVIII

THE PRISON LABOR INVESTIGATION

IN FEBRUARY, 1887, the special legislative Prison Labor Reform Commission appointed in 1886 made its report, the result of inquiries which, according to legislative instructions, were to cover very comprehensively the various systems of employing convicts, — the effects and merits of each; the introduction of a system other than the contract system of prison labor; what experiments ought to be made and under whose direction as to the grading and classifying and the moral improvement of convicts; and "what abuses, if any, obtained in the management and discipline of the convicts in the several prisons, penitentiaries, and reformatories of the state, and what new method, change, modification, or improvement should be adopted in their behalf."

This wide-scoped inquiry was committed to three men: Mr. Bookstaver of New York City, a fair-minded, not very aggressive man; Mr. Blair, of the same city, a local leader there in anti-prison-labor agitation, and Mr. Barnes, editor of a country newspaper. So much of the investigation as was conducted in Elmira related alone to the reformatory. It was not free from the antagonistic influence of the discharged employes and the newspaper which I have previously mentioned. It was dominated by prejudice and, on the whole, the report reveals inadequacy of appreciation of the underlying principles of prison management which we had adopted at the reformatory. Our managers' published estimate of the ratio of reformations was rudely questioned; the salaries of reformatory officers were thought to be too low and there were too many changes of officers. The monitor system the commission could not understand and so disapproved. The report, as it related to the other prisons, contained fifteen counts of criticism, all commonplace, antiquated, and very familiar. The commissioners presented the draft of a bill so manifestly incomplete and disproportionate to the magnitude of the interests involved that no action was taken by the legislature. The objectionable temper, inadequate appreciation, and inconsiderateness of this investigation exerted temporarily an injurious general effect upon the more than eight hundred prisoners then in confinement, and a more serious and permanent injury would have followed but for our habitual complete control and the use of prompt effective measures.

This is the explanation. At the first visit to the reformatory an attaché of the commission while visiting, with the commissioners and newspaper followers, the foundry, where more than a hundred sturdy prisoners were engaged at that heavy work, asked one of the prisoners if tobacco were allowed him. Being informed that it was not, he remarked in the hearing of the prisoners, "If I were here and were refused tobacco 'Rome would howl.'" This remark proved the seed of a small insurrection of the molders. The next day when the melting iron began to flow from the cupola and the exciting work of carrying it to the molds was on, quite a number of the prisoners refused to carry iron unless they were promised tobacco. The keepers without much trouble removed the insurgents to their cells and others managed to receive and pour the molten metal. The next morning I took up the matter and by argument induced all but seven to return to work. The leader, known as "big Charley," who had only a few weeks of his definite sentence to serve, would not be persuaded until his mood was changed by the application of an appropriate physical shock. With Charley's surrender all the others, at their own request, were allowed to return to their accustomed work. This leader, on his release a few weeks later, responding to my inquiry of his future plans said half seriously, "I am going to steal," to which I made only a humorous reply. Two years afterwards, when I visited a great stove foundry at Louisville, Kentucky, I was pleasantly surprised to see my "Charley" working among the molders. He greeted me cordially. The foreman said he was one of their best workmen and had been many months in their employ.

The state legislature of 1888, the year which concluded this six years' epoch of the reformatory, closed for us the antagonistic agitation of the prison labor question; for the Yates Law of that year prohibited productive work by prisoners in all the prisons, including the reformatory. This legislative action was then believed to be disruptive of the whole penitentiary system of prison treatment; and, for our reformatory, a disabling stroke at the very plexus of our plan. Of the gross maintenance cost to date, $1,024,431.06, the prisoners had contributed by their earnings close to 60 per cent, or $606,299.35. Thereafter the entire cost must be provided in appropriations annually by the legislature, which was thought to be unfavorable to the ready supply of sufficient means. It was also feared that the disintegrating influence of idleness or aimless occupation would be disastrous. It was not then clearly foreseen how completely and more usefully the prisoners could be employed without regard to income to the state from their labor. Some of the incubus of solicitude to produce income remained, so that the co-operative scheme for organizing the industries seemed to be thwarted. The plan included diversification of productive industries suitable to the several classified needs. There was to be technical training, and the prisoners were to be credited with their actual earnings and charged something for their subsistence. At that juncture the breadth of technical and manual training and the minutiæ of the perfected marking system, with its average earning and monetary features, which were subsequently introduced and developed, had not been so clearly conceived as to afford relief from a sense of calamity. This is evident from the following published remarks of the managers to the legislature.

"The plan on which the managers, previous to the Yates Law, were building up the reformatory industrial system is outlined in the general superintendent's report. It is asked that all obstacles in the way of this plan be removed as speedily as possible. Even if the ruinous suspension of productive labor is to be continued, authority to sell the products of the trade schools should certainly be conferred. The managers believe that the inmates should be employed at mechanical or other productive labor chiefly for the advantage of training as a preparation for their return to society, and indirectly for the wage-earning of such labor."

Fortunately, the management was never again hampered by any demand or care to earn income for the state by the labor of the prisoners. Thus the legislative anti-prison-labor policy which was at first deemed a calamity was soon turned to advantage, and became for the reformatory system as "the stone at the head of the corner."

Idleness in the state prisons gave rise to grievous complaint because of an increase of insanity, imbecility, and other disorders among the prisoners, occasioned by it. But at our reformatory such evils were obviated by quick resumption of differently directed activities, and, without income from prisoners' labor, means for current support were liberally supplied.

Within forty-eight hours after the Yates Law took effect sixty first grade inmates (intended to form the nucleus of a regimental organization that should embrace all the inmates) were selected and placed under instruction in the primary principles of military tactics. In less than a month a regiment of eight companies was well built up. Times of drilling were so arranged that each man had from five to eight hours a day of that exercise, a part of it in the open air. Very soon, battalion movements were executed on the parade ground, followed each day with the formal dress parade. The regimental band which began with simply a drum corps, developed to a full band with brass musical instruments, each with its prisoner in practice. Merit and demerit marks were given here as in the departments of general demeanor and education, effecting, ere long, a high degree of general military proficiency and unusual perfection in the exercise. *

In addition to the uniform previously in use, the rank and file of the regiment were supplied with tasteful insignia and dummy muskets † scarcely distinguishable at a little distance from the Springfield army muskets then or earlier in use by the regular army. The prisoner military officers were designated by their bright blue dress, the usual military shoulder straps and chevron, and for their command were supplied with veritable swords. It was not expected that the military exercise would replace productive labor as a means for reformation, but it proved so excellent a substitute in view of all the circumstances, in its experimental stage uniting the attention of the men and giving them sufficient healthful physical action, that it was continued after the industrial education system became again active, and it was permanently adopted as a most valuable feature of the reformatory

---

*When the members of the International Prison Congress visited the Elmira Reformatory they were greatly impressed at the dress parade by seeing the Reformatory regiment go through the most accurate evolutions without one word of command.—I. C. B.

†These dummy muskets were made in the shops by the prisoners. The present writer was once going through the Reformatory with Mr. Brockway a few days after an attempted escape, when the would-be fugitives were re-taken. As we passed a man busily at work on a wooden gun Mr. Brockway stopped, looked pleasantly at the man and asked, with a twinkle in his eye, " Johnny, why are you like that gun?" " I don't know, sir," was the respectful reply. " Because you can't either of you go off." The convict's lips betrayed a faint smile, and as we passed on Mr. Brockway whispered to me, " He was one of the boys who tried to elope."

—I. C. B.

system of training. It made possible a degree of perfection in administering that could not be attained without its useful aid; and for disciplinary efficiency and custodial safety while operating, the military system was finally adjudged to be quite indispensable. Indeed it is no exaggeration to declare that in some exigencies of after years, under other managers, the military system, which was originally introduced only as a temporary expedient, was the central binding force that preserved the reformatory from ruinous disintegration.

Any account of the introduction and early development of this military feature would be imperfect in the absence of some mention of the interesting inmate whose good agency so successfully accomplished it. The only child of forehanded cultivated parents living in New York City, he entered college at about the age of his majority, but did not graduate for he was dismissed because of some misbehavior, not for failure in his classes. The distress occasioned by his expulsion from college is said to have hastened the death of his father; and, may be for other fault, completely alienated the affection of his spirited mother.

After leaving college he became a newspaper reporter on one of the best metropolitan papers, and his news assignments were of the highest class both at home and abroad. He was sent to England to return with the first racing yacht coming over the Atlantic Ocean, and assigned to write up the voyage for his newspaper. But while in the newspaper reportorial service he forged pay orders, for which offense he was committed to the reformatory.

He was nearly thirty years of age, a very personable

DRESS PARADE, ELMIRA

PHYSICAL CULTURE, ELMIRA

man, of pleasing manners such as are common in good society; the countenance open and confidence-inspiring; yet, closely scrutinized, the real soul of the man seemed screened from view, not secretive but simply with the margin of reserve maintained by educated men who have much contact with others. Indeed, the total personality of this man was excellent as compared with the average habitué of gentlemen's clubs.

Now, coincidentally, almost at the moment of my own mental decision, he proposed precisely the same plan. I at once assigned him to select from the records and to nominate sixty inmates for military officers, and himself to take up the duty of training and organizing the regiment, of which he was made the colonel in command.

Afterwards, when in due course he had earned and received his parole, he voluntarily entered our service on pay. Then again, after the lapse of a few months, he was permitted to visit the encampment on the Hudson River of the N. Y. S. N. guard and to convey a message to the commander of the National Military Academy at West Point. All his obligations were completely fulfilled until on a Sunday morning in New York while on his way to the train for home he met an acquaintance who advised him of an eligible opening in Maine. Following the bent which his mother had once mentioned to me, to always choose the wrong of two courses, he now again did the wrong thing, — went to Maine without our permission or knowledge, violating thus the condition of his parole. He remained hidden from us a number of months. The employment did not last, so he removed to another city, engaged himself to a newspaper there, and was living, we were told, with one he represented to be his wife. In order to remedy as far as we could the damage of his recreancy, known to all the inmates of the reformatory, and in accord with our legal duty, he was arrested, returned, placed in the third grade, and clothed in the distinctive red dress of that grade. He was assigned to editorial work on *The Summary* and as teacher of one of the school classes.

His manly demeanor under the embarrassment of his grade situation, his good tempered helpfulness, and the change for the better of his subjectiveness, which on close acquaintance was clearly manifest, at once elicited our sympathy. Inquiries made in the city where he had been found disclosed that he was a valued member of the editorial staff of a leading newspaper there, that his domestic relations were altogether proper, and that in all respects he was behaving as a respectable man should do.

Unobtrusive, uncomplaining, and devoted as he was to his duties at the reformatory after his return, he impressed us all that his real self was essentially renewed; the thin veil which hitherto had seemed to screen his real character no longer hid the inner shrine of his genuine personality. Most interesting it was to note the effect of his changed subjectiveness upon the instinctive attitude toward him of officers and men, their respectful gentle approach and intercourse. The sincerity of the man could not be questioned; his native amiability attracted and his unaffected gentlemanliness restrained too familiar friendliness. The new impression his changed character then made upon us all remains in memory another markedly illustrative instance of inevitable revelation and instinctive recognition of the real inward character of a man — notably of goodness. Exceptional action as to his progress and his release was naturally and properly taken. Since only the effect upon others need be considered, he was advanced to the second, the reception grade, in one instead of the usual three months; admitted regularly to the highest — the discharge grade — in six months; and instead of the usual six months in that grade and six months more on conditional release, he was immediately absolutely discharged. Supplied with an outfit of good clothes, suitable for his chosen vocation, and $50 for immediate expenses, he returned to the East, resumed the interrupted family relation and the newspaper reportorial service, being at once placed in charge of the united staff of reporters on duty where the legislature was in session.

Now what of it all? This errant capable man saved from the stigma of a state prison convict by his committal to the reformatory instead, his proper self-respect not only conserved but stimulated and his ambition excited by the occupations and opportunities afforded him at the reformatory; really ennobled by his marriage, his associations and employment during the interval of his unauthorized absence; brought completely into line again and benefited by the incidental discipline of his re-arrest and return; encouraged by considerateness after his return to the institutional custody, easy promotion, and exceptional release, the man was regenerated and rehabilitated.

But, sad to relate, within two weeks after his arrival at home and resumption of his employment he was seized with fatal meningitis and suddenly died.

Other activities this year contributed to the obviation of the evils of idleness such as were suffered at the other prisons of the state: new classes from the dullards among the inmates were organized for systematic physical training by means of gymnastic exercises, baths, massage, and specially prescribed dietary. The experimental classes of two years previous were enlarged, a growth and advancement towards the permanent physical culture department, which, a little later, was perfected and recognized as a necessary fundamental feature of the reformatory training. The physical exercises and the special diet of these pupils were in the immediate charge of Dr. H. D. Wey, the physician, who entered enthusiastically upon the work. His published monographs on physical culture for the purpose of mental quickening afterwards attracted wide attention and were received as authoritative on that subject.

Trades school instruction was also much extended and improved. Twenty-two trades and branches of trades were even then established and pupils taught in them all. The floor space devoted to these classes and to the mechanical drawing class was 35,000 square feet. And besides the previous evening trades teaching day classes were that year formed. In short, not to unnecessarily enumerate, it may be said that all the several departments were pervaded with a new activity; and recovery from the derangement of the disturbed and interrupted industries was so complete that, then, every inmate during all the waking hours of every day was kept up to the proper physical and mental tension, quite equal to and much more useful than the tension when productive prison work was the vogue.

The story of this last year of what I have ventured to term the epoch of adolescent institutional advancement must sufficiently refute the nescient contentions of the so-called Prison Labor Reform Commission the previous year, and effectively controvert the incredulity of that commission as to the accuracy of our published estimate of the probable ratio of reformations achieved.

In the course of the year 1888 a competent clerk was assigned to make a searching inquiry as to the outcome of all the paroled prisoners during the whole period of the reformatory to that date. The result of the inquiry is given in the published report, or year book, of 1888; and was made on the same basis of calculating the probability as the basis of the previous annual estimate and statements. The inquiry shows that after the severe test of endurance for so many years 78.5 per cent lived self-supporting and orderly lives. Such an examination should never again be made. The inquiry reached not only to all the prisons of the United States; to the neighborhood and relatives of paroled prisoners; but to the paroled and discharged men themselves whenever their addresses could be obtained. The inquiry was conducted with the utmost delicacy and consideration, but it painfully uncovered to the men themselves and to others who knew them a remembrance which had in many instances become encysted within the consciousness of the man and his community and should not have been disturbed. Some of the replies received from the men themselves complained bitterly of what they felt to be the cruelty of the inquiry.

It may be fairly claimed for the inquiry and the

result shown, however, that it is as creditable to the efficiency of our reformatory training and the parole practice as is to a college or university the creditable useful career of its graduates; that it is quite possible to make the parole paper of a properly trained and released reformatory man as reliable a token of reasonable confidence as the college diploma of a college graduate is reliable as a token of culture and acquired capabilities.

CHAPTER XIX

THE PROBLEM OF REFORMATION
A PURELY SCIENTIFIC PROCESS
1889-1893

THE ensuing five years' period at the reformatory was one of advancing maturity. It was a stressful period, and for myself the experiences were intensive, alternating from the agreeable to the disagreeable. Expansion, unification, and intensiveness characterized all the institutional activities.

The size and costliness of the reformatory now compelled more public attention and consideration while more and better information disseminated as to its methods secured for it greater public approval. The number of inmates, which in 1889 averaged 922, increased year by year until in 1893 the average reached was 1470. The total outlay for plant and maintenance to date was $1,855,546 and though the per capita per diem cost of maintenance was only 40.8 cents, the appropriation required of the legislature that year for maintenance alone was $150,000, while other items for extension made the aggregate demand $405,000. The whole amount was unhesitatingly appropriated on the motion alone of Senator Fassett.

Previous covert and open opposition of certain prison officials throughout the state was now quieted if not dispelled. A certain prejudiced public sentiment, consequent upon the erroneous notion that our reformatory methods were merely sentimental, had disappeared as the real facts became known. Indifference of legislators and of some executive state officers, because the reformatory management precluded any political partisanship, was now changed to attention by the growing importance of the institution within the prison system of the state.

The favorable public attitude and legislative appropriations enabled building extensions to be carried on to early completion, and improvements were made which became important permanent features of the reformatory system. The extensions at this time included a thousand lineal feet of high inclosing yard wall which increased the enclosed space to 16 acres; 500 additional cells and their housing building, known as the new north wing, which contained also a lecture hall with seating capacity for 600; and a school building of three stories containing 28 modern class rooms, a trade class basement, and a drawing class room. The domestic building was raised and extended so as to give space for new and complete culinary conveniences. Separate refectories for the several grades of prisoners and for the officers were constructed, and officers' rest and lodging rooms. A great central smoke stack or chimney was built, a coal storage building and new steam boilers supplied, and the heating and lighting apparatus was thoroughly overhauled. A bath house with 90 spray baths, each enclosed in a slate stall, was provided. The main auditorium was enlarged so as to hold 1600 theater chairs; and it was handsomely decorated and supplied with a large pipe organ and a grand piano.

The gymnasium building, which was completed that year, was furnished with every item of modern apparatus, and the physical culture department, under the supervision of Dr. Wey, was soon brought to the standard of best scientific use. The building itself covered 80 x 140 feet of ground space with an open trussed roof over the whole. The exercising hall is 80 x 100 feet and has, suspended upon the walls, a gallery for pedestrian exercise. A space 40 x 80 feet is devoted to baths — hot, warm, and plunge — with rooms for massage. For the sake of cleanliness and attractiveness these rooms were finished in marble.

The intention was to invigorate by means of physical culture the entire prison population and, particularly through specific scientific physical renovation, to improve defectives and dullards in their mental and moral habitudes. When the total number of prisoners was about 1500 the gymnasium was used daily for about 500 of the men. During this five years' period the close relationship between corporal conditions and mental operations was so completely demonstrated and unquestioningly recognized at the reformatory that physical education as a means of reformation of social delinquents became not only a permanent but an indispensable basic procedure for approximately 10 per cent of the prisoners, who without it would remain incorrigible. For these the usual gymnastic exercises were insufficient, and special processes were prescribed and adapted to the individual need. Examinations and measurements were made every month and suitable variations of exercises were ordered. The thoroughness of this procedure is indicated by the fact that fifty-six separate bodily measurements were always taken and the changes noted and recorded monthly.

The military system introduced the previous year, when placed in command of Colonel Bryan, who had the advantage of previous cadetship at the West Point National Military Academy, quickly produced precision of military organization and movements with corresponding benefits to the entire disciplinary régime. The reformatory became like a garrison of a thousand prisoner soldiers; more of the prisoners were utilized in the details of management, and prisoners to the number of nearly a hundred were given some military rank. They were assigned to participate in governing by service as monitors, instructors, inspectors, patrolmen, record clerks, etc. The military control was, at one time, so completely by the prisoners that on one occasion at the evening dress parade of the regiment, with a thousand men in line (no citizen but myself was present to observe it), the whole command from colonel to corporal was composed of prisoners.

The court martial and the civil court procedure were both used for the trial of offenders against rules and regulations. The courts were a mixed composition of citizens, employes, and selected prisoners. Juries were impaneled, sometimes prisoner counsel was allowed, and always full stenographic reports of the trials were made and preserved and the right of appeal was conferred. The courts served well for a time, but they became too cumbersome, so that later the trials were held before a permanently assigned examining judge from whose decisions appeals were allowed to the general superintendent, thence to the board of managers. Appeals for clemency to the general superintendent, upon whom alone devolved the duty of imposing penalties, were frequently made, but rarely an appeal for a new trial; and never except in one instance was an appeal for a new trial or review of judgment made beyond the general superintendent to the board of managers.

In that exceptional case the prisoner had been convicted of an offense that involved the penalty of six months' delay of progress towards release. The offender was an experienced criminal, more than thirty years old, though certified as twenty-nine. He possessed more than the ordinary mental capability and he persistently denied his guilt in the face of very conclusive evidence. The board of managers, the court of last appeal, affirmed the previous judgments, yet the prisoner insisted upon his innocence. But the painstaking trial and the right of appeal left the prisoner's mind in a good attitude. He said: "I must acknowledge that I have had here a fair trial with all the opportunity for my defense that I could have had in a court outside; but, after all, I am not guilty, and the judgment is wrong." To this remark I made the reply, which he complacently accepted, that if innocent as he claimed and possibly might be, he could while enduring the consequences of his conviction have the satisfaction and salutary self-discipline of suffering patiently the injustice as he thought it, and by sharing such a common experience get into closer touch with us all and particularly with those who feel the injustice of losses and injuries occasioned by crimes.

A very important event of far-reaching consequences, at the beginning of this period, was the enactment by the legislature of 1889 of Act 382, which settled permanently for the state of New York the vexed prison labor question, enacted into the general penal laws much of the spirit and some practical features of the Elmira system, and induced subsequent legislation by which there was extended to the state prisons a phase of the indeterminate sentence and parole plan of our reformatory. Both the reformatory law of 1877 and the act of 1889 are marred by limitations, but they embody advanced penological principles of the greatest importance which, in their fullest significance, are not yet, at this writing (1912), completely grasped by the managers of our prisons, the judiciary, and intelligent public sentiment. The act of 1889 establishes for New York the "state supply system" of prison employments, makes industrial education of the prisoners the supreme object, directs their classification, gradation, and education, permits the conferring of pecuniary rewards, and authorizes the conditional release of such prisoners as properly qualify themselves for safe inhabitancy.

In fairness, as well as for the sake of the historical record, it should here be stated that this act (1889) which is so elaborate that it contains 13,000 words; so minute in particulars; so wise and well considered that for twenty odd years it has stood without an important amendment and has been administered without serious friction; so pregnant of reform in prison treatment and the public attitude towards offenders — this law was framed and fathered by Mr. C. A. Collin, lecturer, law professor, governor's adviser, and statutory revision commissioner. Undoubtedly Mr. Collin's interest in prison matters and much information regarding practical requirements had been acquired through his contact with the reformatory, and some useful suggestions may have been gleaned from the rough draft of a similar bill which I myself had prepared for other use and placed in Mr. Collin's hands. But the state and country are chiefly indebted for this important measure of penological advance to the active, able mind, legal learning, and broad philanthropy of Mr. Collin, its author and promoter.

This legislation had an important immediate effect upon the workings of the reformatory; it relieved the management of embarrassment and contributed to my personal enjoyment. All the manufacturing industries, with their attendant perplexities and anxieties, were immediately discontinued and our system of trades instruction was at once expanded and perfected. Henceforth the whole time and our best administrative work were available for the one purpose, the training and releasing of prisoners to their safe free inhabitancy.

In review it seems surprising that there could have been in existence, twenty years ago, a state establishment devoted to the care and cure of male adult felons, such as our reformatory had grown to be. It was beautiful for situation, and of convenient, though possibly too costly, construction. It was the pioneer of six somewhat similar institutions in other states, and was the pattern for new general reformatory laws, notably in New York and Ohio. Remarkable training facilities were already in hand and there was no hindrance to additional facilities as new occasion should arise. Neither was there any hampering of freedom for new invention and continual experimentation. Abundant means were supplied for current support and for expansion. Already nearly a thousand inmates were in hand under application of the various means of reformation. The staff, or directors of the several departments, were remarkably capable men, earnestly interested and painstaking; and the hundred and more of subordinate assistants were young, active, efficient and loyal men.

The operation of the several divisions of the reformatory régime was well balanced and the whole was stimulated and dignified by clear consciousness of the central aim and the activity and reach for excellence in every part of the system; not merely mechanical activity and accuracy, but a personal interested effort for each specific object as well as for the general aim. In this unusual general situation I was not subjected to the weariness of a fixed routine — a tiresome sameness, but being free to act, experienced the magical effect of anticipated and from time to time actual achievement. The situation brought to me again a joy akin to that of youth exploring unknown realms.

Under the propitious circumstances new confidence came that, by means of prison science, most of the prisoners committed to the reformatory could and would be so changed in their habits and tastes as to become suitable inhabitants of a free community. The work of forming and reforming human character was felt to be a very exalted sphere of action but not beyond the realm of science. The profundity of the problem was itself inciting, the intricacy of the processes enticing, and the conscious exercise and control of something close akin to creative power was indeed a captivating vocation.

The memory of my exhilaration at the beginning

and during the early years of this period, clearer now, in retrospect, than at the time when in action, can never be completely effaced and quite compensates for later disagreeable experiences.

The movement of all departments at this period was a unified, accelerated, masculine activity which attracted the admiring attention of observant visitors and necessitated close managing attention. Compared with the other prisons I have known, the individual prisoners differed in animal activity as oxen and reindeer, while the mass movement differed as the singing speed of a lightning express railway train from the lumbering motion of a freight. But the motion of men and the mass — the check and swing of things — was, by the aid of the indeterminate sentence and its marking system, as readily regulated from the central office as the movement of the railway train is controlled by lever and airbrake from the engineer's cab. Assiduousness had passed the stage of painful strain and become inspiriting, so that conscious or unconscious complacence characterized the mood of most of the prisoners. The strong swift movement of things swept along in the current numerous sodden and erratic characters to their own permanent betterment, but some sank and grounded. The few intractable, recalcitrant prisoners could wrest the powerful rational moral motives to their own detriment and to the damage of the others. Considerations of safety for a community to which sometime they must be discharged, collective advantage of the other prisoners, and their own future welfare, gave to the problem of their reclamation the sense of great if not of greatest importance.

The sustained stress of the place differentiated, as nothing else could do, the social-moral state of the prisoners, first into three distinctive divisions or grades of nearly equal numbers; then into subdivisions of the three divisions according to more specific needs as ascertained; and brought out to easy observation and needful prescription the individual faultiness of every prisoner. This effect was uniform, apparently automatic, and was unceasingly stimulative to reformatory management. It should be here remarked that with such prisoners as composed and compose the Elmira Reformatory's population regularly recruited and only properly released, proper stringency will always divide the population into three nearly numerically equal divisions. Whenever it is disclosed that, barring extraordinary extraneous influences, the numbers in the divisions or grades are numerically very much out of proportion, the reformatory administration is faulty. The fault is likely to be either hurtful relaxation for the sake of comfortable institutional tranquillity, superficialism intentionally or unwittingly allowed, or a narrow excessive self-regard for the official situation, unappreciative of the important intended public benefit.

The problem of reformation — so long obscured by mediæval superstition, beset modernly with false or excessive sentimentality, discouraged by doubts, and hindered by faulty administration — was conceived to be a purely scientific process, the modification of character by the wise use of rational means and methods. The proceedings at the reformatory during those years were by observers perhaps a little presumptuously entitled "Prison Science," but more and more in our estimation the processes for forming and reforming human characters, the product of knowledge gained and verified by the most careful study, methodically arranged in a rational system, seemed worthy of the title others had bestowed.

The daily study and operation of the system, or science, if it may be so called, was within the three radial terms: governance, training, and adjustment of the men for their appropriate environment. It was my high privilege under unusually favorable circumstances to test again and again in actual practice with the thousand and more men then (1889–1893) in custody and thousands of others to be afterwards received, the actual and maximum efficiency of our theory of reformation, which, to put it epigrammatically, is socialization of the anti-social by scientific training while under completest governmental control.

Neither in theory or practice was there ever any notion of administering justice in the sense of visiting upon offenders retributory pains — equalizing mere deserts. Nor was governing made use of to effect a fancied absolute interior moral state not related to earthly conditions. And no direct attempt was made to deter from misconduct by means of intimidation. The inward intention, manifested in the spirit of the governing scheme throughout every detail and also in the practical direction of the institution, was determined by and held accordant with the foundational purpose — the reclamation of individual criminals. Specifically, and in the order of precedence, the purpose was a threefold one: the public security and benefit, the integrity of the instrument — the institution, and the essential welfare of the inmates.

The outward form or polity of the governance grown to fit the situation and, it is believed, always best for such an institution, was not exclusively autocratic, oligarchic, or democratic. It was a blend of the three traditional systems.

None will question that in view of the slumbering or repressed impulsiveness of such a community, and to insure safe custody and the necessary insistence upon improvement, more or less absolute control must be vested in the governing authority; this power to be exercised either positively or leniently as exigencies and individual cases require. On the other hand, a certain range of personal liberty and participation in the governing must be allowed inmates for the sake of the desirable civic training.

By means, mainly, of the military organization already described, the general tone had gradually changed from that of a convict prison to the tone of a conscript fortress. While sustaining the relation of militiamen, the inmates were allowed, and exercised, some civil functions. Singularly, it was a convict community under martial law garrisoned with its own inhabitants.

Vigorously and thoroughly the grand object of the reformatory was pursued; every incipient disintegration was promptly checked and disinclination of individual prisoners to conform was overcome. The régime was planned to both arouse and restrain; to enkindle interest in the better, though out of hand, prospective good in preference to the present transitory, doubtful indulgence; to enkindle a disposition and ability for endurance; to awaken vision-forecast and good ambition; to restrain at the same time, and so diminish,

310

violent, individualistic impulse such as disqualifies a man for associate activities; and to train intelligent submission to wise and proper guidance.

All the prisoners had gone wrong before their arrest and committal, while at liberty in a free community. They had not maintained the standard of behavior tolerated by the statutory laws and interpreted by the courts. Yet a majority of them satisfactorily responded to the constraints and intensified appeal of their present situation. Many who at first faltered reached, by the impulsion of circumstances, gain or loss of liberties and creature comforts, — progress or retardation towards their final release; but some others did not advance or properly conform until more powerful moral and positive inducements were brought to bear. There was no neutral ground. The prisoners must progress or move down and out of the way. To such as could not or would not respond the powerful moral motives were not only unavailing but proved degrading. The self-respecting sense, with these, conditioned what was evil; the public approval motive — commendation of one's fellows — sought approbation of those who are base as a reward for debasement; and the privileges we conferred as reward of merit were put to perfidious use. And, too, the deprivations — the antithesis of privileges — on which the privileges depended, contributed to or confirmed their degeneracy.

The government of the reformatory treated such default as the resultant of generally rectifiable defectiveness rather than as voluntary depravity; defectiveness rectifiable by scientific treatment. The voluntary co-operation of the faulty subject was of course felt to be desirable but not altogether indispensable, for it could be otherwise secured. That is to say, being at first compelled to act in accord or conformity, the habit and the rewards cultivate conformability, which of itself is easily transformed into co-operation. Such untamed characteristics of criminals are by Lombroso, the scientist, attributed to atavism — reversion to the racial primitive type; and he stoutly declared them incorrigible. But General Washington, patriot and father of liberties, by his remark that some "are so constituted that they cannot adopt and carry into execution measures calculated for their own good without the intervention of coercion," implies the belief that there is corrective effectiveness in some compulsion. Bagehot says: "The first condition of crudest society was the formation of a cake of custom. This foundation of society had to be learned to make any effective society possible, and, in the crude conditions of all things human, this had to be reached and maintained by force. The first lessons could not well have been given otherwise. . . . Thought, reflection, criticism, ideals, were to come later, after the cake of custom had been formed." The management of the reformatory had come to recognize the reign of the law of custom, the commanding formative influence of common usage, the manner of doing or acting whether of and for a community, a body of persons, or a person. The Baconian principle, that "There is no trusting in the force of nature nor to the bravery of words, except it be corroborate of action," commended itself to the reformatory management as sound philosophy, and the conviction was confirmed by individual observation and experience.

Moreover, since the conformity and co-operation

demanded should unquestionably be classed as a virtuous exercise, and since concededly the perfect practice of virtuous energies is a constituent of happiness, all the more the management was inclined to insist on exact observance of the established reformatory régime. This theory of things effectually carried out as it was, — a theory and practice so different from, I may say so far in advance of, the current superficial ideas of the time, and so misinterpreted as it afterwards was, — demands the following additional statement of the attitude of the management.

The personnel of the reformatory management, in which is included each individual of the managing board, the general superintendent himself, the men at the head of each of the several departments, the instructors, lecturers, and preachers, were each and all possessed of average humaneness, as compared with their contemporary fellow citizens. Every one was regardful of the comfort or discomfort of the prisoners, but, in proportion to their intimate knowledge, esteemed the prisoner's welfare more than his momentary indulgence. None was insensible to and some were exceptionally appreciative of existent noumenal or spiritual influences which seem, sometimes, to mold the human character; nor was the management unbelieving or unmindful of possible benefit to minds prepared for such a ministration of powerful moral persuasions. Suitable human agency was always supplied to wield the mystic influence for the benefit of such as proved susceptible. And for the few irresponsive and insensate prisoners, whenever the alternative — abandonment to incorrigibility or use of drastic measures — was presented, then unhesitatingly resort was had to a more direct appeal through bodily sensitiveness.

This measure, though so necessary and salutary for our use — hundreds have been reclaimed by thus initiating their advancement — was, we knew, generally unpopular, made so by its liability to abuse and by historical misuse. We knew, too, how a certain nice sense of very worthy persons was easily offended, and the likelihood of unfair criticism, both from those who could not and those who would not appreciate the beneficent intention and the important benefits of the harmless parental discipline. The risks were deliberately assumed and the measure greatly aided reformation during this five years' period, the best and most serviceable years of the institution.

But in 1893 and 1894 an attack was made upon the reformatory management which continued for the most of the two years. At first the investigation, directed against myself, was conducted by one committee man of the state board of charities, but this was followed with a second investigation, directed against the board of managers, which was conducted by commissioners appointed by the governor. Both investigations covered practically the same ground. The final result was a dismissal of the accusations by the governor of the state. Any adequate account of the attack and trials would fill a large volume. In respect to the powerful influences arrayed against us, the large monetary expenditure and the methods of the prosecuting procedure, and the attention the trial attracted throughout the whole country and abroad in Europe, it may safely be said that the assault on the reformatory management was never equaled by any other attack on a penal or charitable institution. The salient features of this remarkable occurrence are dealt with in the following chapter.

Governance then, at its best estate, attained the happiest blend of two principles; apparently opposite but in reality, in the last analysis, of the same identity: goodness, not the sentiment so much as the purposefulness; and severity, not exercise of harshness but thoroughness of treatment.

The spirit and procedure of the training which may be considered the middle syllogistic term of the whole system, the second premise together with governance, is well expressed in the motto seen by John Howard and by him reported in 1779 when he visited the work house at Amsterdam, Holland. Over the outer gate were inscribed the words:

"Fear not: I mean not vengeance but your reformation. Severe is my hand but benevolent is my intention."

The motto translated into its modern interpretation, as at our reformatory, after the interval of a century and a decade, should read:

"Here ends your customary thoroughfare and to you opens the new and narrow way which leads on to happiness by way of welfare. The wise will choose the path and follow in it: the wayward remainder will be constrained."

The eighteenth century severity directed to subjection of the will had become with us at the reformatory in 1889 the exaction of habitual proper conformity of conduct; and the reformation sought was changed from religious asseveration to the desirable social habituation. The utmost importance was attached to the development of prudence. We were impressed with the ancient philosophy that "Prudence is the beginning and the greatest good, for all the other virtues spring from it"; that "it is not possible to live pleasantly without prudence"; and that "pleasant living based on prudence is connate with all the virtues." This virtue was sought and taught by nature's method, the culture of consequential experiences. It may be formulated thus: Primarily, pain or unpleasantness prompts to prudence; practice of prudence thus promoted breeds good taste and forms habitual preference; prudence when confirmed by practice becomes the ruling impulsion, the dominant characteristic, the essential character. On the low plane of our population instinctive habitual prudence gave promise of the desirable reformatory result.

Our own estimation of the reformative efficiency of habit is well expressed by President W. C. Hyde. He says: "Habit is the great time-saving device of our moral as well as mental life. To translate the moral laws which the race has worked out for us into unconscious habits of action is the crowning step in the conquest of character." However, we reversed the order. Instead of translating principles into unconscious habits, the habits were formed in accord with the unconscious principles.

On admission to the reformatory most inmates were unaccustomed to orderly meditation; were incapable of intelligently appreciating ideal morality. For this reason, practical rather than preceptive training was made the immediate requirement. It had been discovered that pressure of precept on such minds often dazed them; directed the attention from the immediate demand of duties; put luck, or Providence, in place of proper personal effort; disparaged the rational reformatory progress. On the other hand, whatever might be the impulsion, however mundane, it was observed that habits of action which involved energy, integrity, thoroughness, honesty, accuracy, conscientiousness, faithfulness, and patience, — all of them essential to economic efficiency and containing the element of prudence, — tended strongly to create and confirm good social moral character.

In order to accomplish the new and better habitude it was necessary that wrong and heedless habits should be replaced with scrupulousness. To effect this, the entire life of each inmate — his bodily and his mental activities, must, to the utmost, be noted, recorded, and appropriately channeled. The minute knowledge of the outward and inner life of each inmate was obtained and recorded by means of the marking system, the details of which were perfected during this period, and a new channeling of the proclivities and improved habits of mind and behavior was well wrought by the perfected intensive administration. For instance, every day from the early morning reveillé to taps at nine o'clock at night — every waking moment — each prisoner felt the pressure of some care or duty the observance of which gained a credit, or neglect of which involved a loss; the effect being a help or hindrance towards release, increase or decrease of current creature comforts, and a relaxed or straitened sense of the actual disciplinary grasp. Briefly illustrated, acts grossly disregardful of the regulations caused a month or more of loss, or, if clearly criminous, can-

317

celed the previous advancement — carried backward, so that the path of progress must be retraced with better footing. Three demerits — misdemeanors — in any month, canceled temporarily, at least, that month's advance; and such demerits continued through three successive months spoiled all progress, as did the criminousness alone just mentioned. And as to neglects, ten neglect demerits in a month marred the progress to the same extent as did three misdemeanors.

Open accurate records, full and in detail, were kept by a corps of inmate clerks in charge of a citizen chief clerk, all in closest communication with the general superintendent's interior office. The reports and records covered not only all demeanor, but also the ever-changing mental quality and the industry. The record, too, contained memoranda of every reproof, admonition, or coercion, that was administered. The organization was so complete, in the systematic connection and co-operation of the parts of the whole establishment, of the official staff, employes, and the hundred or more participating inmate military subalterns and monitors, that nothing of importance could escape observation and record; and, as to every effect of the system, it had the final determination of the general superintendent's particular personal attention.

This single vital feature of the administration of itself afforded a fascinating daily occupation of unceasing close attention and intensive application. This superior central interest was affected, of course, by every other interest and activity of the institution, so that these too must have similar close supervision and particular personal direction by the general superintendent. He was the chief provider and *entrepreneur;*

he arranged and inspected the educational work of the schools of letters and of trades; he was censor of the library work, the editing and publishing of the weekly newspaper, *The Summary*, of the other current publications, and of the annuals; and he directed in considerable detail the building operations, the farm, the manufacturing (until it was discontinued and replaced by the trade-schools). He was always on the spot, personally accessible to officers and the individual prisoners; and he bore the brunt of the misunderstandings, misrepresentations, investigations, and of occasional annoying newspaper assaults. All this together supplied an absorbing, as it was a captivating, employment which, by its variety, the ever recurring novelty, and its stimulus to research, was sufficiently recreative without vacations.

It was extremely interesting to note and to treat the diverse and variant mental attitudes of individual prisoners when they were face to face with the remarkable array of motives brought to bear with force and precision.

We were confronted with the contradiction of two motives, both of them good. And we learned the inefficacy, for such minds, of deferred benefits, whether tangible or moral, contrasted with the motive of a present and pecuniary advantage. Loyalty to the government was contradicted by the demands of the virtue — fraternity. Fraternity among the prisoners bred cabals, with concealment of perfidy and disloyalties to such an extent that communication was at first absolutely prohibited, then restrained, and afterwards only somewhat regulated. This conflict operated to develop castes or grades, yet without actual or apparent positive class fraternity. This contradiction was keenly felt by men who after reaching the higher grades were assigned to monitorial and military duties. Loyalty and faithfulness in their sphere involved for them a certain contempt of others who esteemed them "squealers"; the very conflict that occurs in schools and colleges. When loyalty triumphed, as with our men it so often did, the individual effect was ennobling and gained plaudits from the management and the men of their grade and rank. Friction occurred as was natural, and in our estimation desirable, for friction in the reformatory procedure is proof of effectiveness. Clearly, under our American system, obedience to the constituted official authority is desirable and a proper habit to be inculcated in a reformatory. The effect and success of the monitor and military governance — strongly supported as it was — soon broke down the hot convict opposition to such control, kept in honorable prominence the worthy exemplars of loyalty, and practiced the prisoners in obedience to and in exercise of proper authority. Invaluable service was rendered by some strong, true, sensible men thus selected and assigned, for whom now in memory I retain the respectful regard and personal attachment which their co-operative aid and their worthiness then engendered.

A considerable number had such abnormal self-conceit that opportunities for securing benefits, prospective or present, benefits beyond an immediate sensuous indulgence, were powerless as motives. They felt themselves to be the victims of some vindictiveness or ill luck. They could not connect the imprisonment and their crime as cause and consequence, natural, probable, and indeed, rightly conceived, inevitable. Some of this class indifferently observed the established routine, but mainly occupied themselves, as definitely sentenced prisoners do, counting the divisions of the passing time, looking to their final release at the expiration of the maximum term and their return to their former haunts, associates, and indulgences. Some settled to the lowest institutional condition and there, stalled, remained. It is but just to say that many of the indifferent and stalled men were of the short sentenced class, the two and a half years' men. Like Dante's purgatorial subjects, these did not view their imprisonment as a divinely appointed means of betterment nor did the imprisonment produce a sorrowful sense of the sin or folly of their deeds. Such states of mind were not, could not, be appreciated by the men themselves. Their mental condition is habitually lethargic, their conceptions are vague. This unfavorable state is more contributed to than corrected by stereotyped, alleged moral persuasions. The best remedies, let me again repeat, are those within the material business of living, where results come quickly and are easily comprehended.

When it was seen that the ideal of simple merit and demerit befogged these men, that mere time value was ineffective, an important change was made by translating time values into monetary terms. This was more tangible and, joined as it soon was to the wage-earning system, brought and kept the men in touch with the essential thing — the economies of personal earning, expending, and saving for future needs. The change from the abstract to the concrete proved most useful for its lesson in motives, as an improved test of character, and for the practical beneficial effects that followed. The change perfected the theory of a marking system, and simplified and made clear, both to prisoners and to managers, what is meant from the state's point of view by reformation and the intended reformatory training. The following concise description of this new departure is by a prisoner, an editor of *The Summary*.

. . . "It is in reality but a modification of the existing marking system by which dollars and cents are made to stand for debits and credits in demeanor, labor, and school; and the penalties for misbehavior, carelessness, and deficiencies are fines instead of loss of marks, the effect upon gradation being exactly the same. Under its terms a man is forced to make his own living by industrious application to his assigned labor, by studious habits and proper regard for the rules enacted for his government, and along such a path journey to the confidence of the management and to the opportunity to put to the test in the outside world, with oversight relaxed, the principle of reliance on self-exertion and self-control thus inculcated in him. From his induction the prisoner is put in the position of a wage-earner and, with the exception of his first suit of clothes and his first meal, he will be called upon to pay for his board, clothes, and all items of expense incurred, out of his own earnings, and will be required as one of the essentials to early release to maintain a credit balance."

Then giving in his account additional explanation of the working of this scheme the writer concludes:

. . . "It is proposed to make the conditions surrounding the inmates more closely approximate those applying to free laborers, allowing them to earn in

322

proportion to their capacity, paying them on a basis of the lowest wages for similar work outside the walls, instead of a fixed sum for all classes of employment; requiring them to pay for their subsistence and clothing a fair price, and permitting them to expend a reasonable amount under certain necessary restrictions for indulgences which otherwise could not be supplied."

The perfected marking system and intensive administration disclosed faultiness of the prisoners which previously had not so clearly appeared. Malingering proved markedly a characteristic of those who were least responsive. For pretended, fancied, and trifling ills, put forward as a reason for relief from the routine, calls on the physician in 1889 reached 13,779 and in 1890 reached 19,811. But when the wage and monetary marking system came in, and the medical consultation became a personal expense, the number of calls on the doctor greatly diminished.

Mendicancy, too, prominently appeared, a fault not so easily corrected. Indisposition to earn progress toward liberty when it could be gained by begging off the debits, long clung to the men in the lower grade divisions. The superintendent's interview hours were crowded with petitioners for favors as children tease for toys. During this period of five years the records show that 23,000 private, often confidential, interviews were held at the superintendent's evening interview hours. And the records also show that 18,695 superintendent's personal notes of reproof, of warning, and other written communications were dictated and delivered to prisoners; and that additionally 1,668 careful oral personal admonitions were made. The malingering and the mendicancy both were closely associated with mendacity, unscrupulousness, and bald dishonesty. Reproofs, admonitions, coercions were always utterly devoid of any quality of retribution; administered not for penalty but for amendment. It was not, of course, easy to make this most important disciplinary principle plain either to the subjects of the ministrations or to the average thinker.

The placing of eligible prisoners in the community after their course of training at the reformatory, at first conditionally released and, if they stood the test, to be afterwards absolutely discharged, is the third term, the conclusion, of the syllogistic problem. A brief statement of the principles of this adjustment will conclude this chapter. The minimum parole period was fixed at six months, for the reason that a longer period would be discouraging to the average paroled man, and a shorter term insufficiently steadying.

The preferable place to which a prisoner should be paroled is the place from which he was committed, or the place of his usual habitation. Recuperation from a smirched reputation and recovery of public confidence are easiest in the community where the misconduct occurred. Paroled prisoners should not deny nor fraudulently conceal the fact of their history when they are confronted with it; and emphatically let it be said, they should not exploit their reformation nor adopt the rôle of the reformer.

Almost without exception — and this should always be the case — the prisoners were provided with pre-arranged employment to which without delay they were required to proceed. And the employment was and would naturally be that for which during their imprisonment they had been trained and prepared. The employer and the parole supervisor were always made fully acquainted with all the facts; this for the sake of honesty, safety, and for a salutary mutuality of the confidential relation it involves. Monthly reports certified by the employer and the supervisor were required. The most satisfactory for supervision of paroled men is the chief of the local police; not the average policeman in the ˙great cities, nor indeed a religious or philanthropical organization or private individual. Certified pecuniary prosperity, the result of legitimate industry and economy, was the prized favorable indication of rectitude.

During the parole period the reformatory was available for asylum whenever urgent need occasioned, and was sometimes so used. It was expected and desired that in due time reformed prisoners dwelling in a community would themselves retain only a dimmed consciousness of the blemish of the erstwhile offense; and that the changes, the absorbing occupations, of our American communities would effectually obscure it.

The total number of prisoners released on parole during the seventeen years from the opening of the reformatory to the close of this five years' period was 3,723, of which number it was estimated that 81.9 per cent had not returned to crime. Of the 279, or 7 per cent, who were returned to the reformatory for violating the conditions of their parole, 110 were treated and then paroled the second time, and 10 were paroled the third time. With the above statement should go the remark that this surprising ratio of probable reclaimed men was achieved during the initiation, experimentation, and early embarrassed conditions of the system that was then being developed. It is based on reasonably reliable information as to all except about 475 of those who were either discharged at the expiration of the maximum of sentence, or were sent out of the state beyond our jurisdiction, including a small number who prematurely ceased the correspondence and were lost sight of. The 475 is one-half of all such cases, and our belief that these also are doing well is justified by facts of our own investigations, and is confirmed by the experiences of the parole system in other states where the circumstances are less favorable than in New York.

Mr. Pettigrove, of the Massachusetts Prison Commission, before the American Prison Congress at Pittsburgh in 1891, said:

" In connection with the supervision which we exercise over our men (paroled convicts), I went over our report and took off 100 names of men who have not reported and gave them to the agent, and directed him to investigate the cases. I found in *every case* that failure to report was merely due to the fact that the men had grown careless about writing because they were doing well."

The vigorous adult condition of the reformatory is convincingly shown by the year books of 1892 and 1893 with their typographical and mechanical excellence, exclusively the work of the prisoners; and the remarkable contents of the books, altogether edited and considerably written by one of them. The former — that of 1892 — includes the photographic facsimile and synopsis of the records of each of the 100 prisoners who consecutively were paroled during that year. It has also 75 half-tone illustrations, statistical and descriptive accounts of the evolution of our reformatory, and similar progress elsewhere; and a description of the state of the reformatory movement throughout the United States at that time — all completely indexed and properly bound in our book bindery. The year book for 1893 produced in the same way, is an equally remarkable and valuable publication. It is a document of 150 pages profusely illustrated. Fifty of the pages are devoted to the technological instructor's report, 23 to the school director's report, 31 to the managers', superintendent's, and other departmental annual statements; and 46 pages contain contributions about a scientific dietary experiment, notes on anthropology, and an account of innovations for the year written by the prisoner editor.

CHAPTER XX

UNDER THE HARROW

TWO INVESTIGATIONS AND THE RESULT

1893–1894

THE years 1893 and 1894 were marked by the newspaper attack already referred to and the consequent investigation, followed by a second which was the natural result of the first. The injury to the reformatory which might have been expected was resisted at the time, but efficiency was somewhat impaired, as might have been foretold; for criticism even when unjust is bound to have an injurious influence, and when exploited by the daily press it bears bitter fruit in any institution.

The attack upon the reformatory and its administration in 1893 originated in the untrue statements of a man paroled from the reformatory who broke his parole but was not returned to the institution for six months, owing to various devices which his means enabled him to command. The stories he told were eagerly seized by the press and exaggerated. They became so widespread that the managers of the reformatory asked for a thorough official inquiry into all the methods and practices at the reformatory. The state board of charities had annually reported upon the reformatory for eleven years, and when the president of that board suggested that it should conduct the inquiry the managers acquiesced. The reports which they had made to the legislature previously had been uniformly favorable. Their published reports to the legislature from 1882 to 1892, inclusive, refer to the reformatory as follows:

An earnest invitation was extended to me (Oscar Craig) to come and spend a week, interviewing the inmates, one by one, without the presence of officers, which I hope to accept and accomplish during the coming year. There are many points which at this late date must be reserved to a subsequent report. There is one distinguishing feature of the administration which should be mentioned, namely, the personal treatment to which each convict is subjected. Indeed, it is evident that the secret of success of the superintendent is in this power to treat convicts in their individual as well as their collective capacity............ In my opinion, the objects of this institution are accomplished, and the laws in relation to it are fully complied with. (1882. Pages 161, 162.)

Several hours one evening were employed in visiting, unattended, the cells after the men were locked in for the night. At this time we had private interviews with most of the men in the third grade (new second), omitting those only in bed and apparently asleep. Few of these men were unoccupied. Most of them were engaged in preparing their lessons for the succeeding evening. Some of them were reading the Bible. We conversed also with several of the members of the second grade (lower first) in their respective cells. These men were likewise generally occupied — some in study of lessons. . . .
. . . And we add that we are of opinion that the complaints with regard to labor are in the main owing to want of attention or effort on the part of the convict, and that the requirements are graduated in theory for the best results to each convict. . . .
. . . In walking through the shops we were accompanied by the superintendent, and we could not fail to notice the cheerful looks and smiles with which the men of all grades responded to his notice or first greeted him on entering.

Corporal punishment is inflicted in no other form than "paddling," and is administered by no one but the superintendent. It is believed that the punishment is never unduly severe. We invited, but received no complaints from the convicts on this score. The theory of the superintendent seems to be that in rare and exceptional cases such discipline is not only justifiable but necessary as a substitute for longer detention in the third grade. Your Committee find a singular unanimity among the superintendents and superior officers of all the reformatories of the State on this subject. . . .

. . . We believe that the government is as purely personal and paternal in adaptation to each inmate as would be consistent with a proper regard for the general rules of the institution and equitable adjustments among fellow-convicts, or with the cultivation of a due sense of the authority and obligation of law. (1883. Pages 113 et seq.)

This institution continues in a very satisfactory condition, and the intelligence and faithfulness of its management is creditable to this State.

Your Committee was greatly pleased to notice the freedom with which the prisoners addressed the superintendent; his pleasant, cordial manner in speaking to them; and the fact that he was able to call each man by his name; indeed, everywhere among the men, Mr. Brockway was greeted as if they were certain he was their friend. This your Committee finds is unusual in penal institutions.

In conclusion your Committee is of the opinion that the work which the Elmira Reformatory is intended to do, in caring for prisoners between the ages of 16 and 30, sent there upon a first conviction, so that they may be reformed and sent again into the world as law-abiding, self-respecting men, is admirably done. Your Committee congratulates the State upon the intelligence and wisdom everywhere manifest in the government of the Reformatory. (1884. Page 31.)

The Reformatory continues under the same enlightened management and is a credit to the State. (1885. Pages 255–263.)

Health and general conditions satisfactory. The prisoners looked hardy and but three were in the hospital, suffering from fistula, pleurisy, and sore finger. There were but two deaths during the year, one from consumption and the other from meningitis. . . . The discipline of the prisoners was admirable, and offenses against it are promptly and intelligently punished. (1886. Pages 149–150.)

All in all, the State Reformatory is one of the most satisfactorily conducted institutions subject to the visitations of this Board.

Prison officers and students of sociology from distant states and foreign countries visit it for their information and instruction, and the inspection of it by your Committee is one of its most agreeable and gratifying annual duties. (1887, Pages 45–46.)

This institution is in admirable order, full, and, in the interest of the prisoners, should not be enlarged. A modification of the prison system of the state, which would admit of the transfer of the more incorrigible and hardened criminals to either of the state prisons, in the discretion of the superintendent and Board of Managers, is recommended by your Committee. . . . (1888. Page 306.)

It should always be remembered, furthermore, that such institutions were not established for the purpose of money making, to be a source of revenue to the state, but rather as reform schools where the unfortunate inmates may be prepared to struggle with the world after being released. (1889. Pages 126–127.)

The institution was found in admirable order, and its management is highly commended as intelligent and humane. A great variety of trades and industries are taught, and a large measure of self-government allowed the inmates. (1890. Pages 39–40.)

Science rules in the Reformatory. . . . (Page 128.)

The large measure of self-government allowed the Reformatory prisoners (the monitor system) cannot fail to raise their moral tone. (Page 129.)

The value of the work of the Reformatory cannot be overestimated, and it should have the generous support of the State to which it is an honor. (Page 130.)

The superintendent of the State Reformatory is admittedly one of the ablest penologists of his time. (Page 131.)

All penologists admit that the Elmira system of prison education and reformation has passed beyond the experimental stage and is a complete and assured success. (1891. Page 78.)

It has been successfully managed from its inception under the same active superintendence, and in its administration, discipline and distribution of the time of the inmates between hard work in the shops and the mental development in the class room, in many respects, is a model of its kind, and as such is annually visited by many officers of charitable institutions of other states and countries, and by others interested in the subject of penology. (1892. Page 43.)

The investigation was therefore committed to the management of the state board of charities. It dragged along from September, 1893, to March, 1894, with twenty-five days of sessions. The two volumes of the report contain among other things more than nine hundred letters from prisoners, procured in one evening at the reformatory.

To facilitate the work of securing evidence from the resident criminals, I made the following offer, which to the committeemen seemed risky, even astonishing, but was so favorable to the prosecutors that they could not reject it. I proposed to assemble all the prisoners in the auditorium, half an hour in advance of the evening school gathering, when, publicly in the presence of the committeemen, I would explain to the prisoners the purpose of the pending investigation proceedings. Then each man should be given a half sheet of note paper, a pencil, and a gummed envelope addressed to the chairman of the committee — Mr. Craig. On Tuesday evening, September 26, 1893, the evening preceding the formal opening of the investigation for the taking of testimony, the proposal was carried out, being only varied by the admission of a newspaper agent on the personal motion of Mr. Craig, the chairman of the committee. I hazard nothing in affirming that the occasion is unique in the history of prisons and prison investigations. The entire prisoner population of the reformatory, more than fourteen hundred felonious convicts, were at night time brought from their cells to the assembly hall and there publicly told that the prison government, especially their general superintendent, was undergoing an investigation on charges of injustice and cruelty to themselves, the prisoners. They were invited to express themselves, freely and confidentially, in the sealed communications addressed to Mr. Craig; and I assured them that none of them would either suffer or benefit by anything he should thus communicate. Mr. Craig then addressed the prisoners, reiterating in substance my own remarks.

The men were then dismissed from the assembly hall to the several class rooms, each receiving as he passed out the promised stationery. At the close of the evening school the envelopes were collected, and the next morning all were delivered to Mr. Craig. There were a few more than nine hundred notes, none of which, judged by the after effects, contained any serious complaints.

The two hundred witnesses examined during the inquiry were mainly convicts transferred to the reformatory from the state prisons, discharged convicts from the New York slums, and resident reformatory criminals. Of the three members of the state board of charities who were to have been responsible for this investigation one died in January, 1894, and one was in Europe. To the third alone was entrusted the making of the report, and it is not strange that under the circumstances, — which with proper self-respect I cannot go into here, — the finding was against the accused.*

Immediately afterward the board of managers of the reformatory protested against the findings, took upon themselves all responsibility for the conduct of the reformatory, and petitioned for another and fairer investigation, concluding their memorial in the following language:

"If the board of managers were convinced by the testimony, that they had been, even through an excusable oversight or natural misapprehension, responsible, collectively or individually, for any injustice, cruelty, or maladministration of any kind, — none of which they emphatically affirm ever existed under their management, — they would not hesitate a moment to return to the executive the commission of their arduous, unrecompensed, and thankless tasks, but as they are not so convinced and as they know that they have neglected no duty in their office, they protest unanimously against the recommendation of their removal. . . .

"The charges were instigated for a sensational agency that boasts it has expended over $10,000 in its unscrupulous work, abetted by criminal revenge, and the report thereon was sustained by a board that never heard or read the testimony. The charges were made against one officer and the report was made against five others, four of whom were never heard in their defense. The investigation was long conducted and finally reported on by one committeeman, who

---

* See Report of the State Board of Charities in the matter of the Investigation of the New York State Reformatory at Elmira, transmitted to the Legislature, March 16, 1894.

was grossly biased, and persisted, both in violation of the explicit directions from the board and against the protests of the accused, in holding on to a place designed to be occupied by three fair, honest, and competent men. His report was illegal, untrue, and unjust."

The managers then petition as follows:

"The managers therefore, for the vindication of their honor as men, and in protection of their reputation as faithful servants against a great wrong,' ask for an investigation by members of your Honorable Body, for the discovery of the truth and the rectification of the wrong."

The memorial was signed by every member of the board of managers, which was then composed of William C. Wey, M. H. Arnot, James B. Rathbone, William H. Peters, and B. L. Swartwood.

The publication of this memorial to the legislature was followed by numerous other vehement published and public protests, with commendations of the reformatory. The high character of our defenders is sufficiently evidenced by the following partial list out of the large number. Among the defenders were such newspapers as the New York *Sun;* New York *Times;* New York *Tribune;* New York *Evening Post;* New York *Journal of Commerce;* New York *Recorder; The Outlook* (New York); New York *Observer;* New York *Medical and Legal Journal;* Harper's *Monthly Magazine;* New York *Life;* Long Island *Weekly Flag;* Brooklyn *Eagle;* Brooklyn *Transcript;* Albany *Argus;* and the three daily newspapers of Elmira — *The Advertiser, The Gazette,* and *The Echo.* Outside of New York we were championed by such newspapers as the Chicago *Interocean*, *Volunteer Press* (St. Paul, Minnesota); the *Christian Register* and the *Christian Leader* of Boston, Massachusetts, together with most of the secular newspapers in Boston; the Hartford *Courant*, and the New Haven *Register* of Connecticut, and others.

The local (Elmira) public sentiment was almost altogether in our favor, represented in the public expressions of clergymen: Thomas K. Beecher; President Cowles of the College; Dr. McKnight of Trinity Church; Reverend Messrs. Isaac Jennings, I. I. Keyes, E. M. Mills, C. C. Wilbur, and Allen DeCamp. Our defense was particularly publicly espoused by Mayor Collin, as also by Judge Seymour Dexter, Judge Sylvester Taylor, Judge Gabriel L. Smith, and indeed almost everybody of any prominence. The Prison Association of New York defended us by published articles by Mr. Eugene Smith, then the secretary and now the president, and by Mr. William M. F. Round who was the active agent of the Prison Association. Mr. John Bigelow, ex-secretary of state, once minister to France, publicly denounced as false an alleged hostile interview with him published in one of the New York newspapers. The same kind of public denial was sent out by Lewis G. Janes. Israel C. Jones, retired after twenty-five years of successful management of the New York House of Refuge, publicly complained of the attack upon our reformatory. Frederick Howard Wines, sociologist, also defended us.

To me personally came letters from a number of discharged prisoners who had obtained their absolute release and were prospering, letters expressing indignation at the accusations and assuring me of their cordial confidence; and from other discharged prisoners, expressions of gratitude for the benefits they had received at our hands.

It is not possible to express adequately my appreciation of the open advocacy, in newspapers, magazine articles, and in public address, of Frank B. Sanborn and of the late Charles Dudley Warner, author and orator. Mr. Warner's monograph entitled "The Elmira System," which he read at the Saratoga meeting of the American Social Science Association, before its jurisprudence department, September 6, 1894,* during the heat of the second investigation, is perhaps the clearest and most succinct exposition of the system that has ever appeared. It is also a convincing defense of the Elmira phase of prison science, of the reformatory and its procedure, and of myself and my management.

Referring to the then recent attacks, he says:

"The Elmira Reformatory, after running for many years as the most interesting object lesson in penology, and with increasing approval of experts and of the general public, has lately been attacked. The attack is due to three causes:

(1) The hunger to make money and notoriety by exploiting a sensation.

(2) The determination to bring the reformatory into the control of the political machine, that it may be used as the state penitentiaries are used, — to give places and profits to partisan workers.

(3) The sentimentalists, who are the most discouraging element in any robust reformatory work."

After dealing with the sentimentalists, who, he says, have a disease which is common in this country, and

---

* See Journal of Social Science, Vol. VI, No. 32, pp. 53-66.

which may be scientifically described as moral mushiness, — speaking pathologically, a fatty degeneration of the heart, — and who have no conception that the true and divine altruism lies only in the enforcement of law and in the discipline of the human race, he concludes his monograph as follows:

. . . "To reform diseased bodies and crooked minds is the work of experts; it is scientific work. Such an institution as Elmira affords an opportunity for the exercise of the highest talent, the best scholarship, the investigation by the most interested students of the laws of the human mind and body. To rectify the bodies, to develop and train the abnormal minds, — this is glorious work. When we go at it seriously, we shall begin to deal adequately and intelligently with the refuse and slag of our civilization.

"The attack upon the Elmira Reformatory is not altogether to be deplored. It is a sign that the work tells. This work has aroused the active opposition of the criminal class and of those who pander to it. It shows that we are moving in the right direction against an intrenched position of the enemy, — the enemy of orderly society, of law, of discipline. If we were having no effect, we should not be opposed. There is little opposition to the soft-shell institutions either of reform or of religion. The work will go on and go on all the more vigorously, owing to the clamor and detraction. It will rally to it the clear-sighted well-wishers of humanity. The fight will be a long one and mainly an individual one. Our forefathers looked for an Armageddon, a field whereon the forces of good and evil were to meet for a final conflict. There will never be an Armageddon. The powers of evil will never risk all on a single fight. Nor is it in nature. For the conflict of good and evil is in every man's heart. But daily we get a little more light, and the area of darkness withdraws. Let us have courage."

338

The second investigation began in May, 1894, and continued until the submission of the final report on October 31 of that year. The three commissioners having it in charge were Hon. William L. Learned of Albany, a retired justice of the supreme court, Dr. Austin Flint of New York, one of the foremost physiologists of the times, and Hon. Israel T. Deyo, an attorney of acknowledged ability who had served honorably in the state legislature and was familiar with our state prison system. The inquiry took on at once a true judicial tone. It covered the same ground as the first, the same witnesses were heard and others to the number of one hundred and fifty. A thorough inspection of the interior working of the reformatory was made and interviews with prisoners were had. On the report being made to Governor Flower he at once dismissed the charges.*

---

*See opinion of Governor Flower, report by Dr. Flint and Mr. Deyo, and minority report by Judge Learned, transmitted to the legislature December 10, 1894. The full text of the opinion and of the majority report is printed in the Nineteenth Year Book of the Elmira State Reformatory, 1893–1894.

CHAPTER XXI

CLASSIFICATION AND DISCIPLINE

1895–1898

A YEAR and a half under the harrow of prosecution, which not inappropriately may be
termed a persecution, was a distressful experience that made a heavy draft on my vitality. Notwithstanding my inward stay of conscious rectitude
and the fact that I was somewhat inured by previous
investigations, the tension so far beyond the strain of
the usual cares of the situation could scarcely have
been endured but for the staunch support that I
received. The board of managers, to a man, stood
firm.* Every one of the one hundred and thirty
officers and employes was completely loyal, despite
attempts to suborn them. The local and other approving public sentiment was also a comforting and sustaining influence. The effect upon myself, now retro-
spectively viewed, was conducive to good endurance
of contradictions; contributive to abiding confidence
in the inherent preservative quality of the truth; and
confirmed my belief in relying for proper justification
upon the deliberate collective public judgment.

---

* It is thought that the death of the noble minded, sensitive president of the board, Dr. W. C. Wey, in 1897, was hastened by this
attack on myself and the reformatory.

Throughout the United States and in Europe the attack on our reformatory attracted much attention; but the effect of the turmoil upon the progress of prison reform as it is typified at Elmira cannot, of course, be precisely traced and stated. But it is confidently believed that the effect was not only not harmful but helpful.

For instance, the Howard Association of London, England, always inclined to advocate the cellular separate system of prison construction and treatment, and whose published bulletins were widely distributed, often criticised unfavorably the "Elmira System," mentioning our reformatory as a "palace prison" where the discipline was too indulgent. Mr. Tallack, the secretary, had often declared that in his opinion the improving opportunities and creature comforts of the Elmira prison were enough to induce crimes by a certain class of hard-pushed free inhabitants. Mr. Tallack seemed not to know that the class of free inhabitants he referred to, if they were inclined to commit felonious crimes, would not be anxious about their own self-improvement or be willing for the sake of it to submit themselves to the strenuousness of the Elmira Reformatory training. Nor did Mr. Tallack seem to reflect that no class of the community was so desirous of the intellectual and moral advancement insisted on at Elmira as to voluntarily incur the stigma of a criminal conviction and of imprisonment. They would surely seek such culture elsewhere, and by the opportunities society so lavishly supplies. The investigations served to considerably correct this erroneous estimate, and at the same time stimulated the publication and circulation of correct information about it.

In England, France, Germany, and in the United

States, a booklet called "The New York State Reformatory," by Alexander Winter, was published in the different languages and widely read. The German edition appeared in 1890, the English in 1891, and the French edition in 1892. The investigation made a strong call for the booklet. The corrected English opinion is indicated in a series of six able articles which appeared in six successive issues of *The* (London) *Law Times* of 1895. The articles are entitled, Our Criminal Law; Reclamation of Criminals; Improved Prison Treatment. They are chiefly devoted to a description of our reformatory and the system, but they also discuss incisively and approvingly the principles on which it is based. Agitation of the prison question in England was, we know, quickened both within and without Parliament by our perturbation; and while the reform moved slowly, as is the wont with England, an advance was actually made. The salient features of the Elmira system are said to have been adopted at the English Borstal and in another English prison.

Throughout our own country and in Europe there was an increase of articles in booklets, pamphlets, and magazines, on criminal law reform and prison science. Officials, delegations, and distinguished foreigners and Americans came in greater numbers to inspect the reformatory; and the legislatures of several states took up the matter. The annual congresses of the American Prison Association were occupied with discussions of the indeterminate sentence system and the American reformatory prison system as it was exemplified at our reformatory; the international prison congresses held at Paris, 1895, at Brussels, 1900, and at Budapest, 1905, discussed the indeterminate sentence; and at the International Congress in Washington, D. C., 1910, the system was formally approved, as will appear by the resolutions adopted.*

The attack upon us proved to be an effective advertising instrumentality and greatly increased the influence of the reformatory which the attack was intended to defame. The effect of the assault upon the interior operations of the reformatory will appear, at least between the lines, in the remainder of this narrative. I may, however, now say that the delicately balanced, firm, steady pressure of the reformative agencies was disturbed, and a gradual deterioration took place. But, so well in hand were the agencies and processes, so powerful was that which may be termed the momentum, that the jostle and slackening occurred so slowly as to be scarcely realized except by those who were in intimate relation with it. To such it was indeed very apparent. The injurious effect was most noticeable in the general relaxation of tension throughout the schools of letters and of trades. As to this, the school director, Professor J. R. Monks, in his published report said:

"It was to be expected that the deplorable circum stances which stimulated in so many cases a rebelliou- and recalcitrant spirit should have affected seriously the conditions of instruction the past year. But this evil has been kept at a minimum by excellent organization, by the substantial value of instruction, and the official faithfulness of all. . . . It is gratifying to report that in spite of these unfavorable conditions — without a parallel in the history of schools — the work has moved on smoothly and successfully. . . . The fact . . . speaks eloquently in praise of the

*See Appendix III, p. 417.

discipline of the institution, whose influence, even when impersonally exerted, so steadied and supported and stimulated our school work of the year."

The following, relating to the effect on discipline, is taken from the published report of Commissioners Flint and Deyo.

"During the five years preceding September, 1893 (the month of the beginning of the Litchfield inquiry), the average number of prisoners reported for fighting, each period of six months during that time, is 37.3; while during the six months immediately following . . . the number reported for the same offense was 172, or four and a half times as many as the number reported during any corresponding period of six months within the preceding years."

Referring to the physical treatment which, though they can find no other term than "corporal punishment" to designate it, they well knew and conceded was never administered at the reformatory as a *punishment*, they add:

"Corporal punishment under proper regulations is preferable to the other modes of punishment which must necessarily take its place if corporal punishment is abolished."

The following facts are also striking. While the average inmate population in 1894 was 10 per cent less than in 1893, there was an increase of "lost time" by inmates in several ways. Malingering was more prevalent and successful: 776 days additional were spent in the cell or room, out of the routine, on the claim of illness; 6002 more days in rooms for idleness; 1560 days more in "rest-cure"; and 2038 days additional in cellular seclusion for serious or persistent disregard of the regulations.

The year book of 1894 cites from the prison report of punishments in the English prisons the records there which, in comparison with our reformatory records, show strongly in our favor, and concludes its communication with the following optimistic paragraph:

"Notwithstanding the recent newspaper fusillade the reformatory retains, as there is the very best evidence for stating, the same high place it has always occupied in the esteem of the best and best informed of public sentiment both at home and abroad. The application in its organization and administration of sound principles of prison treatment of its criminals, its methods and results of reformation, serve to give the institution its honorable rank among prisons and reformatories. Its mission for good is not yet concluded. Its principles may be still better applied, old methods perfected, new ones discovered and treated, a larger ratio of reformations may be expected; and its influence promotive of rational prison reforms will be still further extended."

Despite the disturbances and difficulties, indeed because of them, every possible effort was directed to preserve the good status and gain progress. In 1893 the great drill hall, 250 x 300 feet, was constructed, which made possible thereafter the continuance of daily military drill and parade through the inclement season and stormy weather, perfecting thus the military organization then and since the disciplinary safeguard. Some increase of exactness was achieved with the wage-earning and the monetary-marking system which had become and has since proved so valuable an aid for practical permanent reformation.

345

The study of dietetics was given special attention that year. The long felt need of a more scientific dietary for prisoners had led to correspondence with experts relative to the function of foods in nutrition, and the impression had deepened that, possibly, a more scientific arrangement of the constituents and quantity of foods, to meet individual idiosyncrasy, might, in connection with other means, be found very serviceable. The year book of 1893 contains in concise form an argument, tabulated analyses, diagnoses, and interesting suggestions on this subject, together with short notes by Dr. H. D. Wey, well illustrated. The interest of the management in this scientific forelook was deferred but not relinquished. In 1899 an interesting experiment in dietetics was actually made. The completion and occupancy of the new domestic building in 1893 at once greatly improved the methods of preparation and distribution of food. In the same year five new classes were added in the trade school and in the school of letters; nature studies for the higher classes and natural history for the lower classes were introduced; and separate denominational religious services were permitted for the first time in the history of the reformatory.

A most interesting event of the year was the application of new methods for selected dullards designated in our institutional parlance as "the kindergartners." This experimental class was the object of special interest on the part of the school director, the physician, and myself. Everything relating to this class was regulated with scrupulous exactness: the hours of physical exercise, hot and cold baths, the mental effort called out; and so far as was then practicable the quantities and qualities of their food were prescribed. Calisthenics and massage were in every day's program and effort was made to normalize their bodily proportions and their weight and strength. Regard was had to their clothing for the effect on the mental state; it was of good fashion and fabric, and perfect cleanliness was required, as contributing to proper self-respect. Cleverly devised appropriate tasks and exercises for the hands and eyes were planned as an aid to brain education. Every process was closely observed. Measurements and estimates were frequently made, compared, and recorded. These were tabulated and published in the year book with other interesting information.*

---

* An item in the year book of 1895 that relates to the only prisoners who, during my incumbency, were committed and held under an absolute indeterminate sentence, should not be omitted from this account. Four prisoners had been admitted at different dates whose sentence, had they been committed to one of the state prisons, as it was within the discretion of the court to do, must have been life imprisonment. But at the reformatory they might be detained for life or be discharged by the board of managers when they could properly qualify according to the regulations; three were committed for arson and one for murder in the second degree. The three committed for arson were all released on parole: one after thirteen months, another after twenty-three months, and the third remained seven years. None of the three was ever heard from after his release from the door of the reformatory. The belief is that all of them fled the state. The murderer remained at the reformatory four years and one month. He faultlessly fulfilled his obligations and after six months obtained regularly his final discharge. Years afterward we learned that he was living in the same place to which he had been paroled, and was still working and earning well at the trade he learned at the reformatory; also that he was married, the head of an interesting family, and a respectable and respected member of his community. These four cases seem to point to the conclusion that under the absolute indeterminate sentence system, released prisoners will either by their own act rid the state of their presence or will remain and properly behave themselves. Moreover, when, between the several states, there shall be established mutuality of exchange of identification and information as to delinquent offenders at large, then the discharged prisoners will be obliged to cease from crimes or with great certainty they will be apprehended.

347

In the next year, 1894, we were gladdened by the erection in the auditorium of the sweet-toned powerful church organ, which afterwards in the hands of the master organist and musician, Mr. Carter, was so serviceable, mellowing acerbities, moving the higher emotions, and incidentally contributing to the formation of more correct musical taste.

The New York constitutional convention of 1894 adopted by a majority of only one vote the amendment included in Article VIII, which when the new state constitution took effect November, 1895, changed the state supervision of the reformatory from the state board of charities to the newly created state commissioners of prisons.

The transfer of supervisory authority was hotly contested in the convention, but the change was made in spite of it. The reformatory originally was not subject to the inspection of the board of state charities and it was now felt that the supervision of the discipline of felons might better be under the prison commission. In the year 1899 the complexion of the board of managers of the reformatory was entirely changed through the appointment by the governor of new men.

In the month of February, 1895, occurred the death of Professor Monks, who for twelve years had been a non-resident regular lecturer and for a part of that time the school director at the reformatory. He took service with us on his retirement after a long and honorable record as the principal of the Elmira Free Academy. Professor Monks was a remarkably successful general educator; and he was peculiarly well

348

fitted for the particular educational work at the reformatory. He made the lecture method of instructing such minds a complete success. While his manner of address was never oratorical but quiet, and his speech colloquial, he enlisted close attention and the absorbing interest of the prisoner pupils. His genuine interest in the prisoners and in the topic of discourse; his complete mastery within the wide field covered by his lectures; and very notably his simple yet felicitous use of the English language, gave to his lecture service a peculiar charm. Present as I myself almost always was, I never observed in his audience of hundreds of prisoners a drowsy auditor, not even in the evening lecture classes in summer time when the pupils had put in a full day of physical exertion. The following incident is illustrative of his successful work.

On a general examination evening, at my own suggestion, as a test of the genuine educational efficiency of Professor Monks' lecture method, without a moment's warning the regular examination questions were laid aside and all the pupils put to the task of preparing impromptu a "news item" report of the sermon delivered in our auditorium by one of the city preachers. The result showed that out of the three hundred pupils of intellectual grade ranging from grammar school to academy pupils, more than ninety wrote off-hand productions which on examination were adjudged worthy of acceptance by any newspaper willing to publish such an item. Professor Monks, more than any other man I have known, demonstrated the superiority of oral teaching over the usual printed lesson study method, and demonstrated, too, how effectually common minds may be interested and instructed in the higher range of topics by well-prepared, simply phrased, open discourse.

On another occasion Professor Monks prepared at my request a syllabus on the evolution of the family home for use in an experiment in oral teaching with a selected class of a hundred or more of the dullards. The syllabus, when printed, was illustrated by simple wood cuts of domestic scenes, but the main excellency of it was the chosen words and short sentences in which he had carefully clothed it. He had become so deeply interested in the experiment that he divided into halves his Sunday rest and luncheon hour to get time to try the experiment. It proved a delightful success and went far to confirm the pedagogic view we both were inclined to — that the best of teachers should be assigned to instruct the dullest pupils.

That Sunday Professor Monks remained at the reformatory the entire day and late into the evening. When he came to my office for the usual adieus, standing beneath the lighted chandelier, his countenance and personality were aglow with benevolent satisfaction. Was the appearance possibly the presage of his death, which occurred early the next morning from heart failure? He had during that year written for the *American University Magazine* the very best condensed account of the educational work at the reformatory that has ever appeared in print. The article is copied into the year book of 1895, the interesting contents of which I have already mentioned.

If now — 1912 — I were to name some one particular occurrence and deep personal experience that marks that year in memory, I should mention the death of Professor Monks. The delight of our friendship and of our co-operative efforts, after the lapse of sixteen years, still exhales its sweet, sad savor.

This mention of tender memories quickens now in the consciousness another sorrowful recollection which also has the tinge of grateful fellow-feeling. It centers in prisoner No. 6826, his character, career, and our mutual contact. He was received at the reformatory in May, 1894, convicted of forgery, second degree, the limits of his imprisonment under our law and system being from one to ten years. By his frequent lapse in conduct he was detained at the reformatory nearly five years — until 1899 — when he was released on parole. He was an excellent stenographer and immediately on his admission was assigned to my inner prison office for my individual stenographic service. The time of his admission was just at the conclusion of the Litchfield-Charities investigation and the opening of the second inquiry by the governor's commissioners, so that he was brought into daily association with myself, and under the existing circumstances, into very confidential relations in which he was entirely faithful. He was about twenty-four years of age, native-born but of German parentage, with fair complexion and delicate physique, a frank open countenance, gentle of manners, genuine and winsome. Our daily close association could but incite, on my part, a good measure of personal attachment. The native and acquired mental endowment of the man was of a superior order; his mind was clear-sighted and unusually discriminative. His disposition was habitually good. I do not believe he ever harbored an intention to do evil. He was spiritually susceptible. I have seen his face illumined in the great congregation, with the light that was never seen on land or sea, when he was under the play of noble thoughts eloquently proclaimed.

The forgery for which he was committed to the reformatory was but one of many uses he had made of his father's forged signature. The limit of parental forbearance had been reached and his father, for this last offense, surrendered him to the law and to imprisonment. The father's sensitiveness to the stigma of a criminal conviction and the feeling of family disgrace created a chasm of alienation between father and son which was never completely bridged. His repeated forgeries and the lapses that kept him so long in the reformatory were the product of sporadic impulses; not of conscious wickedness nor the surrender to weakness, but of momentary eclipse of judgment. In a manly way he uncomplainingly acquiesced, accepting the consequences of such faltering, not, I judge, with philosophical resignation, but instinctively, as we accept resignedly the unavoidable accidents of life. Adjudged not fitted for safe free inhabitancy because there yet appeared the symptoms of his recurrent aberrant impulses, I did nevertheless at several different times explain to the father and urge that he receive again his son and renew his parental guardianship. But the father was always inexorable.

Once, when the physician had discovered incipient tuberculous affection of the lungs, I wrote more urgently that the father receive and care for him; but in answer got only the reply, — "If my son has consumption and, as you say, needs the best of hospital care, then, in my opinion, the hospital in your reformatory is the very best place for him." However, in due time, with some regard to his delicate state of

352

health, under pressure of our determination to try him on parole with or without his father's consent, we did obtain his father's conditional promise of aid and he was sent home with the understanding that with a suitable outfit and sufficient means for temporary support supplied by the father he should go to England and engage in his calling. This he did, but previous to his departure it is said he committed another forgery. After expiration of the usual six months' parole period, which he had spent in London, teaching the stenographic art, he piteously begged for absolute release, that he might return to his home in Brooklyn. To this proposition the father objected, which induced us to delay the discharge, hoping ultimately to secure his father's favor and a better situation at home. While we were thus hesitating and negotiating he, overcome, no doubt, by nostalgia and profound dejection, closed his own career by suicide in June, 1900.

This young man was outwardly, in the ordinary sense, a criminal, yet his inner character was not essentially criminous. He would be rated incorrigible, for in all probability he never would or could become quite safe as a free inhabitant; yet he was neither vicious nor insane. Retributive penalties were not required for penitence, for he accepted with Christian resignation the natural undesirable consequences of his misconduct. Persuasion with him was valueless for he was already quite persuaded. Religious conversion was not called for because his soul lay open and receptive to spiritual influences. Education was not a special need — he possessed sufficient for his day and occupation. Economically, he was well provided, and could command by his skill wages enough for a good support. He had no harmful personal vices which were in need of reformation. There was nothing about him outwardly discoverable which was menacingly dangerous. On the contrary, he was attractive and confidence-inspiring. Yet, as I frankly told him, on an appropriate occasion, I believed him to be one of the most unsafe prisoners whose release I had been called upon to consider. Due protection from such a character can only be had under the absolute indeterminate sentence plan and the rationally reformed prison system that inseparably belongs to it. This man should and could have been utilized by the state, in its prison department, to the advantage of both the state and the prisoner.

It was natural and unavoidable that, incidentally, the commotion of the two years' conflict should incite the managers of the reformatory to a reconsideration of every item of the management, especially with reference to coercive measures. This scrutinizing review did but confirm our wonted estimation of the desirability, propriety, and preference of our disciplinary measures and proceedings over any other.

At the risk of some repetition, I must give a condensed account of the conclusions reached and verified on this much mooted and greatly misapprehended topic. There is no custodial establishment — penitentiary, reformatory, or reform school for juvenile delinquents — where, sometimes, for some inmates, some compulsion is not required and used. The worst disciplinary measure — the one commonly in use — is long confinement on a restricted diet in seclusion cells. Whenever personal physical compulsion must

354

be used it should be without passion, remedially intended, skilful, and effective.

In prisons where simply custodial security is the object there is less occasion for coercion than in a reformatory where the object is to successfully train the prisoners for safe free inhabitancy. Where earnest effort is not made to change the character by formation of new habits and preferences little occasion arises for sharp coercion. Indulgence and relaxed requirements diminish friction and smooth the surface but at the same time detract from efficiency of training. Yet even under such a relaxed régime — indeed in spite of it — some exceptionally constituted prisoners derive desirable benefits, but a strict disciplinary régime is better for them and is essential for the improvement of the others. Contrary to a common notion, stricter control is required in a reformatory and for the comparatively younger men, than in an ordinary convict prison for older criminals who are confined for the mere punishment of the imprisonment. The early lesson of the reformatory process for criminals is quick and accurate self-adjustment to a uniform requirement, habituation to the yoke of established custom. Exactness of observance is of the greatest importance. But when, as was the case at the reformatory, the organized standard requirement comports with satisfactory free associate behavior, the exactness possesses a double value, for, according to Huxley: "The conscious actions are by practice organized into more or less unconscious or reflex operations" so that the newly formed habit of precision calls up the instinctive impulse to social orderliness quite independent of conscious volition.

It is not easy to break away from a habitual individual proclivity and form a new one, and it is especially difficult for prisoners who possess strong passions and weak reasoning, who are inclined to short spasms of greedy indulgence, and whose sense of morality is either absent or unavailing. These need some very positive extraneous assistance. The necessary aid was sufficiently supplied by the indeterminate sentence and a strenuous régime such as existed at the reformatory during the strenuous years we are considering, for perhaps 80 per cent of the prisoners. These almost automatically adjusted themselves to the requirements, and only 20 per cent or so needed particular personal attention. This one-fifth of the prisoners constituted a special field for reformative endeavor. Many of these were reached by the personal attentions of the general superintendent at the evening interviews and elsewhere; by persuasions, reproofs, admonitions. Others were recovered after experiencing imposed temporary inconveniences, deprivations, the "rest cure" treatment of enforced idleness (complete seclusion for a short time with or without artificial restraints as seemed suited to each case). But some others, the few, were so constituted, or habituated, that they could not, or at least did not — and such characters generally do not — properly respond to the training methods without the aid of some physical collision that suddenly disturbs the existent prevalent objectionable mood.

Of three measures which are effective for such a purpose, namely, the douche, electricity, and a quickening slap, the last alone was used at the reformatory, and for the following reasons. The difficulty of regulating, with precision, the effect of a dash of water to the variant sensitiveness of the different persons, debarred the douche from our service. Electricity was excluded for the same reason, and also, because of its use for the electrocution of criminals, it has acquired a certain stigma; while the slap, or spanking,—offensively named "paddling,"—was chosen for this remedial use because of its safe, easy, accurate adjustment. Since the three instrumentalities have each and all of them been used and become known as means of punishment, and since the notion of punishment is, in the common conception, so associated with them, I venture to repeat that the use of physical compulsion in our reformatory was never for punishment; never used for measuring demerit; nor was it ever used with intent to directly affect the subject's free will —"to subdue him." No doubt the effect was, sometimes, educative of the judgment, suggestive of what is good or bad policy to pursue, but even that object was not directly in view. Indeed, the conscious immediate object was scarcely an appeal to the intellect at all, or only indirectly so. The immediate purpose was to effect some change in the channels of the mental activities. Any such eruptive change must be helpful to the subject to break away from the bad mood; and might initiate a good change of the habitual conduct. But it is fair to say, as no doubt will be suggested, that the means *might not* produce the intended effect. However, the management felt themselves recreant to their duty until the effort had been made — the experiment had been tried; and so many and such signal successes had been already achieved by this means that there could be no longer any doubt of their duty in the matter.

357

Moreover, the turmoil of the two years and the reconsideration it induced served to decidedly strengthen the growing opinion of the management that great importance should be attached to defectiveness and derangement of the organic substance of the being as a subjective cause of anti-social and criminal conduct. The proper sphere of our corrective efforts must begin and include, if it should not be comprised in, the renovation and reformation of the material human being. The mutual reformative relations of body and mind could not in the present state of science be completely compassed, but healthy mentality was most likely to be had in connection with soundness of the body; therefore the latter should be kept in the best possible state. And since our access to the mind of the prisoner must needs be by way of the avenues of its abode — the body, it was seen that the intellectual and so-called moral results might best be promoted after removing diseased bodily impediments by education of the mind, largely through the functioning of the body, and that in addition to the attention already devoted to that theory, more and more scientific manual training should be introduced.

It is certain that none of those on whom devolved the reformative procedure denied or consciously depreciated the belief that the superhuman agency might, noumenally, effect the change in the individual character; but we had grown to be less assumptive of the possible human control of a direct-acting spiritual force. I myself, at least, had come to have what I believed to be the larger and more reverent view, — that the purposefulness of the infinite Wisdom coupled with the infinite Power cannot be either thwarted or facilitated by the volitional withholding or doing of any mere human.

This view much relieved a former painful vague sense of a certain responsibility, and at the same time intensified and deepened a certain sense of duty that centers in that limited field of seeming volitional activity which relates to earthly welfare and happiness, apparently affected for good or evil by the degree of wise self-adjustment to external circumstances.

I will now conclude my account of this period down to 1899, by summarizing some of the conditions that were affected, and to some extent brought about in the administration of the reformatory by the cessation of the storm, when a new order of things was inaugurated.

The trades school remained under the direction of Mr. Clark, who was a graduate of the mechanical engineering department of Cornell University. With the advantage of the thirteen years of its existence he selected, adopted, and developed industrial arts to meet the individual needs of the prisoners. In the year 1896, thirty-six trades and branches of trades were taught to the resident population of 1500; and the entire enrollment, 2111, received trade instruction. The thoroughness and practical value of this trades instruction at the time is shown by the published statement of 1896. Of the 329 men paroled that year, 324 went to the trade or employment acquired or arranged at the reformatory; four had trades on their admission to the reformatory; only one was discharged without trades training. Closely co-ordinated to the trades school was the manual training department organized in 1896, which when it was fully developed embraced 500 of the 1500 prisoners in confinement. The class was composed of the prisoners who, during a trial period of six months, did not keep pace with the progress made by the others in the regular institution régime. They were either exceptionally stupid or deficient in a single faculty such as the arithmetical; or they were incapable of the ordinary prudential self-regulation of their demeanor.

In respect to the number of pupils, the completeness of control, the analysis of capacities, the diversity of exercises, the precision of adaptation of the tool and other processes to group and individual needs, and the ability, energy, and devotion of the director, Professor Bates, probably no other manual training experiment anywhere was ever so well equipped and worked.

The work of the physical training department and of the school of letters, which have been already sufficiently described, was closely united to the manual training, so that for the pupils a threefold potency urged improvement by means of physical, manual, technical, and good pedagogical education. These pupils, too, were included in the general educational effect of the kaleidoscopic interchangeable classifications of the prisoners throughout their regulated association which were then maintained and afterwards perfected. The following is a simple enumeration of the interchanging classifications:

(1) Five grade divisions based on the character as it is determined during the imprisonment.

(2) Three school grades and 28 school classes governed by the ascertained intellectual quality and proficiency alone.

(3)   Thirty-six trade divisions looking to industrial efficiency and economical engagement on or after the release.

(4)   Four battalions and sixteen military companies which embraced all the able-bodied prisoners.

(5)   Five religious divisions according to the denominational affiliation.

(6)   Three general divisions and 75 subdivisions, interchangeable, of the manual training class.

(7)   Six designated groups of the very defective prisoners arranged on the basis of the physician's opinion of requirements.

Thus there were one hundred and fifty groups of the prisoners changeable and interchangeable, kaleidoscopically, as would and did best promote the reformative educational efficiency.

Classifications were not haphazard arrangements but were based on ascertained actual differences. The differences and changes were all recorded and readily accessible, and the records were so complete that by means of them the differential characteristics and circumstances of each prisoner were closely seen; and from the central record office there could be quickly called together for any desired purpose, any grade, group, school, or trade class, religious persuasion, or any individual prisoner. There were fifty biographical and conduct record ledgers, two pages or more of which contained the record of each inmate. On more than 16,000 pages of these books was to be found exact information relating to fully 8000 prisoners. Such of these books as contained the records of resident prisoners and men on parole were in constant use for reference by the general superintendent and his assistants, by heads of departments, and by the eighteen prisoner clerks engaged in keeping the records.

The biographical record books give succinctly the diagnosis and treatment prescriptions made personally by the general superintendent, when the prisoner was first received at the reformatory, and afterwards, and the notes made from time to time of progress and changes. These biographical records reveal at a glance the incentives to the criminal acts for which the prisoner is committed; show specifically his defectiveness and the prescribed outline of the proposed treatment. From this continuous record can be traced the degree of accuracy of the first examination, the wisdom or otherwise of the original prescription, the prisoner's reach of preparation for release, his performance while out on parole, and other known facts of his history after he received the absolute discharge. The records supply the severest possible test of the correctness of the judgment about the prisoners made upon their admission to the reformatory and of the wisdom or otherwise of the prescription and the procedure; and it is gratifying to be able to say that the accuracy and efficiency revealed by these records prove the practical value of the system as it was then administered.

The last year of this period, extending until May, 1899, the date when the new managers were appointed, is typical of the sustained good status of affairs, with the possible blemish of a too restrained use of physical contact coercion. The satisfying remembrance remains a present consciousness and is reinforced by reference now to the year book of 1898 and the remembrance of the things attempted during the first few months of 1899.

362

CHAPTER XXII

THE CONCLUSION OF THE WHOLE MATTER

1899–1900

M Y CONNECTION with the reformatory was concluded within this period. During the few months of my continuance as superintendent, unremitting effort was made to maintain and to ripen the methodical movement of the selected and active reformatory agencies, and keen research was kept alive for other possible aids; but after May, 1899, the interference of the newly selected managers checked the movement and it lost verve. Of three then most promising methods, two were abandoned; and inventive enterprise, when thus discouraged, quite ceased. The manual training department was arbitrarily discontinued; and of two dietary expedients, but one remained in use, which has become a permanent important feature of the reformatory procedure. Both were planned to make an effective appeal by means of a scientific dietary to animalism for the desired social and moral betterment: the one an appeal to degenerates and motiveless men for a better nervous state — more susceptible to mental and moral impressions; the other directed to the prisoners who were nearing their conditional release, for the cultivation of personal economy. The former,

363

the very interesting experiment which was abandoned, shall be duly explained, but attention is now invited to the abiding experiment.

One hundred and fifty of the best grade of inmates, who had acquired a credit balance under the operation of the monetary marking and wage system, were privileged to select their meals from a properly limited menu of considerable variety of priced food. This was skilfully cooked and served at small tables of four persons each, and with better table furnishings than the others had. The original additional cost of this dietary régime over the cost of the regular fare was only 5 cents per man per day. This additional cost was provided for in the general appropriation for maintenance, made available for prisoners by the increased daily wage rate fixed for men of the advanced grade when, and only when, the wage was actually earned under the required conditions of earning a credit balance. Three times a day, at meal times, these prisoners, besides the general economical prudence, practiced to gain their grade advancement; and this dietary privilege exercised the particular regulation of self-indulgence based on a proper expenditure of their individual legitimate income from wages. It was not only a most valuable economic training for their prospective freedom, but valuable also as a test of fitness for release.

The plan worked out well for the participants, and the effect on the non-participants was also favorable. As would be expected, some of the men who enjoyed the privilege over-indulged themselves, exhausted their credit balance, and lost the privilege. Such men "failed in business"—that is, failed in management of themselves and their individual economies — and so showed their unfitness for the exigencies that must confront them immediately when they should be released. The failure of itself often supplied the needed lesson — the privilege being regained and afterwards sustained by exercise of wiser economy. There were, indeed, some prisoners, a small quota, who over-stinted themselves in order to increase the credit balance required by the regulations as a condition of the parole. These, too, were then shown to be faulty in self-regulative judgment. This plan, in its con-nection with the wage-earning system, held taut the details of management; for privilege or advancement, if improperly gained or given, was at once disintegrating to the individual and the collective welfare. When we were assured that the plan was worked out with good integrity, the sight presented to a thoughtful observer—the dining hall with one hundred and fifty men seated at small tables spread with white cloths and good plain crockery; the diners clad in neat blue clothing, each studying the menu, regulating indul-gence according to his resources and prospective needs — was very impressive and most hopefully inspiring. The appearance and the fact were in striking contrast to the usual arbitrary feeding of convicts on a coarse uniform prison food, all at the public expense, without any sense on the part of the prisoners that they them-selves were in any way interested in the expense of it. The old ordinary way of prison feeding can but con-tribute to a subjective sense of pauperism, which is close akin to criminousness.

The other prisoners, those who could not or did not avail themselves of the privilege, the mass of the men who took their common fare at long tables in an adjoining apartment, were affected by the appetizing odors and buzz of cheery conversation nearby, and thus somewhat stimulated to good exertion. Of course the arousing influence accentuated differences — some men were beneficially quickened, while others, indifferent when driven from cover, became acute instead of habitually chronic patients.

The other dietetic experiment, which was devoted to degenerates, was confined to a small number of selected decadent inmates and bore promise of such good practical results as would warrant its considerable extension to others. It was a new departure in reformatory prison treatment and very interesting, but it proved to be short-lived, partly because of the generally depressing or inhibitive influence that consciously or unconsciously emanated from one of the new and not friendly managers, and partly because the expert leader, Doctor Elliott, resigned to take a better professional position elsewhere. He reports about it substantially as follows:

"I set out with the purpose of ascertaining whether any tangible change of character could be induced in the young adult criminals by special feeding. I wished to bring a new force to bear on that small minority of prisoners in whose case our many excellent reformative measures were not producing desirable and adequate results. I was to deal with the failures, so to speak.

"Thirty men were accordingly selected from this class and divided into three sets of 10 each. The first set of 10 were deficient generally; they were run down in health, and their records in school and discipline were altogether bad. A careful study was made of their regular fare for the purpose of comparison and they were prescribed a menu scientifically worked out to meet the physiological requirements of young adults doing light work. Their food was changed each day in the week, but uniformly contained for the day's food, protein ¼ pound, fat ¼ pound, and carbohydrate nine-tenths of a pound. The total heat units consumed amounted to 3250 daily. Though this was about 1000 calories less daily than their former allowance, a gain of 54 pounds at the end of one month for the 10 men showed that their bodily wants were fully met. This gain was not made each month, but a permanent advance was maintained to the end of the experiment. The food was specially prepared and served, which no doubt added something to the net result. The daily cost per man was 12 cents.

"But the alteration in character sought was not so well realized. As before stated, these men were among the worst in the prison and the discipline necessary to hold them in line kept them in a pretty constant state of perturbation. Besides, they were frequently absent from the table for days at a time undergoing punishments for misdemeanors. This was especially so after the cellular confinement took the place of the more active forms of coercion. Had I obtained the results I looked for under these circumstances, I could safely place this dietary before the public as a specific against crime.

"The second set of men was composed of undersized, ill-developed weaklings. They had little inhibitory power and were controlled chiefly by the animal instincts. Their wretchedly constructed nervous tissues were still further weakened by masturbation. In elaborating the dietary of this class I endeavored to meet the absolute needs in the matter of proteins, and to retain a full allowance of fats and carbohydrates. They had a change of food each day in the week, of which fresh vegetables always formed some part. Although the number of calories was reduced to 3050 a day per man, the average gain for the first month was 2½ pounds, and at the end of the experiment there remained an average gain of 2 pounds over the weight at the start. The adaptability of this dietary is thus shown.

"Mentally this group brightened up some but the same distracting influence spoken of above did much to counteract good effects, and it is feared that proteins, fats and carbohydrates are not mixed in such suitable proportions in this dietary as will stimulate these ill-made individuals to exhibit the virtues and capacities of normal beings. The dietary cost 9 cents per man per day.

"The third set of 10 men were strong physically and of fair intelligence. They failed chiefly in demeanor. Each man was prescribed food capable of generating 3000 calories per day. No fanciful articles entered into this or either of the other two dietaries. To meet the bodily needs and give as great a result as possible, with due attention to economy, were the principles which governed in its construction. A steady gain in weight was obtained as well as improvement in general health.

"Intrinsic change of conduct has been slight. Some apparent improvement took place, evidently the result of personal effort on the part of the prisoners who were intelligent enough to appreciate what was being done in their behalf. The experiment was closed on the first of August, 1899, having been in operation for seven months, as 'impracticable under the *present conditions*.'

"Although the foregoing experiments were not very satisfactory or conclusive, still I am led to venture the opinion that no material lasting deviation in the character of the adult can be induced by special feeding except in so far as it operates through the general health. The feeble organism may be whipped up by stimulants and its capacity increased; but it is exercise which modifies the habit of functioning. It seems to me that the ideal prison dietary ends its work when it has inexpensively brought the prisoner into the state of health which will best enable him to withstand disease and maintain constant and intense activity of the functions along normal lines."

Doctor Elliott, the conductor of this dietary experiment, and each of the directors of other departmental reformative agencies, naturally esteemed his own particular province to be of pivotal interest. This attitude gave efficiency to their efforts, and when the general management directed all these divisions into harmonious action, the entire reformatory scheme reached its best effectiveness. The importance of a scientifically arranged dietary as an aid to rational reformation of degenerate criminals is emphasized by Doctor Elliott's concluding remark, that it can produce sustained *"activity of the functions along normal lines."* It is regrettable that the experiment was necessarily discontinued.

During this year, 1899, the manual training department was also discontinued. This was done at the instigation of one man against the mild protest, at first, of the other newly appointed managers, though with their ultimate acquiescence, and in utter disregard of the views of the older members of the board. The pretext for discontinuing the manual training school was a trifling fault of Professor Bates, the remarkably efficient director, a fault not germane to his general usefulness.

In November, Mr. Ansley Wilcox, the manager appointed shortly before from Buffalo, resigned his office. In December, Manager M. H. Arnot, who for so many years had rendered most valuable service, a high-spirited man who would not brook the new régime, refused to attend the monthly meetings, and resigned. Henry G. Danforth, the other new appointee from Rochester, also withdrew from the board early in 1900.

The board of managers as constituted anew from time to time enacted inhibitive measures which produced between the board and myself an open breach. When, after a while, the preposterous suggestion was made that the standard of reformatory requirement be lowered, that the fine swift movement of affairs be slackened, I could not consent to the proposition nor permit myself to participate in the proposed change to a superficial, and therefore less effectual, administration of the reformatory work of this expensively supported state public institution. The consequence was that the already strained relations reached the rupture which resulted in my resignation and withdrawal from the reformatory management in July, 1900. The inconsistency of the new notions and actions in relation to the proper reformatory discipline, will appear from the following recital of what had actually taken place under the inhibitions instituted.

Instead of the former and proper remedial coercion of certain insusceptible, therefore unamenable, prisoners, since the use of coercion was interdicted, and they could not, or would not, adjust themselves to the established standard of requirements, they were necessarily withdrawn from the usual associated contact. Each prisoner so withdrawn was left to himself in his ordinary cell situated in a division of the general corridor. He was limited to two instead of three full rations a day. These prisoners in solitary confinement were not at first supplied with reading matter nor with any means of occupying themselves, and they did not *permissively* converse from room to room. They were not under punishment but simply relegated to idleness apart from the crowd, analogous to their detrusion from the community by their imprisonment.

The number of prisoners thus separated gradually increased until after a few months a round hundred of them were withdrawn and so situated. They occupied the rooms on an upper gallery of the general corridor overlooking from the windows on one side the interior yard inclosure, surrounded by the school and factory buildings with the stir of activities within them; the yard where the awkward squad was drilled and where, at evening time, the regimental dress parade with its band and banners was held. Through the windows on the opposite side of the corridors the beautiful landscape of charming valley, the moving railway trains and the highway traffic were in full view; and occasionally from the public recreation park came pleasing strains of instrumental and even vocal music. No wonder that the entire release from all effort and the entertaining prospect kept the number large. But note the additional inducements.

Soon the physician reported that these secluded prisoners appeared to be but insufficiently nourished and immediately the three full prison rations were supplied them. Then the doctor became solicitous about incipient scurvy, when at once they were furnished with fruits in addition to abundance of fresh vegetables. Apparent deterioration continued and was attributed to famishment of mind, which was sought to be remedied by supplying pictorial papers and sensational novels suited to interest such low and perverted minds. To cap all, it was thought necessary in order to check the apparent growing decadence, that these men should have a daily airing which was provided by an hour a day of leisurely promenade in the open attractive park or garden situated within the sixteen acres of the inclosure.

The result of this new policy was that the intractable men of the prison population were not subjected to the improving means and processes of the reformatory régime. They were not only relieved from all work and educational effort, but they were supplied with an extra diet, with sensational reading matter, and were privileged to saunter in the flower bedecked grounds lined with graveled walks and to enjoy their shady nooks. These recalcitrant prisoners after their abundant meal of excellent food and fruits; after the pleasant outing in the park and the after snooze; could, stretched upon their cots, peruse the literature supplied them, enjoy the cool breeze through the open windows and slatted doors, the while contemptuously regarding the better men who in the buildings beyond were striving to improve themselves in preparation for their honorable discharge and intended corrected career. It was bad enough to surrender these men to their own destructive devices, yet as a choice of evils, it was preferable to the alternative of lowering the entire régime for all the inmates to the level of this lowest element of the prison population.

But ere long the hundred seriously disturbed the quiet and progress of the mass. Protected as they were from all coercive measures these men soon grew tired of the quiet of their isolated room life and, though against the regulations, openly conversed from room to room. The talk was mostly bawdy and profane. It grew boisterous and was interspersed with ribald songs.

The disturbers were then removed to a remote division of the cells where their behavior disturbed the other inmates less, but could be heard by neighbors living near the institution. This had the tendency to lower the tone and reputation of the reformatory, both within and without the inclosure, from that of an orderly and useful educational and reforming establishment to the level of a common jail and abode of bawdry.

That the evil tendency of this policy and attendant disorder were so well resisted by the orderly men, that the contagion of it was confined to so small a contingent of the large population of prisoners, is surprising and is, of course, a gratifying recollection. Like the appeal to the good sense of the bulk of the men at the very commencement of the first investigation — that remarkable transaction of the September evening in the auditorium with all the prisoners and the investigators — it was another severe and successful test and proof of the prevailing powerful moral control exercised: and it gives clear evidence of the efficacious influence of the then existing momentum of affairs.

After my retirement in July, 1900, my immediate successor, who in important respects was unsuited for such a service, ventured on no intentional innovation during the three years of his superintendency; but it was soon evident that good pivotal regulation was lacking. He was wise enough to resign his office in time to save himself and the reformatory the injury of threatened hostile public criticism.

The appointment in 1903 of Joseph F. Scott, for many years superintendent of the Massachusetts reformatory for men, a man of high character, good capabilities, and large experience, undoubtedly saved the reformatory from impending collapse. A binding force which supplemented Mr. Scott's management was the military organization established about the year 1888, kept up by the salutary martinetism of Mr. Maston, the military instructor.

In June, 1911, Governor Dix appointed Mr. Scott to the office of superintendent of state prisons with his office at Albany. Mr. Scott was succeeded as superintendent of the reformatory by Mr. Patrick J. McDonnell, who since July, 1900, had been assistant superintendent.

Not only has there been a change in methods of administration but in the inmates as well. The present and prospective need of wiser, therefore more effective, reformatory treatment of imprisoned criminals is suggested by the more criminous character of the prisoners in confinement. The prevalent complacency about crimes and tenderness towards accused offenders; the lenient, loose, and inconclusive court practice in criminal trials; together with the operation of the probation and parole laws, leave at large the less criminous of the offenders, imprisoning only the very defective and more difficult. The type of reformatory prison to be required, therefore, is less that of a reform school for juvenile, venial, and accidental derelicts, and more a scientific training place for degenerate adults. It may be feared that unless the reformatories for adult male felons meet this need more effectively and supply surer protection to the public against fresh crimes committed by men discharged from the reformatories, the costliness and comparative uselessness of these establishments will lead to their abandonment and to the

374

ultimate return to the former punitive penitentiary system.

My opinion of the principles and procedure of such a reformatory as will fairly meet the newer need is presented in my article prepared for and published in the souvenir volumes which were presented to the foreign delegates at the International Prison Congress of 1910.*

I now offer the following synopsis or concise restatement of this newer point of view:

The common notion of a moral responsibility based on freedom should no longer be made a foundation principle for criminal laws, court procedure, and prison treatment. The claim of such responsibility need neither be denied nor affirmed, but put aside as being out of place in a system of treatment of offenders for the purpose of public protection. Together with abrogation of this responsibility goes, too, any awesome regard for individual liberty of choice and action by imprisoned criminals. Their habitual conduct and indeed their related character must needs be directed and really determined by their legalized custodians.

While yet because of much nescious common opinion about it, some regard for alleged equity remains, the administration of justice is no longer the aim of imprisonment. Requital of goods or evils, so-called, becomes but incidental to welfare; temporary wellbeing is made subservient to the larger and more permanent benefits. The individual self-interest of each prisoner is considered to be merged in the communal or collective good.

Reformations formerly sought to be accomplished

---

* The American Reformatory Prison System. By Z. R. Brockway. (Page 88 of Prison Reform and Criminal Law.) Correction and Prevention series. Russell Sage Foundation Publication. New York, Charities Publication Committee, 1910.

by means of the direct appeal to the mind and emotions; instantaneous permanent change of proclivity, magically wrought responsive to ministerial influence, now are held to consist in increase of active powers, improved habitudes with consequent change of tastes and choices. It is estimated to be a gradual, natural, and preferably an unconscious, change of character, induced by use of desirable and disuse of objectionable mental and bodily engagement. Exactitude of performance and the persistence which this rational procedure requires, go beyond common satisfactory orderliness, to minute matters of the common life. Managing, then, means complete repression on the one hand and effective arousing on the other. The waiting, shirking, superstitious managing attitude is necessarily replaced with awakened interested endeavor, using scientific research and methods — it is the faith that is made perfect in works. The perfected reformatory will be the receptacle and refinery of anti-social humans who are held in custody under discretional indeterminateness for the purpose of the public protection. Legal and sentimental inhibitions of necessary coercion for the obdurate, intractable element of the institution population will be removed and freedom given for the wise use of unimpassioned useful forceful measures. Frequent relapses to crime of prisoners discharged from these reformatories will be visited upon the management as are penalties for official malfeasance. The change will be, in short, a change from the reign of sentiment swerved by the feelings to a passionless scientific procedure pursuing welfare.*

---

* Extracts, including forms of procedure, from the paper here referred to, will be found in Appendix IV, p. 419.

The Author's Study in His Elmira Home

CHAPTER XXIII

AFTERWARDS

AS RELATES TO MYSELF

ON leaving the reformatory Mrs. Brockway and I removed to our house in Elmira, where we have since lived with our widowed daughter, Mrs. Blossom and her children. The change from the superintendent's house at the reformatory, which we had occupied for about twenty-five years, the severance from our familiar apartments, was of course a little disquieting; and the complete surrender of what had been and was essentially the formative work of my own hands and heart, was an impressive experience — but neither is worth mentioning. But the sudden let-go of the lifelong tension incidental to responsibilities and duties — the absolute cessation of all demand upon my time and energy — could but be a trying personal experience. Happily I was delivered from the untoward effects, indeed from the common calamitous effects both to body and mind of such a transition in the experience of men of my age, by several engagements which quite unplanned, and entirely unsolicited, soon came to me,— requests to discourse on penological topics, to examine and report on the condition of jails, and after a time two years' engagement in the duties of the mayoralty of Elmira.

377

I venture to mention particularly some of the engagements that served so well to prevent injury from harmful ennui. The lively local interest in the reformatory and in my retirement therefrom brought out a very large audience at the Park Church on the annual Prison Sunday, which that year was on October 28, to hear my address on Crimes and Punishment. There is little likelihood that the exceptionally large audience on that occasion was attracted either by interest in the topic or in myself; but after the turmoils and the infelicities of the administration of the reformatory, there was doubtless public expectation that my address would contain reference to what had occurred. All such reference was carefully avoided; and while the crowded assembly sat patiently through the hour of my address, and though the newspaper notices were commendatory of it, no doubt the bulk of the audience was disappointed not to hear the denunciations that were expected. The following January (1901) I went to Boston, Massachusetts, on the invitation of the Twentieth Century Club, and met in the afternoon the Society of Municipal Officers for discourse about misdemeanant offenders and their treatment. The evening of the same day, in the Tremont Temple, before the members of the Twentieth Century Club and friends, the Massachusetts Prison Association, and the Associated Charities — a large audience — I made an address on The Prison of the Present and of the Future. The same subject was presented the next day to the undergraduates of Brown University at Providence, Rhode Island, and some time later to Professor Lounsbury's students of the Sheffield School of Yale University at New Haven, Connecticut. In April and May, the same year, at the request of Professor Jenks, I gave five lectures about prisons and prisoners before his political science classes at Cornell University at Ithaca. In the autumn after, I gave three lectures at the theological school at Meadville, Pennsylvania. I attended the annual congress of the American Prison Association at Kansas City, Missouri, in November; spent two days at the State Charities and Correction convention at Topeka, Kansas; and visited three days with Major R. W. McClaughry, superintendent of the United States Penitentiary at Fort Leavenworth, Kansas. Journeying homewards I spent a week in Indiana visiting, with Amos W. Butler, secretary of the Indiana State Board of Charities, the charitable and correctional institutions of that state, and incidentally, the Butler and Bloomington Universities; and finished the tour of the state at the Jeffersonville Reformatory as the guest of Superintendent Hert on a Sunday which particularly remains in my memory as a most delightful occasion.

These things served to carry me safely into the year 1902. Depression of relaxation was overcome. In the winter of that year, I had requests to which I gladly responded for addresses under the auspices of literary and men's church clubs. I also made notes for this narrative. The monotony of the remainder of the year 1902 was relieved by the service gratuitously rendered to the Prison Association of New York, in inspecting a number of jails and penitentiaries located in the central and western part of the state, and formulating special reports thereon, together with observations and conclusions of a more general character relating to the jail and penitentiary

379

system of the state. These reports are published entire in the fifty-eighth (1904) annual report of the Prison Association of New York to the legislature.

The trying crisis of a sudden disengagement of the mind from the absorbing occupation of a lifetime, was avoided for a while by the request from Samuel J. Barrows, the commissioner for the United States on the International Prison Commission, to prepare for the proposed discussion at the Seventh International Prison Congress, held in September, 1905, at Budapest, Hungary, a paper on the Best Means of Securing the Moral Classification of Prisoners. The monograph was translated into French by Mr. Barrows and in that language published in the proceedings of the congress, and again in English in the report of the commissioner, and in the sixtieth annual report of the Prison Association of New York. Fortunately, too, for the diversion of my mind, I was in 1902 made a member and in 1903 and since, president of the board of managers of the Arnot-Ogden Memorial Hospital. The connection accords with the desire I have long felt to be of some service to the suffering sick; and it supplies a new associative interest. Notwithstanding such fugitive and isolated engagements during the five years of my retirement, I was in 1905 quite conscious of the reactionary effect of diminished personal vitality. But any serious permanent loss was averted by my election in November to the mayoralty of the city. The duties and activities incident to the office, a two years' term, greatly revived my energies. Like the other relieving engagements this office came unsought. The political episode is so unique in my life and the partisan hypocrisy is so plain that the story should here be told.

I consented to become the fusion candidate for mayor at the solicitation of the two men who locally controlled the two principal political parties. I was not selected as the fusion candidate because of any supposed particular personal popularity nor for any previous political activity, but rather because of my habitual political inactivity and independence of any partisan relation; and perhaps because of my supposed fitness to confront a municipal condition then the result of political partisanship and perhaps inadequate management.

That year was the time, and the fusion movement the occasion, of the famed "Elmira Compact" — the signed solemn agreement of the principal leaders of both parties to faithfully restrict the use of money in the elections to the bare necessities of proper expenditures, and thus endeavor in all good faith and earnestness to purify local politics. The sequel casts doubt on the moral sincerity of the compact, for it was only transitorily adhered to. It is said and is probably true, that during the campaign when at one time it seemed possible that the opposing candidate of a third party endangered the success of the fusion movement, the leaders who had signed the compact held a conference and seriously considered whether it was not advisable to use money with "floaters" as usual. Since the compact was ostensibly, at least, for moral benefit, the conference presented the anomaly of proposing to buy votes in order to confirm prohibition in that respect. The only reason the proposal was not adopted was that assurance was had that the fusion movement would succeed without it.

In reality the total controlling motive was the desire of both parties to side-step and unload on a reform administration the onus and involved unpopularity of the necessary increase of taxation and friction of "cleaning up" after their faulty partisan management, and then, after a two years' period of unpopular reform, to resume the usual exploitation of municipal affairs for their personal or partisan advantage. The return to power of partisan government in 1907, accomplished as intended, was by means of electioneering methods not only disregardful of the compact, which never since has been observed, but by the usual misrepresentations, trickery, and humiliating personal soliciting of votes, — means which the fusionists did not adopt, for they scorned to use them. The fusionists made no active campaign and would have been retained in power except, as the returns show, for the vote in the floater wards. The partisan candidates even ventured to put forward as an argument for their return to office, the increased tax rate of the first year of the fusion control which was made necessary by partisan management!

The public benefits believed to have been derived during the two years of my service as mayor are generally recognized to be substantially as follows:

The improperly accumulated floating debt was liquidated; city bonds that fell due were paid, not refunded; the bonded debt was slightly reduced, notwithstanding the issue of $55,000 of new bonds for the Lake Street Bridge; an improved system for collecting delinquent taxes was initiated; pending damage suits were tried and disposed of; exorbitant demands of the Utilities Monopoly Company for water and gas and electric light supplies were vetoed, but by the usual control of the councilmen were carried over the veto; the pay of the rank and file of policemen and firemen was increased; systematic inspection and sanitation of the contiguous milk-supply dairies were instituted; 130 miles of streets and 69 miles of sidewalks were improved or built; the parks and parkway trees were renovated and defects treated; a new river bridge was built at Lake Street, the others were repaired, and the usual stretch of sewers was laid, etc., etc.

The city charter was revised, collated and published, the number of the council being changed from twenty-four to twelve men; biennial instead of annual city elections were established; the governing commissions were reduced from five to three members each; the granting of franchises was guarded and perpetual franchises prohibited; overdraft by the commissions was made a misdemeanor offense as against the commissioners; and the mayor's veto power was again restored. The poor department was reorganized; outdoor relief from public funds prohibited; a municipal loan association established; and other minor yet not unimportant improvements in the organization and personnel were effected. In this connection I venture to add, justified by the prevalence of the general impression publicly proclaimed, and frankly avowed by an intimate attaché of the succeeding partisan mayor, that a certain salutary, but to the partisans a troublesome tone was carried over and remains.

To myself, personally, the official term of office was beneficial in increase of vital energy and so probably in the duration of my life; and incidentally it was gratifying as a rebuke to the erstwhile newspaper attacks and the proceedings of the reformatory investigation towards myself; and it was a pleasing after expression of local neighborly respect and regard.

The revived vitality derived during the mayoralty was preserved through 1908 and 1909 by the natural persistence of interest in public affairs aroused by my official service; by new and necessary attention to arranging for a final disposal of some personal affairs; and devotion to the home life to which my wife from habit and preference chiefly confined herself. Our evening hours, after taking up our residence in the city, were uniformly spent together with books and reading aloud to each other. It is now a source of painful remembrance that during our twenty-five years at the reformatory — owing to the extreme occupation of my time both days and evenings — I did not devote myself to her pleasure as much as I ought to have done.

Early in 1910 the trend of the preparations for the quinquennial International Prison Congress to be held in the fall of that year in the United States of America attracted me, and as the year progressed, more and more engaged my attention. Knowing that I did not possess the necessary qualifications for the active presidency, and feeling physically unequal to the demands of preparation for the congress, I asked that my name be not mentioned for the presidency, as friends told me was intended. Gladly, however, I promised to prepare for the souvenir volumes for the foreign delegates the article on the principles of the American reformatory prison system previously mentioned, and another, a thesis on prevention of crimes,

ZEBULON R. BROCKWAY, 1911

one of the topics set for the discussion of the congress. The preparation of these papers, correspondence and casual conferences relating to the congress; the anticipation of meeting foreign officials and authors who, by their writings or by interchange of letters, were already pleasantly known to me; together with the knowledge that the official international prison commissioners had already, at their preparatory conference at Paris, designated me as the honorary president of the congress,—all these together contributed to the swift and agreeable passage of the time until in the autumn the foreign delegates actually arrived in New York, and came on to visit the reformatory at Elmira. They afterwards toured the eastern and middle states in their special train as guests of the United States, and then on the first of October convened at Washington, D. C. My attendance at Washington at the closing session of the American National Congress, with the renewal of fellowship and cordial greetings with longtime acquaintances; my attendance on the opening session of the International Congress, and the honor of being elected the honorary president thereof, seemed to finish, not inappropriately, my career in its connection with prisons and the prison reform movement. For at this meeting the International Congress endorsed and adopted, for the first time, resolutions approving of the indeterminate sentence.*

On leaving Washington, accompanied by my daughter Caroline — Mrs. Butler — I proceeded to Hadlyme, Connecticut, my childhood home, where for the nine years previous I had not been. The death there in the April preceding our visit, of my sister Mary; the

---

* See Appendix III, p. 417.

disposal to Mr. Seymour of the parental homestead, the farewell to my sister, Mrs. Comstock, eighty-six years old, and an afternoon at Wethersfield, where in my youth I was clerk of the state prison (the commencement of my service in prisons), and where my wife, Jane Woodhouse, was born and lived until our marriage, seemed fittingly to supplement the termination of my prison career. It closed, or rounded out, my family connection there, by severing the strong bonds which attached me to the place of my nativity and by the probably final separation from my aged sister.

The weeks after our return to Elmira in October sped on winged feet until February 8, 1911, when suddenly came the calamity that must irrevocably overshadow the remainder of my existence: the death of my wife.

At this writing, March 13, 1912, the eighty-fifth anniversary of the birth of my lifelong companion, I am indeed bereft and sorrowfully tarrying to meet my own last summons.

APPENDICES

APPENDIX I

THE IDEAL OF A TRUE PRISON SYSTEM FOR A STATE*

PRACTICAL reforms come from actual contact with the classes considered. A prison system devised by the philosopher, may or may not be practicable; but a system drawn from experience is likely to be true; and such is the ideal I wish to evolve.

The prison system of a state should partake of the *same spirit* of the other parts. The true interests of the individual are always identical with those of society. Whatever may be his character or conduct, this remains ever true. Disregard of this principle is sure to bring disaster. Legalized degradation of any criminal inflicts injury upon the whole social organism, while efforts for the highest and best welfare of any person promote the general good.

Not only should there be unity of spirit in the general government and the prison system of the state, but *identity of aim*. The central aim of a true prison system is the protection of society against crime, not the punishment of the criminal. Punishment, the instrument, protection, the object; and since it is clear that there can be no real protection against crime without preventing it, *prevention* must be placed fundamentally in the principles of a true prison system.

---

*Condensed from the paper of the same title delivered before the National Prison Congress held at Cincinnati in 1870. The views in this paper as relate to self-support of prisons by the prisoners' labor, and the estimate expressed as to systems of employment of prisoners, were by the law of 1888 in New York, and experience at the Elmira Reformatory, considerably changed.—AUTHOR.

The causes of crime are primarily in the person; secondarily in the circumstances that surround him. The science of man forms the foundation of all systems for his government. A true prison system, therefore, should take cognizance of criminal classes as such, to bring to bear such forces as may modify the common character, thus diminishing the tendency to crime. Not only does there devolve upon the department of criminal administration the gathering and arrangement of social statistics that bear upon crime, but the duty of generalizing them. No sound prison system can be devised until examination is had of antecedent social phenomena.

The current opinion as to crime is twofold: That all men are absolutely free to do or not to do; that they voluntarily elect and deliberately do wickedness, or, at least, that all men are *born* free, and if the chains of captivity now bind them, it is by their own folly and free act; that they might have prevented it, and if suffering comes as a consequence, it is but just; and that, if crime is committed, the public punishment should be such as to recompense them fully in anguish and pain for their wickedness, and strike with terror those who know of their fate.

On the other hand it is maintained that our individual liberty of action is limited by the bias with which we are born, or by that arising from the circumstances of our early life (both beyond our control); that the quality of the physical organism, as well as the condition of health, at any given time, influences our impulses and desires, and bears upon the possibility or impossibility of self-control; that election itself is determined in great degree by the natural tastes and those that come by cultivation and habit, without our special volition; that any line of human conduct, good or bad, is governed much by the balance of power in the will or passions; that society should not punish the criminal, but impose upon him such restraint and treatment as shall secure protection to itself, and conduce to the further and higher development of the wrong-doer himself.

The advocates of this latter view hold that vengeance has no place in a true prison system. Nor should punishment, they maintain, be inflicted on the perpetrators of crime that others may be deterred from a similar course, for this is unjust, and breeds antagonism to the law and its executors. They further affirm that, in the history of jurisprudence, the deterrent force of punishment is found practically a failure for the purpose in view. Nevertheless, they demand the most thorough treatment of criminals. They espouse no sickly sentimentalism. They are not mere popular philanthropists, but urge upon society the obligation to treat the great company (of criminals) constantly coming to the surface *in such a manner that they shall either be cured, or kept under such continued restraint as gives guarantee of safety from further depredations.*

There is a wide difference in these two views of crime; a difference so wide that every prison system must be founded on one or the other of them, and not by any possibility upon both; for a system, so founded, would be divided against itself, and could not stand. If punishment, suffering, degradation, are deemed deterrent, if they are the best means to reform the criminal and prevent crime, then let prison reform go backward to the pillory, the whipping post, the gallows, the stake; to corporal violence and extermination! But if the dawn of Christianity has reached us, if we have learned the lesson that *evil is to be overcome with good*, then let prisons and prison systems be lighted by this law of love. Let us leave for the present, the thought of inflicting punishment upon prisoners to satisfy so-called justice, and turn toward the real objects of the system, viz: *the protection of society by the prevention of crime and reformation of criminals.*

Crime cannot entirely cease until we have a perfect society, but crime may be diminished by the progress of civilization, which, within the sphere of our influence, we may help or hinder. The throng of European emigrants coming annually to our shores, seems to have something to do with the volume of crime in our own country and may be regulated so as to secure a more rapid and sure absorption of immigrants among the native population; and something may be done to distribute the dependent and dangerous classes, thus doing away with many incitements to crime. The large proportion of criminals living out of the family relation suggests the thought of some governmental control of marriage, to make it honourable and desirable for the poorer classes, and to prevent such unions as necessarily propagate disease and dangerous tendencies; also to require and maintain suitable sanitary conditions for the growth of a healthy people, with pure impulses. The latter seems more possible, from the fact that so large a majority of criminals are under thirty years of age, and therefore susceptible of improvement as a class. The labor question, in its numerous ramifications, bears directly upon crime. The prevention of crime seems to involve the necessity for better compensation and better facilities for education.

So, too, it would seem a hopeless task to try to prevent crime without regulating and restraining the vending of intoxicating liquors, when it is shown that 82 per cent of criminals admit themselves to be intemperate. The department of prevention also involves the compulsory education in common schools of those children now excluded by incorrigibility or indifference, and the neglect or disregard of parents and guardians; also of the children and youth in jails, almshouses, and dependent families, who are wholly or in part the wards of the state, for here are found the seeds of much degradation, and the source of much criminality. The iniquitous common jail system must be stricken from the face of society, and some safe place be provided in each county for the isolated imprisonment of alleged criminals before trial, and also district industrial reformatories for the treatment of those convicted of misdemeanors.

The prevention of crime involves a change of public sentiment as to these matters. There must be such an advance of civilization, such virtue and intelligence in the state, that its chief officers, the legislature, and its courts, shall have real regard for society. The influence of society at large and of the government must be enlisted in aid of efforts to interpose barriers to the growth of crime, preventing, so far as possible, the crop of criminals now gathered as a harvest with every returning court session and restraining, educating, refining, reforming such as sift through these preventive means, and come into prison establishments for cure.

The term *reformation*, as here used, has reference to that "correction or amendment of life and manners" that makes those who were obnoxious and troublesome, tolerable, acceptable, or useful citizens. This, society may undoubtedly secure by force, if necessary. The so-called liberty of the citizen may be legitimately restricted; but society may not attempt the forcible adjustment of individual interior relations to the Divine Being nor impose any particular religious system. The change sought in the character of criminals, called reformation, is of a practical nature, and has to do with daily life in ordinary social relations. No particular importance is attached to the welling up of the emotions at particular times, those spasmodic impulses poured forth in passionate utterance from fickle hearts and foolish tongues. All this is but a poor antidote for evil propensities inborn, imbued, or inbreathed from the atmosphere of a lifetime.

Reformation involves such change in the constitutional tendencies, that the impulses and desires are revolutionized and become permanent, with their preponderance decidedly to the right. It involves such added power of self-control as gives always free choice when the mind is drawn by mixed motives; and it involves such favorable situation in society, when restored to it, as shall strengthen the good, and not excite the evil within by a temptation greater than can be borne.

The ideal prison system which I would delineate has three departments, viz: (1) organization; (2) legislation; and (3) administration.

393

The organization may be considered under two heads: (1) the executive force, the governing power, the centralized head; and (2) the institutions and instruments through which it is to act upon society and the criminal.

The title of the organization which is usually board of charities, while preferable to that of prison commissioners or commissioners of correction, is still objectionable; and the term prison should be stricken from our statutes. The language in which the public laws are expressed, the name given to officers and institutions, modifies the idea conveyed and shapes public sentiment. To put into society prisons for the punishment of any class stirs up a spirit of opposition. The true attitude of government is that of guardian; its true function to shelter, shield, help, heal. Therefore I propose the title *board of guardians* for the commissioners who shall control criminal treatment, as well as the direct charities of the state.

The appointment of the board should rest with the governor with the advice and consent of the senate. The term of appointment should be long enough to make the position a permanent one in the esteem of the appointees, and thus to deeply interest and thoroughly educate them and to make available for the state their ripe culture and experience; say from five to ten years.

The right composition of the board is difficult, from the fact that there is little available material from which to select; but when the dignity and importance of the duties are better understood, it is believed the high demand will naturally develop the needed supply. It is a glory of our time that strong men, with sound minds are throwing their plummet with flowing line into the dark depths of society, and are presenting plans for improvement. These men, intelligent, enterprising, ingenious, already interested in the science of society, are to be found in every state, will be multiplied as time goes on, and will form the class from which these boards should be selected. It is desirable that there should be upon the board a physician, an educator, a judge well versed in moral as well as legal science, a mechanic, a manufacturer, a merchant or financier, an editor or man of letters, a man specially distinguished for his "common sense" and independence of character, a matronly mother, of sound sense, and a woman zealous for the rights of her sex — making altogether the number of 10, which is given as the maximum.

These should serve without pay, except for their necessary expenses; for, unless citizens can be found who will give their lives for the good of society and devote themselves freely to the guidance of such interests without compensation, they cannot be found at all. Such men will not sell their services for pelf. Such a board should be literally loaded with power; it is only thus that the position can attain sufficient dignity to secure the gratuitous services of good and great men, and can thoroughly enlist the life interest of noble souls; only thus can they obtain the freedom and independence of action necessary to meet promptly and decidedly the exigencies that will be ever arising in this department of state administration. They should be held to a rigid accountability by the state legislature and the public; the growth of crime should be deemed a disgrace to them; and, after suitable changes are made in the criminal law, the frequent recommittals of the same persons for crime should be their sentence of condemnation.

Their attention should, in a general way, be directed to sanitary regulations for the state at large, for here is found a germ of that physical and mental degradation which gives rise to vicious desires and ungovernable impulses; to compulsory education of indigent or indifferent children and youth, for, by this, much evil may be counteracted; to the encouragement, inspection and general supervision of individual and independent enterprises for the care of all classes of unfortunate and dependent people, which when systematized and rightly directed, will prove an important preventive agency; to the dissemination of much needed information, by publications and addresses, as to the causes that produce, and the means to prevent, poverty and crime; also to direct the ministerial police of the state for the suppression of all public practices and institutions existing in violation of law, which bear directly as causes upon these dark social problems.

This board must have full power, (1) to appoint, to remove for cause, and to affix the amount of compensation of any and all officers in the employ of the state in this department, except sheriffs and those whose duty and authority are of mixed criminal and civil jurisdiction; but so far as such officers have control of criminals and paupers, they should be subject to the board; (2) power to create, annul, alter or amend all rules and regulations for the government and the general and particular management of such establishment and officers; (3) power to transfer at will any ward or criminal from one institution to another, if such transfer be deemed better for his treatment; to release, temporarily or absolutely, reformed persons; and to re-arrest and return to treatment such as relapse into vicious or criminal practices, of a public nature.

The relation of the board to these establishments should be like that of shipowners to captain and crew. They should shape the policy to be pursued, leaving their executive officer to carry into effect their own particular plans; the former supervising, reporting and recommending modifications and measures; and the latter being required to carry out the plans practically, and to *achieve success* as the condition of continued official position. For this purpose the executive should have the selection of his assistants, and power to dismiss them at pleasure.

The institutions and instruments through which the purposes of the board of guardians may be realized are:

(1) *A state police or constabulary* with power to direct the sheriff, or deputy sheriff, in each county, for their particular work, which is an easy and economical way of affording them indispensable aid.

(2) *Primary schools* for the education of the children from the alms-houses, who are three years of age and upward, away from the contamination and taint of these miserable places, where they shall be fed, clothed, and trained for good citizens, instead of criminals as now; also *schools of a compulsory character* in large cities and towns, for the control and culture of the incorrigible, who are now expelled from the public schools or brutalized by corporal punishment.

(3) *Reform Schools* for juveniles, older and more advanced in wrong development.

(4) *District reformatories* for the treatment of those who are now confined in jails for misdemeanors; reformatories in which persons living vicious lives, when arrested and convicted, may be cured, and thus saved from a life of crime. The whole vile system of common jails for the imprisonment of convicted persons must be uprooted and blotted from existence, and the structures for detaining alleged offenders be made suitable in all respects for the custody of witnesses, with large, well-lighted, cheerful apartments, strong and secure against escapes, entirely isolating their occupants from each other. Solitary abode for all in common jails should be invariably enforced. The treatment of early offenders, who almost always commit misdemeanors before felonies, is entitled to much greater prominence than it now has in any prison system in the world. As a rule, the inmates of municipal prisons are only in the edge of the maelstrom, while the inmates of the state prisons unreformed, as too many of them are, usually plunge at once into dissipation and become "disorderly persons" whose prompt arrest and treatment would save them and society from the effect of fresh felonies. These intermediate or district reformatories may, therefore, form a part of

(5) *A Graduated Series of Reformatory Institutions for Adults.* These should consist of three grades:

(a) *The House of Reception.*— Here all prisoners should be received and retained, until reliable information is obtained as to their ancestral history, their constitutional tendencies and propensities, their early social condition and its probable influence in forming their character; and until, with this aid, an examination is had and a careful estimate made of their physical, mental, and moral condition, upon which basis a plan of treatment may be outlined. Here the incorrigible must be detained in solitary or safe custody, and experimental treatment applied to all, for the purpose of finding those who can be properly transferred to the next grade.

(b) *The Industrial Reformatory.*— The special office of this grade is to cultivate the germinal faculties of the intellect and the moral nature, discerned during their stay in the house of reception. Prisoners coming into this institution with good physical health will be here so trained to labor as to insure their productive employment thereafter, and their perseverance and self command will be developed and subjected to appropriate tests. Such of the prisoners as thrive under this training may be removed, with great hope and confident security, to the last of the series for male prisoners, viz:

(c) *The Intermediate Reformatory.*— This grade of establishments may be supplied from present municipal prisons or district penitentiaries, or otherwise provided. Their location should be in the interior part of the state, near some populous town, and, if possible, near some good educational institution. Their construction should embrace a large enclosure, secure in and of itself, and sufficiently removed from apartments where most of the time is spent, to obviate the evil effect of an ever-present and observable physical restraint. This enclosure should contain dormitories, affording to each prisoner a separate room, such as a respectable citizen might occupy; a dining hall, upon the plan of a well regulated restaurant for work people, where, within due limits, any desired edible may be supplied; a library building and public hall, suitable for reading rooms, religious services, scientific and other intellectual exercises of a public nature;

suitable industrial apartments for the branches of mechanical business carried on, which with limited agricultural employment, may constitute the productive industrial occupation of the residents; the whole to be organized substantially upon the co-operative plan.

(6) *Separate Reformatories for Women* are also necessary. These should be under the immediate management of women, and that exclusively. The movement in this direction in Massachusetts and Indiana is worthy of all praise. Wayward women must be won to virtue by their own sex, if they are won at all. Build homes for these, 80 per cent of whom "are what they are through no fault of theirs"; cultivate their natural love for home life; furnish with womanly affection; fit them to earn an honest and sufficient support; find them employment and a friend; follow them with friendly acts and faithful guardianship, and fear not for their future. Full 50 per cent of them (possibly more) may be reformed, when full control, for an indeterminate time, is vested in a suitable board of guardians, and the family system supplants prison houses for females.

The success of the prison system through these institutions will be governed much by the efficiency and intelligence of the state police or agents of the board, to be located in each county; for, the supervision of prisoners discharged conditionally will devolve upon them, and the duty of rendering regular reports of their character and conduct, until absolute release is ordered; also to re-arrest and return to custody such as slip through unworthily, as it is expected some will do.

The department of *legislation*, like that of organization, is capable of dual division, relating (1) to laws for the government of the board itself; and (2) to laws providing for the control and culture of the class from which criminals spring and to all establishments for the custody of criminals, and to laws conferring such custody.

Criminals committed to prison naturally entertain much antagonism to the laws and towards their custodians; and this feeling forms the first and very formidable obstacle to their reformation.

The remedy cannot be had, the public sentiment toward the law cannot be changed, so long as a *determinate* sentence is imposed at the time of trial. The sentence of imprisonment must, of necessity, affect the mind of the prisoner, as too short and trivial, too long and tyrannical, or just adequate to the offense. If the sentence is too light, prisoners are stimulated to deserve a heavier one, that they may be esteemed more daring. If the sentence is too long, they often feel complimented by the importance thus conferred upon them as great criminals, until imprisonment is once entered upon, when they become vindictive toward all in any way connected with their arrest, trial, and custody, and finally fall into apathy and discouragement. If perchance the prisoner's views should be precisely met, and his inward sense approve the penalty, this pernicious effect is produced: he lives with a mistaken idea that he is paying the penalty — expiating his offense; like the others, he counts the days as they go; and, when released, he re-enters society, as he conceives, exactly as when he left it, having, in his own estimation, paid up and put himself right with the community.

Another active cause of crime is the release annually of hundreds of prisoners in every state, who are unreformed by their imprisonment, which must always be the case under the present system of sentences. No man, be he judge, lawyer, or layman, can determine beforehand the date when imprisonment shall work reformation in any case, and it is an outrage upon society to return to the privileges of citizenship those who have proved themselves dangerous and bad by the commission of crime, until a cure is wrought and reformation reached. Such minimum of restraint must be retained as will protect the people from their pernicious influence; and this will be likely to prove more powerfully deterrent upon criminals and the criminal class, than would all the severities of the inquisition. Therefore, as for the other reasons suggested, sentences should not be determinate but *indeterminate*. By this is meant (to state briefly) *that all persons in a state, who are convicted of crimes or offenses before a competent court, shall be deemed wards of the state and shall be committed to the custody of the board of guardians, until, in their judgment, they may be returned to society with ordinary safety and in accord with their own highest welfare.* Of course this board will have control of all the preventive and reformatory agencies of the state as before indicated, and will be charged with the right restoration to society of all prisoners, at the earliest possible date, when this result is reached.

I pass now to the statement of 15 points of argument in favor of the plan of indeterminate sentences.

(1) It supplants the law of force with the law of love, both in the state administration as a fact, and in the esteem of the people, giving the state thus her true place — no longer "*the governor*," but "the guardian." (2) It secures certainty of restraint and continued treatment, which operates to prevent crime, as severity does not. (3) It makes possible the arrest and right training of that whole brood of beginners, before their character is confirmed and their caste irretrievably determined, which is impossible at present; for the public mind, filled with the idea of *punishment*, is opposed to any forcible restraint until great depravity is reached and serious offenses committed. (4) It utilizes, for reformatory ends, what, though ever the strongest motive, is now the greatest hindrance to reformation, in the mind of prisoners, viz: the love of liberty, or the desire to be released. (5) It removes the occasion and so mollifies the feeling of animosity usually felt towards the law and its officers; puts the personal interest of the prisoner plainly in line with obedience to rules; and thus renders safe and simple the disciplinary department. It concentrates the faculty of *finesse* (so common with convicts) and the use of artifice upon the persons charged with their curative treatment, thus securing actual and active contact of mind with mind, and bringing under immediate

manipulation that element of character which should first be reached, an attainment so very difficult ordinarily. (7) When falsehood and strategy fail to deceive, as surely they will fail with a wise board, it secures hearty co-operation of the prisoners for the end in view, an aid without which reformation is impossible. (8) It places the responsibility of fixing the period of imprisonment and the amount of restraint on a responsible head, known to the public, easily reached and reviewed, instead of leaving it to the whim of officers elected by the popular vote, who (as a rule) have neither time nor opportunity to know what is best in the case. (9) While this plan does not necessarily remove the power to determine periods of imprisonment for criminals from the judiciary, it furnishes the advice of experts in examinations, and the advantage of experience not now had. (10) It removes the date of determining the term of detention away from the time of trial, with its excitements, its prejudices, and any influence of popular clamor, and affords opportunity to judge correctly of the real character of the prisoner. (11) It renders possible the speedy correction of errors and of wrongs, often unintentionally inflicted upon first offenders, those who, only once or twice in a lifetime, follow a morbid impulse to the commission of a crime. (12) It accomplishes the return of reformed persons to society at the right moment and at the best point, regulating the amount of restraint as well as its duration. (13) It retains, through the whole life of the prisoner, if need be, such guardianship as protects society and even the prisoner himself from his ungovernable impulses, from persecution by the injured or ill disposed, and from poverty and great want; but in other cases relaxing control from time to time, until the new found purposes and the newly used powers are determined and developed, when absolute release should issue. (14) It is constitutional and competent for the legislature to enact such a statute, as I am informed by the highest legal authority. That it is the only sound legal basis of thorough criminal legislation, both

402

deterrent and reformatory is a growing conviction in legal minds; that it is practicable is demonstrated by the operation of the law in Michigan passed in 1868, known familiarly as the "Three Years Law." (15) The writer's experience of more than twenty years, with the most careful study of the whole question of reformation possible, forces the conviction that a reformatory system cannot exist without it, and that it is quite indispensable to the ideal of a *true prison system*.

The administration of a prison system is the important thing when the system itself is well planned, for its success as a preventive and reformative agency must depend much upon this, and great care will be needed lest the management becomes diverted from these aims. When the popularity of the system or of any of its agents becomes the leading thought, when the results are esteemed more for their value to the pet theory than for their practical good to society, disintegration will sooner or later ensue. . . . No true prison system can be administered for partisan ends in any degree. Personal considerations influencing the bestowment of places of responsibility, also pervert and spoil the best laid plans of management. Men and women must be selected for their real fitness, for their practical value, as any business concern selects its employes.

The general administration will necessitate a secretary in smaller states, and two or more secretaries in larger ones who will constitute the executive officer or officers of the board; also the sub-division of the board into committees, each having special charge of some department of the work.

There should be a sanitary and structural, a financial and industrial, an intellectual and educational committee. Another committee should take charge of the examination and generalization of the facts to be found in society that contribute to criminality, and the cultivation of right public sentiment on the whole question, on which so much depends.

Still another committee, and the fifth, should be devoted

to discharged persons, their favorable restoration, measurable protection, and watchful supervision in society, through the system of agents before mentioned. Thus there will be two members of the board to each department, provided the number of 10 suggested constitutes the whole.

It is true that the reformation of prisoners during their imprisonment is indispensable, for to return to society discharged prisoners unreformed is to poison it with the worst elements possible; and to retain them in prison indefinitely, while affording at the same time protection from their evil influence, would impose a burden impossible to be borne. A fundamental condition of success in this respect is the financial independence of the organization and its institutions.* The importance of this feature cannot well be too prominent. It is too much to expect in our day that citizens generally will vote taxes upon themselves not only to provide suitable institutions for the reformatory treatment of criminals, but to support them in unproductive industry, and to supply them with the indispensables of reformatory progress. viz: good diet, good clothes, good quarters, entertaining educational agencies, and the pure personal friendship of a refined religious instructor. If these are supplied regularly to prisoners, it must come through their own exertions and by levy of excise on the grosser appetites and propensities. The labor of the prisoners, together with income from taxes (for repression) upon traffic opposed to the public weal, must furnish funds for all this, when once the establishments have been erected; otherwise success is impossible for this or any system, designed for the curative treatment of criminals. Then again, there is little hope of reformation for criminals generally, unless they can become self-sustaining through their own honest effort, and this power must be acquired while under tutelage of these guardians. The habits of self denial and productive personal exertion must be imparted, or degradation and disaster will surely follow their return

* See footnote on page 389.

to the normal society. After medical treatment, the first step toward moral improvement is, in many, perhaps most cases, *industrial training*. This involves compulsion as an element of discipline; and as the training is for their own improvement, its use is justifiable.

The administration of a prison system should be characterized by inflexible purpose, based upon a firm foundation of principles. Indeed, every step towards indulgence is fraught with danger.

The employment of prisoners should be at mechanical branches chiefly. Whether they shall be employed with or without the intervention of contractors is an open question, and must be governed much by circumstances. I am opposed to the contract system, but there are times and circumstances when to contract the prisoner's labor is the best thing.

The whole scope of the world's industry should be open for the employment of prisoners; no interference of trades' unions can be tolerated. The statistics show that about 82 per cent of ordinary prisoners have been laborers and servants, only 18 per cent artisans. It would seem that in proportion as laborers become mechanics and tradesmen, their liability to commit crime is reduced; hence, the employment of prisoners at mechanical pursuits is a reformatory measure, and for the best interest of society at large. Shall the small per cent of artisans in society object, or seek to prevent this? It is unworthy of them, and, comprehensively viewed, not for their interest.

The co-operative principle may be applied to the industries of a reformatory prison, where the sentences are upon the indeterminate plan — at least of such a one as the indeterminate reformatory herein outlined. By this is meant that the prisoners may be interested in producing an income sufficient to defray all the expenses of the establishment by the privilege of sharing in any surplus gained, which I believe to be the best, if not the only feasible general plan of giving prisoners a share of their earnings.

In prisons conducted on the best system that can be devised, graduate them as you will, there must always be a mixed company. Only the very worst element can be withdrawn from the industrial reformatory of this series. Were it possible to accomplish a perfect classification upon the basis of conduct, it would be of doubtful utility, for thereby the influence of the better prisoners over the worse would be lost; as also the stimulus to the former, and the test of character, which is found in resisting evil and in triumphing over its influence; and the whole of both classes be deprived of that grand motive for self-improvement — a fair field for self-forgetful and self-sacrificing efforts for the elevation of others. The best behaved prisoner is often the worst citizen; men of whose reform there is absolutely no hope in many cases, will grade out early by the best mark system that can be devised, if conduct in prison is the test; while some, whose reformation is already attained, cannot possibly keep a clean record. The true basis of classification of prisoners is *character*, not conduct. The criterion of character should be uniform throughout the whole system of institutions, and, therefore, should be applied in each case by the same officer or officers. *Good conduct may be assumed but good character never;* men feign insanity and thus get into an asylum, but the insane rarely feign sanity sufficiently well to get out; nor is it easier to put on the semblance of virtue so perfectly as to deceive an experienced judge and sensible man. Reformatory results hinge on financial independence, which is largely dependent upon the wise organization and application of the labor of prisoners; and it will be found, practically, that to classify as is generally proposed, would destroy or greatly impair the efficiency of the force for producing income, and thus work against the object sought, and neutralize any immediate result attained.

After withdrawing the very worst and best elements from an institution, the best method is to have such supervision of each aggregation of all the different apartments, during the hours of actual occupation, as shall prevent corrupting communications, permitting occasionally, and within due limits, such intercourse as is of good effect; and the public sentiment of a reformatory may be so favorable that quite general communication can safely be indulged in at times.

In administering a prison system, the *intellectual education* of all classes must take more prominent place, and the education of adult prisoners must not be neglected. The conviction is gaining ground that Christian character can be cultivated; that it can come *only thus;* that it is a veritable quality of being, inbred and inwrought by Christian culture; that criminals are capable of being changed for the better by this means; and that education, in its enlarged sense is the true title for the process. The absence of mental culture must leave them the blind servants of the animal instincts; and these are both favorable conditions for crime. The effect of education is reformatory, for it tends to dissipate poverty by imparting intelligence sufficient to conduct ordinary affairs, and puts into the mind, necessarily, habits of punctuality, method, and perseverance. By education the whole man is toned up, and not only are the habits improved, but the quality of the mind itself; so that its strength and activity render possible nicely discriminating moral perceptions, whose tendency is to better impulses and acts. If culture, then, has a refining influence, it is only necessary to carry it far enough, in combination always with due religious agencies, to cultivate the criminal out of his criminality, and to constitute him a reformed man. Education helps to secure admission to respectable society, without which permanent reformation cannot be accomplished, and at the same time it imparts an impulse in that direction. Education occupies the time and affords society in solitude, whose tendency otherwise is always deteriorating. It adds firmness to the mind, thus fitting it for the crises of life, constituting fortitude the guard and support of the other virtues. The testimony of those who know is that between 40 and

50 per cent of the prisoners in school are deeply interested in their personal religious relations, while only 6 per cent of the others manifest any special regard to the matter.

The religious faculties, however, are not always the first to feel the influence of Christian culture, though they frequently present the first observable evidence of improvement. A man cannot respond to religious influence till his intellect is stirred to see, and his affections trained to feel, the effect of self-sacrificing love. Christianity cares for the body, the mind, and the soul, and to cultivate it is also Christian. Christianity is more than a system of religion; it is before it, beneath it, above it; religion is included in it.

The ideal of a true prison system, in the great scope of its influence, in the spirit and principles upon which it is based, in its grand twofold aim, in its plan of organization and legislation, and in the details of its administration, is the *Christian ideal*, in all the breadth and blessedness of that term.

Let us then lend our influence and our aid to plant such a system, not only in one state, but in every state, and throughout the world, being assured that when we have found the " philosophy of the plan of salvation" for the feeble and fallen of our fellow creatures we shall have found God's plan for saving the race, and may feel the force of those divine words, "Inasmuch as ye have done it unto one of the least of these My brethren, ye have done it unto Me."

APPENDIX II

MISS EMMA A. HALL

PIONEER IN WOMEN'S REFORMATORY WORK

A S ONE of the most devoted and successful prison
workers it is fitting that a fuller sketch of Miss Hall's
work in Detroit should be given here.

Miss Hall was born at Raisin, Lenawe County, Michigan,
in February, 1837, and she died at Albuquerque, New
Mexico, aged forty-seven years. Her service in association
with myself at Detroit covers a period of five years, from
1868-1872, when her age was between thirty and thirty-five
years — the very prime and fullness of her womanhood.
Well educated, a graduate of the state normal school, a
trained teacher, a faculty member of Professor Sill's seminary
for girls in Detroit, for diminished monetary compensation
and from the noblest motives she surrendered her professional ambition, resigned her situation in the seminary, and
took up this association with prisoners to save them by education and religion, two agencies she wielded with wondrous
skill and marvellous spiritual power. Her friends were
amazed that she should leave her congenial occupation for
the work which they deemed self-denying in its nature, but
she herself did not so esteem it. So lofty was her aim and
so spiritual her character that she felt no sacrifice in such
devotion of herself. An instance well illustrates this. Once
a visitor, a noble wealthy woman of highest social standing,
was visiting the house of shelter, when she noticed in what
manner Miss Hall lived, en famille with the thirty convict
women. She remarked with deep feeling, "Miss Hall, I

could worship at your feet so moved am I at your sacrifice of yourself for these." To which came the quick reply, with a tinge of indignation, "Dear madam, you quite mistake me — a sacrifice! Why here I find my happiness and often chide myself for too much selfishness in what I try to do for this my family."

The interesting life she led with these women, and, incidentally, her own extreme occupation, are given in her own language in the report of 1872. I quote:

"We breakfast at half past five o'clock, spend usually half an hour at the breakfast table, then repair to the sitting room, gather about the organ, and all sing twice or more; then promptly at half past six o'clock enter the sewing room where each resolutely takes her accustomed place at work, or cheerfully accommodates herself to such new place as best will accomplish the shop work of the day. The noise and rapid motion of the sewing machines is of itself inspiriting, the use of them rivets the attention and the expenditure of nervous force to keep the machines in motion diverts energies often otherwise intractable, to a useful purpose. All enthusiastically work until half past five or until six o'clock at evening, save a recess of an hour and a quarter at noon, a half hour of which is regularly devoted to preparation of lessons for the evening school at the house of correction, which four evenings in the week we all attend. Five of the house of shelter girls assist in teaching there, either in a general or writing school, or both. But the most interesting feature of the house, and I am prone to say the most useful, is the Thursday evening exercise and entertainment. On this evening the whole family dress in their neatest and best attire. All assemble in our parlor, together with some of the longer sentence prisoner women from the house of correction as invited guests, and enjoy themselves in conversation and needlework, awaiting the friend who week by week on Thursday evening, never failing, comes at half past seven o'clock to read aloud an hour entertaining stories and poetry carefully selected and explained. After exchange of salutations between the 'young ladies' and madam the visitor, and after the reading, tea and simple refreshments are served in form and manner the same as in refined society. This is followed by evening devotions, departure of the prisoner guests and retirement for the night. It is difficult for us who are or have been accustomed to good social amenities to rightly estimate the pleasure and benefits of this Thursday and a similar Sunday occasion. It supplies a home attraction and home life such as these women are by nature fitted for and of which generally they have been previously deprived. The social occasions supply not only a passing pleasure but a pleasurable anticipation, present in the mind all the time and good for the mind's contemplation and for conversation. On Saturday afternoons we all attend and enjoy the lectures in progress at the house of correction and Saturday evenings are devoted to preparation for the Sabbath.

"Every Sunday at nine o'clock in the forenoon we attend the regular chapel services at the house of correction, at the close of which we — myself, family, and all the women prisoners of the house of correction — repair to a commodious room set apart for that purpose where for an hour a general prayer meeting is held. Then follows dinner, and at half past two o'clock on Sabbath afternoons we attend, all of us, the mission Sunday school located near, where the family forms a Bible class by itself.*

"The Sunday evenings at the house of shelter are devoted to the visit there of the superintendent of the house of correction, who reads to the assembled family from suitably selected literature until nine o'clock when with devotional exercises, as on Thursday evening, the gathering separates and the house is closed for the night."

How by her communicated earnestness, stolid minds were aroused to effort and perverse characters moved to helpfulness, may better appear by the following illustrative incident.

An adult woman of the prisoners' school, gross, dissolute, the habitué of the city slums along the docks, unable to decipher the alphabet, worked hard for weeks with such teaching aid as could be supplied, to learn to read. The alphabet and some one-syllable words once acquired, the pupil was stalled for long at words of two or more syllables.

---

*The mission was then conducted under the direction of the superintendent of the house of correction, and Miss Hall retained there her place as Bible class teacher of her family pupils.

It seemed as though she never could learn to read sentences. Another younger prisoner pupil in a nearby class, knowing Maggie's fruitless efforts and the failures of her teachers, besought Miss Hall's permission to try her skill in teaching Maggie. This little Mary, a habitual offender, young as she was, and a frequent short-term prisoner, had acquired the contagion of enthusiasm and sympathy. Later, on another school evening, attention was directed to the "Margaret and Mary" class by the stir of excitement there, when it was discovered that the prisoner teacher had dissipated the pupil's obtuseness. Both vehemently exclaimed: the one, "Oh, she can read!" the other, "Sure I can read!" This incident, simple enough as I now record it, was at the time impressive. We beheld daybreak in the mental darkness, the awakening of a soul hitherto enthralled by ignorance, to a larger consciousness and to the possibility of a better life. From that occasion and by means of it we possessed a firmer belief in the possible benefits to be wrought by means of wise skilful effort particularly directed to the education of this almost hopeless class of public offenders.

Now in order that the characteristics of this remarkable woman and her ministrations shall more clearly appear and that the regnant reformatory efforts of that period, both at the house of shelter and at the parent institution, — the house of correction — shall not be lost to view, the following excerpts from her published reports are here cited.

"I have found that in order to insure contentment of mind, and persistent voluntary well doing, each member must have a clearly defined object in life, a definite aim in her own mind for which she puts forth her efforts. . . . Eight of my girls are studying with commendable industry and perseverance to prepare themselves for a regular service essential to earn a living. . . . Spare moments have been devoted by my girls to worsted work; it teaches them to do delicate work besides the common work they must also do; it educates a discrimination among colors and, in exercise of good taste in the management and construction of ornamental and sometimes of beautiful fabrics. . . . In this connection I must mention the joy with which we have received the piano furnished. It has already dispelled many a dark hour of doubt, despondency, and dangerous moods; it has proved a constant inspiration in the house, stimulating industry, affording amusement and instruction not only, but spiritualizing the tone of the family. Twelve of the girls are practicing music lessons with regularity and intelligence. . . . Some of the girls are pursuing a course of study with the view to enter, later, the high school or a seminary."

Again she exclaims:

"How can I convey any adequate conception of the myriad influences, social, mental, moral, both good and bad influences which, in the conduct of such a house as this, require to be discovered, destroyed, rallied and wielded, as the case may be? I cannot! 'Tis impossible!"

Her practical good sense is shown in the following:

"I am convinced that the importance of remunerative industry in such houses as this has been underestimated by many. . . . It is, among other personal reasons, of great importance to the feeling of self-respect essential to an elementary growth of good character that the home should be *self-sustaining*."

Referring now more particularly to the religious work at the house of correction, at this period (1872), and Miss Hall's participation therein, it will be noted that there was no abatement of religious zeal; yet more and more a rational tone appears and the recognition of natural means for use in seeking reformations. After commending the change from a resident chaplain preacher, for the public religious services, to non-resident ministers and laymen, delivering each but one discourse; and referring to th e before mentioned agencies adopted, she says:

"It is no exaggeration to say that in the conference meetings during the year, and also with my communication with prisoners in private, there is a manifest growth of religious

413

inquiry, of thoughtful seriousness, and with several this spirituality is betokened by sweetened tempers and increased tenderness of feeling. My experience in the religious work among prisoners impresses me with the importance of some preliminary preparation of them for religious ministrations, such as improved physical health: more systematic educational exercises: and, also, if permanent reformatory results are to be reached, their social elevation subsequent to their release from prison should be regarded and there should be maintained over them for a time, good governmental care."

Concerning the results of the training at the house of shelter Miss Hall said:

"Of the whole number treated to date (1874), I have reason to know that 58 per cent of them are doing right and probably 18 per cent of the remainder also, which would increase the proportion of recoveries to 66 per cent. . . . When it is remembered that those who come to us are sadly circumstanced and largely so by causes beyond their control: that our own sisters might have been as unfortunate (indeed these are our sisters), the incentive to continue our efforts becomes very strong. Here is just one typical case of recovery. A homeless girl, an orphan, the victim of an older wicked girl, had been repeatedly sentenced for short terms, to the house of correction, and at fifteen years of age was considered completely hopeless. Now, for eighteen months after the expiration of our legal control over her conduct she has stood unfalteringly by her resolution to live aright and to become a good woman. This good conduct has been maintained in the very neighborhood of her former evil associates. She is pursuing a course of advanced study and with a spirit of determination that will never yield to difficulties."

After the closing of the house of shelter in 1874, Miss Hall was appointed superintendent of the state public school at Coldwater, a new institution for the care and culture of dependent children out of the almshouses of the state, and dependent children of soldiers and sailors. Having myself had to do as adviser as to the plans of buildings, aim, and organization scheme of this new and noble institution of

414

Michigan, it was with much satisfaction that I saw Miss Hall selected and installed as the first superintendent. She showed here the same executive ability, good sense, and charming spirit that had characterized her efforts previously. The Coldwater school once well organized and launched on its useful career, she resigned the superintendency to accept the charge of the state school for deaf and dumb at Flint, Michigan. Her service at Flint continued from 1875 to 1881 and is abundantly attested as most excellent in every particular. While at Flint Miss Hall was chosen for a member of the board appointed by the state to establish the girls' reform school at Adrian and when it was completed (1881) she was appointed its superintendent. Bishop Gillespie of the state board of control of penal and charitable institutions testifies that her peculiar qualifications and unselfish devotion made the administration entirely successful. Deeply interested in the class under her charge and hopeful in her nature she keenly felt any disappointment in her wards, and the bishop more than once warned her that she must restrain her sympathies or break down. Want of sympathy on the part of some women members of the institution board induced her resignation after a time. From Adrian she was called to the home mission work of the Presbyterian Church and was appointed matron of the Indian School at Albuquerque, New Mexico, where on December 27, 1884, she entered upon her duties. Two months later she died of heart failure.

I am often inclined to reproach myself for introducing to such wearing service as was the reform effort at the Detroit House of Correction and House of Shelter, this delicate and devout soul. There is undoubtedly a close connection, as a cause and effect, between very intense and long sustained tension of affectionate feeling towards irresponsive and difficult subjects and the heartbreak and complete collapse of the vital forces — even the very life, a fact which is mournfully attested by the exertion and death of Miss Hall. Such expenditure of a consuming love has so frequently served to rescue the fallen that its efficacy cannot be doubted, but it is a sacrifice, if voluntarily made, or an unconscious sacrifice, as with Miss Hall, which, I am moved to say, may be unnecessary and so unjustifiable. Lofty as is the impulse that induces this self-destructive exercise it may well be asked if such expenditure may not grow excessive? Not only may perfervid feeling destroy its subject but may divert if not prevent good reason and so subvert the object of it. A loveless scheme for reformations seems inconceivable — well nigh a contradiction; but the love that really saves is much more than what the word itself suggests of sentiment. True humaneness must find expression in true science which does not exclude, but goes beyond emotion; methods more in harmony with human nature in the sway of reason. So Miss Hall had learned to work.

APPENDIX III

INDETERMINATE SENTENCE RESOLUTIONS

Action of the International Prison Congress, Washington, D. C., October, 1910

First Section.

"In the name of the first section, Mr. Gleispach reported on the first question and presented the following propositions:

1. Proposed by the Prseident of the section, Professor Prins:

'The Congress approves the scientific principle of the indeterminate sentence.'

2. Proposed by Professor Prins and others:

'The indeterminate sentence should be applied to moral and mental defectives.'

3. Proposed by Professor Gleispach of Austria, M. Vambéry of Hungary, and others, and amended by M. Castorkis of Greece:

'The indeterminate sentence should also be applied as an important part of the reformatory system to criminals, particularly young delinquents, who require reformation and whose offenses are due mainly to circumstances of an individual character.

'The introduction of this system should be conditioned upon the following suppositions:

'1. That the prevailing notions of guilt and punishment are compatible with the principle of the indeterminate sentence.

'2. That an individualized treatment of the offender be assured.

'3. That the 'prison board' be so constituted as to ex-

417

clude all outside influences, and consist of a commission made up of at least one representative of the magistracy, at least one representative of the prison administration, and at least one representative of medical science.

'It is advisable to fix the maximum duration of the sentence only during such a period as it may be necessary because of the novelty of the institution and lack of experience with it.'

"After prolonged discussion the resolutions were adopted by a large majority with the substitution of the term Board of Parole, or Conditional Release, for the words 'Prison Board.' It was also agreed that the word 'reformatory' should be used in the English version and 'educative' in the French, as expressing best the corresponding ideas in those languages."

(BULLETIN No. 6. Oct. 2–8, 1910, pp. 160–161.)

APPENDIX IV

THE AMERICAN REFORMATORY PRISON SYSTEM*

THE American reformatory system is based on the principle of protection in place of punishment; on the principle of the indeterminate sentence instead of the usual time sentence; and on the purpose of rehabilitation of offenders rather than their restraint by intimidation. This theory works a change of attitude on the part of the state, a change of the relation of the offenders, and involves a different prison procedure. . . . Efficiency of the reformatory procedure depends on completeness of its mechanism composed of means and motives. A mere enumeration of means and motives of the mechanism is, briefly, as follows:

1. The material structural establishment itself. This should be salubriously situated and, preferably, in a suburban locality. The general plan and arrangements should be those of the Auburn Prison System plan, but modified and modernized as at the Elmira Reformatory; and 10 per cent of the cells might well be constructed like those in the Pennsylvania System structures. The whole should be supplied with suitable modern sanitary appliances and with abundance of natural and artificial light.

2. Clothing for the prisoners, not degradingly distinctive but uniform, yet fitly representing the respective grades or

---

*Extracts from article by the author in Prison Reform and Criminal Law, one of four volumes prepared for the International Prison Congress, Washington, D. C., 1910. Russell Sage Foundation Publication. New York, Charities Publication Committee, 1910.

standing of the prisoners. Similarly as to the supply of bedding which, with rare exceptions, should include sheets and pillow slips. For the sake of health, self-respect, and the cultural influence of the general appearance, scrupulous cleanliness should be maintained and the prisoners kept appropriately groomed.

3. A liberal prison dietary designed to promote vigor. Deprivation of food, by a general regulation, for a penal purpose, is deprecated; it is a practice only tolerable in very exceptional instances as a tentative prison disciplinary measure. On the other hand, the giving of food privileges for favor or in return for some special serviceableness rendered to the prison authorities is inadvisable and usually becomes a troublesome precedent. More variety, better quality and service of foods for the higher grades of prisoners is serviceably allowable even to the extent of the *a la carte* method, whenever the prisoners, under the wage system, have the requisite credit balance for such expenditure. Also for some of the very lowest intractable prisoners, a special, scientifically adjusted dietary, with reference to the constituent nutritive quality, and as to quantities and manner of serving, may be used to lay a foundation for their improvement, otherwise unattainable.

4. All the modern appliances for scientific physical culture: a gymnasium completely equipped with baths and apparatus; and facilities for field athletics. On their first admission to the reformatory all are assigned to the gymnasium to be examined, renovated, and quickened; the more defective of them are longer detained, and the decadents are held under this physical treatment until the intended effect is accomplished. When the population of the Elmira Reformatory was 1,400, the daily attendance at the gymnasium averaged 429.

5. Facilities for special manual training sufficient for about one third of the resident population. The aim is to aid educational advancement in the trades and school of letters.

This special manual training, which at Elmira Reformatory included, at one time, 500 of the prisoners, covered in addition to other exercises in other departments mechanical and freehand drawing; sloyd in wood and metals; cardboard constructive form work; clay modeling; cabinet making; clipping and filing; and iron molding.

6. Trades instruction based on the needs and capacities of individual prisoners, conducted to a standard of perfect work and speed performance that insures the usual wage value to their services. When there are a thousand or more prisoners confined, thirty-six trades and branches of trades may be usefully taught.

7. A regimental military organization of the prisoners with a band of music, swords for officers, and dummy guns for the rank and file of prisoners. The military membership should include all the able-bodied prisoners and all available citizens of the employes. The regular army tactics, drill, and daily dress parade should be observed.

8. School of letters with a curriculum that reaches from an adaptation of the kindergarten, and an elementary class in the English language for foreigners unacquainted with it, through various school grades up to the usual high-school course; and, in addition, special classes in college subjects and, limitedly, a popular lecture course touching biography, history, literature, ethics, with somewhat of science and philosophy.

9. A well-selected library for circulation, consultation, and under proper supervision, for occasional semi-social use. The reading room may be made available for worthy and appreciative prisoners.

10. The weekly institutional newspaper, in lieu of all outside newspapers, edited and printed by the prisoners under due censorship.

11. Recreating and diverting entertainments for the mass of the population, provided in the great auditorium; not any vaudeville nor minstrel shows, but entertainments of such

a class as the middle cultured people of a community would enjoy; stereopticon instructive exhibitions and explanations, vocal and instrumental music, and elocution, recitation, and oratory for inspiration and uplift.

12. Religious opportunities, optional, adapted to the hereditary, habitual, and preferable denominational predilection of the individual prisoners.

13. Definitely planned, carefully directed, emotional occasions; not summoned, primarily, for either instruction, diversion, nor, specifically, for a common religious impression, but, figuratively, for a kind of irrigation. As a descending mountain torrent may irrigate and fertilize an arid plain, scour out the new channels, and change even the physical aspect, so emotional excitation may inundate the human personality with dangerous and deforming effect if misdirected; but when skilfully handled it may work salutary changes in consciousness, in character, and in that which is commonly thought to be the will. Esthetic delight verges on and enkindles the ethical sense, and ethical admiration tends to worthy adoration. The arts, which in essence are the external expression of the idea — the revelation of the reality — have too exclusively remained the heritage of the wealthy and wise; they must ultimately fulfil their God-given design — ennoblement of the common people. "We shall come upon the great canon 'art for man's sake' instead of the little canon 'art for art's sake.'" I have sufficiently experimented with music, pictures, and the drama, in aid of our rational reformatory endeavors, to affirm confidently that art may become an effective means in the scheme for reformation.

In addition to the foregoing items the prisoners are constantly under pressure of intense motives that bear directly upon the mind. The indeterminateness of the sentence breeds discontent, breeds purposefulness, and prompts to new exertion. Captivity, always irksome, is now unceasingly so because of the uncertainty of its duration; because the duty and responsibility of shortening it and of modifying any undesirable present condition of it devolves upon the prisoner himself, and, again, because of the active exactions of the standard and criterion to which he must attain.

Neither punishment nor precept nor both combined con-. stitute the main reliance; but, instead, education by practice — education of the whole man, his capacity, his habits and tastes, by a rational procedure whose central motive and law of development are found in the industrial economies. This is a reversal of the usual contemplated order of effort for reformations — the building of character from the top down; the modern method builds from the bottom upward, and the substratum of the structure rests on work.

INDEX

INDEX

Patterson Smith Reprint Series in
Criminology, Law Enforcement, and Social Problems